The Art of Rails

The Art of Rails®

Edward Benson

WILEY

Wiley Publishing, Inc.

The Art of Rails®

Published by
Wiley Publishing, Inc.
10475 Crosspoint Boulevard
Indianapolis, IN 46256
www.wiley.com

Published by Wiley Publishing, Inc., Indianapolis, Indiana

Published simultaneously in Canada

ISBN: 978-0-470-18948-1

Manufactured in the United States of America

10 9 8 7 6 5 4 3 2 1

Library of Congress Cataloging-in-Publication Data

Benson, Edward, 1983-
    The art of Rails / Edward Benson.
        p. cm.
    Includes index.
    ISBN 978-0-470-18948-1 (pbk.)
    1. Web site development. 2. Ruby on rails (Electronic resource) 3. Ruby (Computer program language) I. Title.
    TK5105.888.B4524 2008
    005.1'17 — dc22

                                                           2008012006

For Grace

About the Author

Edward Benson is a Staff Scientist with BBN Technologies in Arlington, Virginia. Edward's work at BBN includes the design and implementation of agent-based logistics and data processing architectures and semantically-enabled data recording and processing environments (often called the ''Semantic Web''). He is a member of the IEEE and has published papers on both grid and agent computing techniques. Edward is an experienced web applications developer and a co-author of *Professional Rich Internet Applications*, also from Wrox. Edward received his B.S. in Computer Science *summa cum laude* from the University of Virginia.

Credits

Acquisitions Editor
Jenny Watson

Development Editors
Lori Cerreto
John Sleeva

Technical Editor
Dana Moore

Production Editor
Daniel Scribner

Copy Editor
Susan Christophersen

Editorial Manager
Mary Beth Wakefield

Production Manager
Tim Tate

Vice President and Executive Group Publisher
Richard Swadley

Vice President and Executive Publisher
Joseph B. Wikert

Project Coordinator, Cover
Lynsey Stanford

Proofreader
Jen Larsen, Word One

Indexer
Robert Swanson

Acknowledgments

My heartfelt thanks go out to the team at John Wiley & Sons — especially John Sleeva and Lori Cerreto — and to my colleague and technical editor Dana Moore. Your insight, feedback, and hard work have been paramount to making the book what it is. Thanks also to Carol Long at Wiley for believing in my ideas enough to convince me that I should write them down as a book proposal.

I could not have completed this book without the help and love of my fiancée, Grace. At times, writing can be a painstakingly slow and all-consuming process. Her never-ending encouragement pushed me to write each chapter with the enthusiasm that prompted me to begin the book in the first place.

Thank you to my parents and brother for their support; to my cousin Emily for her fantastic cartoon renderings of W. Web — they didn't make it into the book, so now we'll have to lobby Wiley together for *The Art of Rails, Animated Edition*; and to Robert Hiedemann for his grandfatherly advice and encouragement to make education a part of my life.

Thank you to the many friends at BBN Technologies who provided help and advice to make this book happen: Pete Pflugrath and Bud Sichler for being understanding of my time constraints and being flexible with my work schedule; Troy Self for providing feedback on early chapter drafts; Rob Battle for being a sounding board for ideas; and Doug Reid, Dave Kolas, Steve Allen, Jeremy Learner, Andrew Perez-Lopez, Tony Stein, Jonathan Nilsson, and Greg Joiner for providing their thoughts, humor, and feedback on ideas over the course of writing. (Steve's reaction to the title: "'The Art of Rails'? Who do you think you are, Donald Knuth?")

Several people on the Internet were kind enough to contribute their advice and code bits. Thank you to Rob Malda for his thoughts on the early days of web application development; Elaine Wherry of Meebo for her encouragement and feedback on the AJAX chapter; and Scott Raymond for allowing me to use his RSS 2.0 template for the XML Builder. Thank you, finally, to the many open source developers and Rails bloggers whose hard labors have advanced web development to the discipline that it is today.

Contents

Contents

Contents

Contents

Introduction

There is a certain state of mind, a certain transient condition that arises, where everything seems to resonate and effort becomes effortless. Athletes call it being in the zone, some others call it flow. Flow has nothing to do with triumph or accomplishment; it isn't the product of your labors. Flow is the merging of a watchmaker and his watch or an artist and her paints.

The dot-com bust was a confusing time for web development, but rising from the burst dreams of instant wealth, something strange and exciting happened. The web development community as a whole reached a kind of flow. In a world filled with duct-tape solutions and proprietary formats, suddenly web developers were clamoring for standards compliance, for elegance and simplicity. And it wasn't just to fend off browser compatibility issues, but because the code looked *beautiful.*

Through the fits and starts, the competing ideas, and the explosion of development frameworks that followed, an identity began to emerge. This identity is as much a philosophical statement about what the web could be as it is a technical statement about how to accomplish those goals. This identity is still emerging, and there are still many problems to be solved, but one thing is now certain: web application development has come of age as a rich discipline of programming that stands up on its own.

Ruby on Rails is just one part of this much larger story, but in many ways it is the symbol of this coming of age. Rails challenged the web development community to rethink what it meant to build a web application. It provided an entire application ecosystem when most developers were embedding their code inside HTML files. It made unit testing not only easy but also cool, and did so at a time when debugging web applications was, at best, a black art. It introduced a new generation of web developers to the ideas of meta-programming and domain-specific languages. And, most of all, it found the voice of the change that was taking place: that the web provides a natural and elegant architecture on which to write applications if only we can create the right metaphors to harness it.

What Is the Art of Rails?

Any programmer knows that an API is only half the story, and with Rails this is especially true. Good Rails development, and good web development, is much more about the design choices you make than the framework you have at your disposal. I wrote this book as an attempt to create the resource I wish I had after settling into Rails development — to pick up where the API leaves off and explain how to take good Rails code and turn it into beautiful Rails code: simple, effective, reusable, evolvable code.

This book is meant to take your Rails development to the next level, and in doing so, it cuts across a wide range of topics. Each of these topics is selected to highlight a particular part of the design and development process that can make the difference between just using the Rails framework and achieving a state of flow with the framework. Throughout the book, the focus is on *the way you code* rather than the mechanics of coding. The book is divided into clusters of chapters that represent the themes listed in the following sections.

Development Philosophy of the New Web

Chapters 1 and 2 discuss the changes in style and focus that have taken place since the web's inception. Chapter 1 presents a brief history of the evolution of web development, with a focus on interpreting that history as it relates to the changes that impact our lives as web developers today. Many aspects of the modern web application architecture were shaped by earlier programming styles that can still play invaluable roles in analyzing your design and code. This chapter gives names to some of these styles, such as code-first development and document-first development, to cast light on some of the design decisions that we are faced with today.

Chapter 2 presents Ruby on Rails as "one part framework, one part language extension, and two parts state of mind." It picks apart Rails from each of these angles so that you can see how it all fits together mechanically, stylistically, and philosophically. When you are starting out with Rails, just understanding the mechanics of writing a Rails application is sufficient, but as you advance in your skill, a deeper understanding of how the framework fits together is necessary. This holistic presentation of the Rails architecture highlights some of the concerns that you should be factoring into your code as you become a more seasoned Rails developer.

Advanced Tricks and Patterns for MVC Development

Chapters 3 and 4 focus on getting the most from the MVC paradigm. Strict adherence to MVC is one of Ruby on Rails' most prominent contributions to web development, but the benefits you get from this code-organization structure can vary widely based on how you choose to organize the code within it. Chapter 3 discusses the MVC design process, including the steps for organizing your design work, a plan for decomposing functionality into the right objects, and guidance on refactoring your code.

Chapter 4 focuses on the implementation side of MVC with the goal of making your code as clear and concise as possible. It provides guidance on how to divide your implementation between the model and controller layers for maximum reusability and seamless error-handling, provides examples of aspect-oriented programming, and shows you how to decompose your HTML code so that you'll never have to repeat yourself, among other things.

Read-Write Web: APIs, Resources, and REST

Chapters 5 and 6 focus on the emerging web application architecture and what this means for APIs, resources, and REST (Representational State Transfer). Chapter 5 shows how to design web applications so that API access is overlaid on top of your web controllers from the very start, and it provides techniques for metering API access and managing multiple data formats. Chapter 6 introduces the idea of resources, one of the foundational metaphors for the future of web development, and presents the REST application architecture. REST both guides your design toward a simple and consistent style and centers your application's operations around a growing standard on the web that supports interoperability and sharing between web applications.

AJAX Patterns

The wealth of full-featured JavaScript frameworks today means that the hard part of AJAX is no longer AJAX itself, but all the design issues that begin to arise after you have decided to go that route with your UI design. Chapter 7 presents five different AJAX design patterns that characterize different approaches to AJAX integration. It elaborates in depth two of these patterns — partial style and puppet style — that are particularly effective in Rails applications, and it shows how to integrate these styles of AJAX into your application without losing the simplicity and reusability of your design.

Advanced Ruby and Meta-programming

Much of the style of Ruby on Rails would not be possible without the Ruby language. Chapters 8, 9, and 10 focus on some of the wonderful advanced features of Ruby that make it so different from other languages. You will learn how to think and design in "blocks" and discover several design patterns that blocks make possible, such as adverb-based programming, creative APIs, and code wrappers. Chapter 9 dives into mixin-based development and monkey patching. You will learn how to change the implementation of an object after it has been loaded in memory and will see how to use this technique to refine the way the Rails framework behaves. Chapter 10 teaches you how to use message passing and the `method_missing` method to create introspective and dynamic APIs such as `ActiveRecord`.

Group Schema Development and Behavior-Driven Development

Chapters 11 and 12 address topics outside the "application" component of web applications. They show you how schema development and code testing can become integral driving factors in your design and development process. Chapter 11 discusses topics in data management, focusing primarily on `ActiveRecord` migrations and how to manage your migrations over the life span of a project and working with a large team of members. It also dives into other database-related challenges, such as techniques for seeding production data and encoding complex object models within relational schemas. Chapter 12 presents behavior-driven development (BDD) and a framework called RSpec that implements it. BDD is a reconsideration of test-driven development that is taking the Rails community by storm. You'll have to turn to the chapter to find out why!

Whom This Book Is For

This book is for any developer who has a basic understanding of Ruby on Rails and is looking to expand his or her skills to become a seasoned Rails designer. Ideally, you have written a few toy applications and have a general familiarity with the key features that Rails is known for — routing, models, views, controllers, associations, validations, layouts, and partials. This book provides short refreshers when these core concepts come up, but quickly moves on to higher-level discussions about how to best use these concepts for effective development.

Although this is a Ruby on Rails-centric book, many of the topics contained within are relevant to any developer who wishes to understand the techniques and design patterns that thrive on modern MVC-style web frameworks. As such, it is a good resource for developers wanting to learn the "Rails style" even if their target platform is something else. As has been said on the web more than a few times, learning Ruby on Rails is a great way to become a better PHP developer.

What's Up With the Stories?

Each chapter begins with a story about a fictional character named W. Web who gets caught up in an adventure that spans the book and ends online at both the book's companion web site (www.wrox.com)

and at www.artofrails.com. Each chapter's segment of the story roughly aligns with the overall topics and themes of the chapter — some blatantly and some a bit more subtly.

I wanted to add a storyline to the book because I believe that a book so heavily concerned with design should be something that you can read cover to cover rather than something that just serves as a reference. Writing each installment of W. Web's adventure was a way I could remind myself of that goal at the start of each chapter. My other, much simpler motive was that it was fun. The most entertaining technical book I have ever read is *Why's (Poignant) Guide to Ruby* (http://poignantguide.net). Although this book lacks *Why's* crazy cartoons and chunky bacon, the stories were lots of fun to write and, I hope, will be fun for you to read.

Conventions

To help you get the most from the text and keep track of what's happening, I've used a number of conventions throughout the book.

> Boxes like this one hold important, not-to-be forgotten information that is directly relevant to the surrounding text.

Tips, hints, tricks and asides to the current discussion are offset and placed in italics like this.

As for styles in the text:

❑   I *highlight* new terms and important words when I introduce them.

❑   I show filenames, URLs, and various code elements within the text like so: persistence.properties.

❑   I present code in two different ways:

```
I use a monofont type with no highlighting for most code examples.
I use gray highlighting to emphasize code that's particularly important in the present
context.
```

Source Code

Good code is concise, sometimes startlingly so, and Rails allows you to program at your best. This book consciously attempts to steer clear of large code examples in favor of small, targeted segments of code to demonstrate a particular point or technique. This keeps the signal-to-noise ratio high, and keeps the focus on what is meaningful about the technique and when you might want to use it.

Any code examples long enough to be run in a stand-alone fashion can be found online for your convenience in the source code files that accompany the book. This code is available for download at http://www.wrox.com. When you're at the site, simply locate the book's title (either by using the Search box or by using one of the title lists) and click the Download Code link on the book's detail page.

Because many books have similar titles, you may find it easiest to search by ISBN. This book's ISBN is 978-0-470-18948-1.

After you download the code, just decompress it with your favorite compression tool. Alternatively, you can go to the main Wrox code download page at `http://www.wrox.com/dynamic/books/download.aspx` to see the code available for this book and all other Wrox books.

Errata

I make every effort to ensure that there are no errors in the text or in the code. However, no one is perfect, and mistakes do occur. If you find an error, such as a spelling mistake or faulty piece of code, I would be very grateful for your feedback. By sending in errata, you may save another reader hours of frustration and at the same time you will be helping me provide even higher-quality information.

To find the errata page for this book, go to `http://www.wrox.com` and locate the title using the Search box or one of the title lists. Then, on the book details page, click the Book Errata link. On this page, you can view all errata that has been submitted for this book and posted by Wrox editors.

If you don't spot "your" error on the Book Errata page, go to `www.wrox.com/contact/techsupport .shtml` and complete the form there to send me the error you have found. I'll check the information and, if appropriate, post a message to the book's errata page and fix the problem in subsequent editions of the book.

p2p.wrox.com

For author and peer discussion, join the P2P forums at `p2p.wrox.com`. The forums are a Web-based system for you to post messages relating to Wrox books and related technologies and interact with other readers and technology users. The forums offer a subscription feature to e-mail you topics of interest of your choosing when new posts are made to the forums. Wrox authors, editors, other industry experts, and your fellow readers are present on these forums.

At `http://p2p.wrox.com` you will find a number of different forums that will help you not only as you read this book but also as you develop your own applications. To join the forums, just follow these steps:

1. Go to `p2p.wrox.com` and click the Register link.
2. Read the terms of use and click Agree.
3. Complete the required information to join as well as any optional information you wish to provide and click Submit.
4. You will receive an e-mail with information describing how to verify your account and complete the joining process.

You can read messages in the forums without joining P2P, but in order to post your own messages, you must join.

After you join, you can post new messages and respond to messages other users post. You can read messages at any time on the Web. If you would like to have new messages from a particular forum e-mailed to you, click the Subscribe to this Forum icon by the forum name in the forum listing.

For more information about how to use the Wrox P2P, be sure to read the P2P FAQs for answers to questions about how the forum software works as well as many common questions specific to P2P and Wrox books. To read the FAQs, click the FAQ link on any P2P page.

1

Emergence(y) of the New Web

W. Web knew immediately that something was wrong. He had suffered stomach pangs before, but never like this. Stumbling out of the taxi cab and toward the hospital, he mopped the sweat from his brow and pushed his way through the sidewalk traffic.

Inside, everything was a dizzy blur flowing past him — nurses, patients, a police officer, and several computer technicians hitting a computer monitor and mumbling something about the Internet going down.

"I know, I know!" Web thought as he struggled past them for the emergency patient entrance.

Luckily for W. Web, this particular hospital uses a triage system, and when you explain to the nurse at the front desk that you are the Internet, you get bumped to the front of the line. A lot is riding on your health.

As Web lay in his hospital gurney, passing other familiar technologies as the nurse pushed him down the hall, he realized that he had made the right decision to stop ignoring the pangs. It was going to be okay.

This book will make you a better web application developer. And if some of the pundits with crystal balls are to be believed, we're all on the path to becoming web application developers. More specifically, this book will make you a better Ruby on Rails developer. It assumes that you have written code using Ruby on Rails and now you are thirsty to understand how to design with Ruby on Rails and how to master the elements of Ruby that make it so successful.

The web is a strange medium for application development. Web applications can't run by themselves, they have little access to a machine's hardware and disk capabilities, and they require a menagerie of client and server software providing them with life support. Despite all this, as you probably already know or are beginning to learn, the Web is a wonderful and exciting place to be developing applications.

Programming for the Web is a blend of art and engineering. Its odd quirks and demands can be harnessed to create applications out of clean, concise, elegant code with minimal waste. This book will show you how.

Programming for the Web is also a task in which good design skills can be the most critical part of a project because of the lack of features such as compilation and type checking found in the desktop world.

Web applications aren't programs; they are ecosystems. For each separate task, a separate language is called upon: SQL for data persistence; Ruby and others for application logic; HTML for UI structure; CSS for UI appearance; and JavaScript for UI logic. Good design skills must extend past the knowledge of each individual area and incorporate the ability to coordinate all areas. On top of all that, the rise of web APIs and RESTful endpoints enable yet another ecosystem of web applications to communicate with each other and exchange services, adding another layer of abstraction that is built upon the ones below.

The Web is here to stay, and its potential will only grow as a development platform. As Internet access approaches utility-like status, as telephone and television did before it, the distinction between your hard drive and "the cloud" will blur to the point that the two are functionally indistinguishable. With the exception of maybe games and media editors, applications on the Web will be every bit as powerful as those once deployed on CDs and DVDs, but these new applications will be easier to code, faster to deploy, and will harness the combined intelligence of swarms of users to enrich their experience.

These changes are already taking place. In 2007, the primary process for both the Democratic and Republican parties included a presidential debate with a new twist: Questions for the candidates were asked via YouTube videos submitted by ordinary people through the Web. Web front ends for our banks, stocks, and bills are now considered requirements instead of features. It is no longer surprising to store data that we own, such as our documents and photos, to web applications such as Google Docs and Flickr — space leased for free in exchange for a bit of advertising. The Web is no longer just about fetching documents; instead, it has become a universal communications medium for both humans and software.

If you are here reading this page, then you see these changes taking place. The question that remains is how to best understand and take advantage of this new development medium.

This book aims to be a blend of design and programming. It takes a critical look at what makes the modern Web tick from the standpoint of Ruby on Rails. The chapters touch on a wide range of topics, from REST-based web design to domain-specific languages and behavior-driven development. All these topics represent the cutting edge of thought about web development and will become cornerstones of the web of applications that will flourish over the coming years.

At times throughout the book, the code will be sparse; elsewhere, it will be frequent. In all chapters, long code examples will be avoided in favor of small code examples interwoven with the text to demonstrate an idea. This is a book primarily about concepts, not syntax.

Rails, Art, and the New Web

No development framework understands the new Web better than Ruby on Rails. In a world of general-purpose languages applied to the Web through libraries and Apache modules, Ruby on Rails was the application framework to speak the Web language as its native language. Rails is both a programming framework and a style of development reflected by that framework.

Ruby on Rails embraces the latest thoughts in web design so thoroughly that in many cases it literally forces you to use them. Most other frameworks don't have this option — they have been around so long that entire industries built around them require legacy support. As a newcomer to the scene, Rails is in the unique position of being able to cherry pick both its features and the way that it exposes them to the developer, unifying the framework around these choices. Remember when Apple ditched the floppy drive? It's like that.

This our-way-or-the-highway approach is a bit brazen, but it has a wonderful effect: It yields a remarkably clean framework that makes writing high-quality code in very little time easy. Most of the "housekeeping" involved in writing a web application is done for you by the framework, and the rest of your coding tasks are assisted by a host of helper functions and code generators (both code-time and run-time). This means that good Rails developers can spend their time focusing on design-related issues rather than writing code, making sure that each line written is effective and appropriate.

But Ruby on Rails is still a tool, and as with any other tool, it can be misused. Tools that make a point of being simple to use often lull their owners into a false sense of security. The quick learning curve creates the illusion that there isn't anything else to it. Rails, and the Ruby language, are known for being concise, but tidy code doesn't come for free.

Art and Engineering

This book will teach you the finer points of designing and coding in the Ruby on Rails environment — the points that will transform Ruby on Rails from an easy-to-use web tool into a methodology of programming in which every design choice you make is purposeful. Ruby on Rails is a particularly good platform on which to practice this type of purposeful, artful programming because of the way it cuts out the fat in web development to leave only your design remaining.

Software development takes on an inherently artistic quality when the developer truly understands the environment he or she is working in and the tools that are available. Conversely, if you have ever watched a watercolor painter work, you know that art has a lot of engineering in it. Watercolor paintings are intricately designed in advance because each brush stroke can only add to, rather than replace, the color beneath it. Intricate protective masks are applied and layered with the precision of an Intel engineer layering the metal on a silicon wafer.

Ruby on Rails operates with this level of attention to the environment of web development — a level that extends beyond engineering and into art. This book attempts to address the higher-level web application design issues with this same level of attention. With a solid framework underneath and good design skills guiding your programming, your development will become both productive and fun, and these qualities will be reflected in the software that you write.

The New Web

The days of version numbers seemed over when Microsoft Windows suddenly jumped from version 3.11 to 95 overnight, and then advanced 1,905 product releases forward to 2000 in the span of just five years. So what a throwback it seemed when the masses collectively announced that the Web was versioned, too, and it had reached 2.0.

Web 1.0 describes the web as a digital version of the traditional publish-subscribe media model in which a few groups produce content while the majority of users passively consume it. Web 2.0 is a correction of this imbalance. Web 2.0 applications provide environments in which users can create and publish their own content without having to create and maintain web sites by themselves. Applications such as Blogger, Flickr, Digg, Wikipedia, YouTube, and Facebook turn over the bullhorn to their users, and in doing so have toppled traditional assumptions about the media industry.

Foreshadowed by the prevalence of APIs on the Web today, Web 3.0, as many are calling it, will bring a layer of automated reasoning and programmability to the Web. Semantic search engines will be able to answer questions such as "which flights will get me to Seattle before lunchtime tomorrow" instead of simply suggesting web sites associated with the topics "flights," "Seattle," and "lunch." These engines will be able to sift through the Web as a data set, piecing together bits from multiple web sites using semantic markup to align the meaning of the data elements of each. This roadmap for the Web is shown in Figure 1-1.

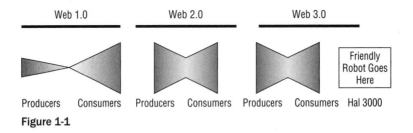

Figure 1-1

Another story is taking place beneath the media headlines and business models, and that is what this book is all about. A true renaissance of web development techniques is making the new capabilities of the Web possible. These advances are breaking long-held assumptions about the way web sites are developed and are introducing a completely new discipline of application development. In the world of web developers, each new "version" of the Web reflects a maturing of the art of web development as a discipline.

On the client side, Web 2.0 represented the push for refinement and tidying up of web formats, turning what once was a document markup language into a full-blown client-server application platform. This new platform was made possible because the web development community chose to place a high value on excellence in coding. XHTML and CSS validation icons were displayed as badges of honor at the bottoms of web sites, and the tutorials filling the Web focused on getting rid of the endless TABLE tags that clogged auto-generated HTML and on moving instead to simple, hand-crafted XHTML designs decorated entirely via CSS.

On the server side, the changes included new ideas about the ways frameworks should interact with developers, new interpretations of how URLs represent a web site's capabilities, and the incorporation of traditional application programming techniques into web development. In the chapters ahead, you will see how Ruby on Rails is at the forefront of many of these changes and how to incorporate them into your own development.

As the technologies of the Semantic Web are refined, Web 3.0 will be made possible by the introduction of resource-oriented development techniques in web development. The REST development style in Chapter 6 will teach you resource-oriented web design, which is the first step in this process. REST-based web design paves the way for formal modeling and reasoning systems to be directly integrated into our web applications, combining modern web design with the Semantic Web vision of an interlinking web of data and logic. So what is the "New Web"? The New Web isn't one particular set of technologies or content models. It is the continued evolution of the art and challenge of web design toward more capability and richer user experience. Web development has come a long way since the early days of CGI scripts and Mosaic, and it is here to stay as the medium through which a new environment of network applications will be born.

The Truth about Web Applications

Unfortunately, these exciting developments on the Web have a catch, and that catch is vitally important to anyone who wants to design good web applications today. The truth is, the Web was not originally designed to be an application platform in the way we are currently using it. As is the spreadsheet, the web is a victim of its own success. It proved to be such a fundamentally simple but flexible tool that its users bent and pried it into increasingly complex roles over the years. Today, we have full-featured web applications displacing the roles of the traditional media and software industry, but these applications are built on top of an architecture that has grown organically over 15 years of development. Web applications are the unexpected child of HTTP and HTML.

This history means that today's applications are still framed and bound by many of the design choices made in the early 1990s when the Web was solely a document publication system. Because we've all been caught up right along in the momentum, many of the oddities created by this fact never received much attention from the scripting community until Ruby on Rails came along; they just seemed to be natural characteristics of the web development environment.

Understanding the unexpected evolution of web applications is essential to understanding how to design a good one. Much of the cutting edge of web design is centered on the idea of returning to the roots of Berners-Lee's original ideas for certain components of web application design while throwing some of our original assumptions out the window in other areas. So although the rest of this book will explore the new world of Rails-based web application development, the rest of this chapter focuses on the evolution of the web from the eyes of a developer.

Patient History: The World Wide Web

For all its short history, the Web has been about *documents*. When Sir Tim Berners-Lee, then employed at the CERN laboratory in Switzerland, created the Web, he was looking for a way to publish and cross-reference project information throughout his lab.

Those were the Dark Ages of computing, when dragons and wizards roamed the net and no two computer architectures could really interoperate. A universal document format that was both hand editable and included the ideas and functionality coming out of the hypertext community at the time would be an enormous improvement to the then-current way of working. Equally important to Berners-Lee's idea was a browser for this new system, which would manage the download and display of these documents automatically, allowing users to follow links from one document to the next.

Berners-Lee had had experience with hypertext before. He had developed a hypertext editor to manage local webs of documents called Enquire, named after a book he received in his childhood titled *Enquire Within Upon Everything*. In his book *Weaving the Web*, Tim Berners-Lee describes his early vision for the Web: an Enquire-like hypertext editing system that was not bound to a single computer.

> My vision was to somehow combine Enquire's external links with hypertext and the interconnection schemes I had developed for RPC. An Enquire

program capable of external hypertext links was the difference between imprisonment and freedom, dark and light ... anyone browsing could instantly add a new node connected by a new link. The system had to have one other fundamental property: It had to be completely decentralized.

To facilitate this architecture, Berners-Lee and his colleague Robert Cailliau developed the two technologies that continue to fuel the Web today:

- ❑ **HTML** — A language to structure documents and the links between them
- ❑ **HTTP** — A protocol for storing and retrieving documents on servers

Equally important, they left us with a legacy of how to think about the web: The web as a distributed document (resource) repository.

Although today the World Wide Web is a virtual world of interaction on the Internet, back then it consisted of two executable programs that Berners-Lee and Cailliau developed for the NeXT system: `WorldWideWeb`, the client, and `httpd`, the server. The `WorldWideWeb` program was a hypertext document editor with a catch: The documents it loaded were specified using Universal Document Identifiers (UDIs, now called URIs) rather than traditional file paths. These UDIs contained both a network host name and a path on that host to specify a file. This meant that in contrast to normal programs, `WorldWideWeb` allowed users to open, edit, and save hypertext documents that were anywhere on the attached network.

The accompanying `httpd` server was responsible for making documents available for remote viewing and editing with the `WorldWideWeb` client. A later version of the `WorldWideWeb` browser is shown in Figure 1-2 (from `http://www.w3.org/History/1994/WWW/Journals/CACM/`) after support for features such as in-page images had been introduced. (The original version could display images, but only as documents themselves, not inline within a hypertext document.)

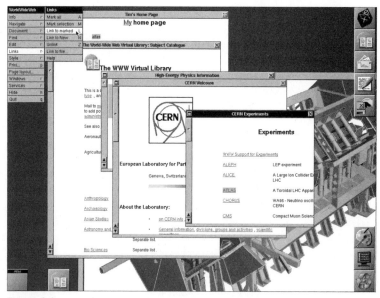

Figure 1-2

The pencil-sketch that Berners-Lee drew in his funding proposal shows a web of concepts, not just documents, interlinked across the network (much like the modern vision of the Semantic Web). But the Web that was immediately needed materialized as a web of published documents. These documents lived on a virtual distributed file system composed of every Internet-accessible computer running the `httpd` server. All that was needed was a URI to specify the server and file path, and any published document in the world could be pulled up, read, edited, and saved back to the `httpd` file server. This basic model is shown in Figure 1-3, a figure that will evolve as the chapter progresses.

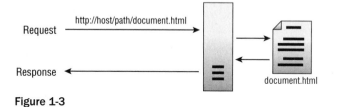

Figure 1-3

If we can characterize the World Wide Web's original behavior as similar to that of a worldwide filesystem, then HTTP is this filesystem's API. The HyperText Transfer Protocol was the mechanism that Berners-Lee designed for performing the operations that one might want to perform on a set of remote files. A working draft of the HTTP specification from 1992 contained 13 method calls in this API, but by the late 1990s, web developers used only two or three with any frequency, and much of these methods' original meanings had disappeared. The following table lists the four primary methods in HTTP commonly used by web developers today — GET, PUT, POST, and DELETE — and includes a summary of their meanings as defined by the HTTP 1.1 specification.

Method	Definition
GET	The GET method means retrieve whatever information is identified by the Request-URI. If the Request-URI refers to a data-producing process, it is the produced data which shall be returned as the entity in the response and now the source text of the process, unless that text happens to be the output of the process.
POST	The POST method is used to request that the origin server accept the entity enclosed in the request as a new subordinate of the resource identified by the Request-URI in the Request-Line. POST is designed to allow a uniform method to cover the following functions: — Annotating existing resources — Posting a message to a bulletin board, newsgroup, mailing list, or similar group of articles — Providing a block of data, such as the result of submitting a form, to a data-handling process — Extending a database through an append operation The actual function performed by the POST method is determined by the server and is usually dependent on the Request-URI. The posted entity is subordinate to that URI in the same way that a file is subordinate to a directory containing it, a news article is subordinate to a newsgroup to which it is posted, or a record is subordinate to a database.

Continued

Method	Definition
PUT	The PUT method requests that the enclosed entity be stored under the supplied Request-URI. If the Request-URI refers to an already existing resource, the enclosed entity should be considered as a modified version of the one residing on the origin server. If the Request-URI does not point to an existing resource, and that URI is capable of being defined as a new resource by the requesting user agent, the origin server can create the resource with that URI.
	The fundamental difference between the POST and PUT requests is reflected in the different meaning of the Request-URI. The URI in a POST request identifies the resource that will handle the enclosed entity. That resource might be a data-accepting process, a gateway to some other protocol, or a separate entity that accepts annotations. In contrast, the URI in a PUT request identifies the entity enclosed with the request — the user agent knows what URI is intended and the server must not attempt to apply the request to some other resource.
DELETE	The DELETE method requests that the origin server delete the resource identified by the Request-URI.

From this early draft specification, it is clear that the Web was designed as a distributed document architecture, and all the action was taking place in the HTTP protocol. This Web did not just fetch HTML documents for display, it natively allowed editing and creating, too. New resources could be created with the PUT and POST commands, existing resources could be edited with the PUT command, and resources could be viewed with the GET command. The WorldWideWeb software served as the document viewer and editor for these resources, like a Wiki implemented at the level of HTTP. For example, the following request might be used to change the text of the welcome page to a personal web site:

```
PUT /welcome.html

<HTML>
<HEAD>
<TITLE>Home Page -- Edward Benson's Site</TITLE>
</HEAD>
<BODY>
<H1>Edward Benson's Web Page</H1>
<P>Welcome to my home page! I just modified it with a PUT request!</P>
</BODY>
</HTML>
```

The Web seemed set to provide a distributed document architecture as it spread across the Internet. What Tim Berners-Lee could not have expected was how interpretations of its features would change as the Web moved into the wild and researchers all over the world began making modifications and additions to the web architecture to meet their needs.

From Documents to Interfaces

The first group to dive headfirst into the web was the National Center for Supercomputer Applications at the University of Illinois. Its team included the gang of developers who developed Mosaic, the first web browser for the masses and who later went on to form Netscape. Although Tim Berners-Lee was responsible for creating and incubating the idea of the World Wide Web, these developers — people such as Marc Andreessen and Eric Bina — are largely responsible for making it a household name.

A great deal of power rests in the hands of whoever writes the interpreter for a computer language because that person or group has unilateral ability to add, remove, or change the way the language is translated into actions by the computer. Microsoft, for instance, is notorious among web developers for single-handedly mutating the way web pages had to be constructed by implementing a flawed rendering engine in early versions of the Internet Explorer browser and then failing to fix the bugs as the versions progressed. The sheer size of the IE market required web developers to treat the exceptions caused by IE's bugs as the new rule. As the web grew in the early 1990s, the Mosaic team had even greater influence by the nature of its role as the keeper of the first mainstream browser.

Two powerful features that the NCSA Mosaic team added to its browser were the ability to display images within HTML documents and the ability to embed forms inside a web page. At the time, these features were controversial in the research community from which the Web came, but their introduction was a result of real-world need rather than research, and they were powerful additions to the web architecture.

Retrospectively, the introduction of IMG and FORM tag support into NCSA Mosaic was a symbolic event that shaped the future of web development. These two tags set the Web down the path of hosting applications rather than just documents. The IMG tag represented the shift of the Web away from an environment consisting only of information and toward an environment in which presentation played a key role. The FORM tag represented the shift of the HTML language as a passive medium for information conveyance toward a transactive medium used to facilitate remote database operations. The transactive capabilities that the FORM tag enabled also marked the beginning of what would eventually become a complete inversion of control between HTML (the application layer) and HTTP (the transport layer). Although HTTP was once the layer at which information was created and modified, forms allowed HTML to slowly take over and become the place where the real action occurred, leaving HTTP as just the transport mechanism to tunnel data between web forms and the form processor.

The Decline of Semantics

The use of the Web to convey rich document layouts and form-based application interfaces shifted HTML and HTTP away from their original use and semantics. Tags such as IMG and FORM allowed web documents to be so much more than just informational documents: They could be company home pages, rich advertisements, magazine articles, or user surveys. Similarly to parents of a growing teenager, the original designers of the web could only watch, sometimes with pride and other times with disappointment, its shifting nature as it was adopted and put to use throughout the world.

The Web, as defined by empirical use, broke from its original design and semantics in both of its two major components, HTML and HTTP. Namely,

- ❑ HTTP was reduced to only the GET and POST commands in popular use.
- ❑ HTML became a display language.

HTML and the Rise of Pages

What began as a language for describing documents quickly became a language used to describe rich page layouts and rudimentary application interfaces. Driven primarily by commercial interests, but also by academics excited by a new way to expose an application's functionality to their peers, HTML proved an effective way to produce a particular visual rendering on the client's screen that conveyed aesthetics and branding in addition to structured information. The Web was no longer a repository for just documents; now it hosted "pages," functioning like a digital magazine.

Until stylesheets were developed later in the 1990s, using HTML as a language for UI layout wasn't pretty. The tags in HTML reflect its intent as a document markup language; they are structures of typography rather than layout, such as paragraphs and headings, boldface and italics. But with no choice other than to use HTML, web "page" developers began hacking their designs out of its original structures. Of all the tags hacked for the purpose of visual design, the TABLE tag became the most important (and abused).

The TABLE tag began as an innocuous way to record tabular data. (Makes sense, right?) But a table and its cells also carry with them a certain spatial presence useful for arranging items on a page. Web browsers also supported the ability to specify such properties as border color, height, and width, and so the TABLE tag quickly became the staple for constructing user interfaces. Oh, was it painful. With sheer willpower, developers used the flexibility of this tag to coax the Web into a visual medium of its own, but at the expense of readability:

```
...
</td></tr></table></td></tr></table>
<br clear=all>
<table border=0 width=180 cellpadding=1 cellspacing=0 bgcolor=#708090 >
<tr><td>
<table width=100% border=0 cellpadding=4 cellspacing=0 bgcolor=#708090>
<tr><td bgcolor=#ffffff valign=top>
<table border="0" width="100%" cellspacing="0" cellpadding="0">
<TR><TD ALIGN=center CLASS=small BGCOLOR=#FFFFDD>
<table bgcolor="EDEDED" border="0" width="100%" cellspacing="0" cellpadding="0"
hspace="0" vspace="0"><tr>
<td align="center"><a href="Link removed to protect the innocent!">
...
```

This use of HTML as a display language created the web page metaphor that we have today, so, without a doubt, it was an important and exciting building block toward current web applications. But it came at a cost: HTML lost its semantic meaning as a conveyer of documents and became nothing more than an ASCII-based serialization for user interfaces.

Following the dot-com boom of the 1990s, a movement swept across the Web to kick the habit of HTML as a display language and return web design to its roots. This movement, made possible by the spread of CSS to all the major browsers and the development of more evolved versions of the HTML language, is why the TABLE tag as a UI structure is now largely a distant memory.

HTTP and the Rise of Forms

Although Berners-Lee's WorldWideWeb browser and httpd web server were designed to comprise a full-featured hypertext editing system, allowing users to read, create, change, and remove network-hosted HTML documents, NCSA Mosaic and other third-party web browsers supported only viewing HTML documents. With only the ability to view web pages, these web browsers did not have much use for the POST, PUT, and DELETE commands as originally intended. The new FORM element created a new mechanism through which the user could send data to the server, though. By transforming the answers to a fill-out form into a series of key-value pairs, the browser could embed additional user-provided information with the web request.

If the form method was GET, then form data would be encoded and appended directly to the end of the URL in such a way that the server could easily separate the parameters from the document identifier, as follows:

```
GET /search?q=rails&display=100 HTTP/1.0
```

If the form method was POST or PUT, then the encoded form data was sent in lieu of what once would have been HTML content created by the web browser's editor, as follows:

```
POST /search HTTP/1.0

q=rails&display=100
```

With the great array of possible uses of the FORM tag came a realignment of the possibilities of what a web page could represent. Instead of serving merely as a way to publish and modify information, a set of web pages now could together form a transactional interface to some server-side application's capability. This FORM-centric realignment morphed the way HTTP commands were used. Instead of using a full set of resource-oriented operations such as PUT and DELETE, web developers embraced a two-operation mindset: Users were either GETting data or POSTing a form. The four primary HTTP commands shifted in meaning accordingly.

❑ The DELETE command slowly disappeared from the vocabulary of web developers, a casualty of atrophy.

❑ The PUT and POST commands ceased to be ways to create and edit web resources and became the mechanisms through which form data was submitted to an application running on the server. Their identical operation made them interchangeable, with POST arising as the dominant choice, arguably because the official definition of the POST command better aligns with form-centric development. Some HTTP servers to this day no longer support PUT by default.

❑ The GET command ascended to reign over all nonform requests. Whereas formerly the GET command was used only to retrieve a resource without making any changes to data on the server, with the addition of URL-encoded form data, GET requests gained the ability to make changes, too, although it was and is frowned upon to use GET for such operations.

Therefore, although deleting user number 3 should officially be accomplished with a DELETE command:

```
DELETE /users/3
```

today, nobody flinches at the notion of "posting a delete user":

```
POST /deleteUser
```

or perhaps even getting one:

```
GET /deleteUser?id=3
```

The form model of programming remains the dominant way to write web applications today. Even the most advanced JavaScript-based applications such as Google Docs are fundamentally organized like a mail-order magazine. Users GET read-only pages from this magazine, fill out JavaScript-enhanced forms on the pages, and then POST that data back to an application running at the magazine's source. In return, they receive another read-only page whose contents may have been affected by the previous POST data. So although web applications such as Wikipedia allow users to create, view, modify, and delete their own interlinking documents in a similar fashion to the original web, they do so at a layer above HTTP commands originally created for these purposes. Users don't ever really edit a Wikipedia *page*; they edit a form containing data about that page and submit it to a script that writes that new data to a database.

In Chapter 6, you will learn about REST-based development, a style of web application development that unites form-based web development with much of the original intent of the HTTP commands. REST represents a whole application architecture defined by web-hosted resources that can be operated upon using HTTP.

Hello, Web Applications

The form-based web development model kicked off the explosion of CGI programs on the Web. Recall that the HTTP GET command returns either a document or the results of an executable script at that document's location. With the addition of forms, these remote scripts were able to receive input from the user, creating a whole new range of possibilities. This new architecture is shown in Figure 1-4.

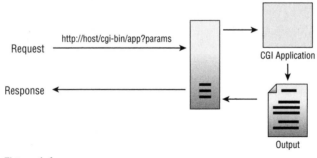

Figure 1-4

In the CGI-driven setup, HTML documents sent to the client represent an interface to a program that resides on the server. These documents contain forms that post to one or more endpoints that the web server knows represents that program rather than a particular file. The nature of the HTTP request is no longer about retrieving a document on the server but instead about sending data to the hosted program and seeing what it has to say in response. The program executed by the web server examines the parameters on the HTTP request, performs some server-side function, and then generates HTML as its output. The following Perl script might be used to process some basic form input, and output a web document, for instance:

```perl
#!/usr/bin/perl
use CGI qw/:standard :html3/;

my $first = param('first_name') || "unknown";
my $last = param('last_name') || "unknown";
```

```
print header,
    start_html('New User Signup'),
    h1('Thank you for Signing Up!'),
    table({-border=>''},
    caption(strong('Below is a summary of your information')),
    tr({-align=>CENTER,-valign=>TOP},
        [
        th(['Field','Value']),
        td(['First Name', $first]),
        td(['Last Name', $last])
        ]
        )
    ),
    end_html;
```

The output of the CGI script is then sent back to the user as the result of the request, usually as another HTML page containing the last operation's output as well as more forms.

And thus dynamic web sites were born. Built on top of the original HTTP+HTML architecture, a form-based programming model that could provide an interface to server-side software was now possible. CGI scripts were usually written in Perl, but any language could do. The only requirement was that they had to take all their input up front as an HTTP-encoded request and eventually produce their output as HTML.

This is a book about web application design, so the exciting result of CGI is the coding styles that developers used to develop for this new environment. Two styles of coding evolved to support CGI programming and the form-enabled web model, one after the other, which I name here *code-first develop-ment* and *document-first development*. Both styles attempted to fix the complications of writing applications that use form-based web interfaces, and the two styles result in very different code.

Code-First Web Development

Code-first development is a programming style that places primary importance on the programming language and secondary importance on the output it produces. The components of a code-first program are filled with functions, classes, and the usual suspects. Any output of the program is assembled using variables, string concatenations, and buffers within the code.

So a Perl program using the CGI.pm module (which is responsible for bringing us such pillars of the web as Slashdot and Amazon.com) would render HTML code using helper functions for all of the tags, such as:

```
h1('Thank you for Signing Up!')
```

Or a Java program might use a StringBuffer:

```
sb.append("<h2>Thank you for signing up!</h2>");
sb.append("<p>You should be receiving your pickled herring shortly.</p>");
```

The key in both is that the HTML document served by the web request is treated as the output of some program. The web developer doesn't write this document — he writes a program to write it.

The early days of CGI heavily favored this approach because it was the most straightforward way to integrate existing programming languages into the Web. Most programming environments (except for a few, such as LaTeX) were, understandably, program centric rather than document centric. The code-first development style allowed developers to write code in more or less the same way as what they were used to, with the only difference being that the code's output had to be assembled as HTML. These programs would be placed on a filesystem available to the web server, and all that the web server needed to do was execute these programs when a URL referenced them and then send the program's output back to the web user.

The code-first approach offers a number of advantages to the web developer, including:

❏ It is essentially the same as traditional forms of programming, making it easy to apply well-understood design patterns and testing methodologies.

❏ It provides complete freedom for the developer, separating the operation of the program completely from the fact that it is being operated in the context of some external service (the web server).

Despite these advantages, its limitations are severe in the context of any nontrivial web application:

❏ **The HTML produced by code-first programming is not easily maintained.** Anyone who has ever written a Java Servlet without using JSP knows this problem: Scores and scores of concatenated strings assembling fragments of HTML like a person rushing through a store filling his arms with piles of goods. The following code contains a serious HTML error. Can you find it?

```
protected String buildThankYouResponse() {
  StringBuffer sb = new StringBuffer();
  sb.append(beginPage());
  sb.append(title());
  sb.append(beginSidebar());
  sb.append(writeLinkMenu());
  sb.append(beginMainSection());
  sb.append("<h2>Thank you for signing up!</h2>");
  sb.append("<p>You should be receiving your pickled herring shortly.</p>");
  sb.append("<p>Click <a href=\"index.html\">back</a> to return to the book.");
  sb.append(endMainSection());
  sb.append(endPage());
  return sb.toString();
}
```

The error is just one of many common ones in this type of code. The output of the begin Sidebar() method is appended to the final response, but an endSidebar() method is never called. The incremental, method-calling approach makes committing this kind of mistake easy, potentially leading to nonsensical HTML. Equally as dangerous is the confusion that these method calls add to the process in the first place: Perhaps the beginSidebar() function cleans up after itself and does not need an endSidebar() counterpart, but without digging into the implementation of each, it is impossible to know.

HTML is a hierarchical, document-centric language, and it quickly stops making sense when small fragments of it are taken out of their context. Scattered across many lines of code and surrounded by quotes and function calls, it is hard to understand, and it isn't any fun.

❏ **Code-first programming combines page design with control logic.** When HTML pages are assembled inside the loops and functions of a program, separating the design of the page from the control structures that decide what a user should see becomes impossible. This means that any visual changes to your web page require modifications deep within your application code. Imagine if painting your car required rebuilding the engine. That is what to expect whenever you run across a program that begins like this:

```
beginPage(sb);
if (user.isAdmin()) {
 sb.append("<h1>Administrative Interface</h1>");
 for (Module adminModule : adminModules) {
        adminModule.toHTML(sb);
 }
}
else {
 sb.append("<h1>Welcome, Ordinary User Not Deserving of Cool Admin
Modules!</h1>");
 }
```

For small applications, this limitation may not be a serious problem, but over time, and with scale, it will inevitably become a big one. Page design shouldn't be about programming, and programming shouldn't be about page design. They are separate concerns that are addressed using separate languages, so making one depend on the other only hinders the ability to be effective in either. Web designers with mastery of HTML and CSS but not programming find it difficult to play an active role in web development and maintenance in this environment, for example. Each change they make must be embedded into the flow of a program, so new designs and updates might have to be applied to the site through a programming-minded intermediary. Ideally, web designers could make visual updates to the site with minimal interaction with the program logic that powers its behavior.

❏ **Code-first programming leads to HTML duplication.** Each code-first program stands on its own, with its own entry point and output, so each is responsible for performing everything required to produce a complete web page. It is possible to organize all these mini-programs so that they share common routines and code, but, in practice, this does not usually happen as well as it could.

So, seven different CGI scripts all might have a routine that checks to see whether a user is logged in. Or the ubiquitous navigation strip at the top of the page might be duplicated for each page with different styling to signal which page the user is currently on. This type of copy-and-paste programming can be more convenient during development in a code-first approach, but it ultimately makes site maintenance difficult.

Document-First Web Development

Not long after CGI programming swept the Web, a new web development model began to emerge that emphasized the HTML output over the control logic governing it. Document-first programming is a style of programming that places primary focus on the formatted output of the program and secondary focus on the control structures that affect it. Document-first code consists of documents in their output format with embedded code that must be processed before the output is considered complete. Figure 1-5 shows the document-first, or active-document, model graphically.

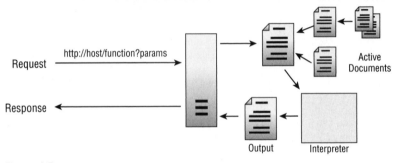

Figure 1-5

For the quintessential example of document-first programming on the Web, look no further than PHP. In 1995, Rasmus Lerdorf wrote a Perl program to help him track accesses to his online résumé. That script turned out to be a bit of overkill, and after two years and a rewrite in C, it became PHP, one of the most successful web scripting languages of all time.

PHP, and the document-first style, presents the programmer with a different environment from the one the first CGI authors were used to. It is an inversion in the primary language used to describe the web application. Instead of writing code that outputs HTML, the programmer writes HTML that contains embedded code. Embedded code is contained within special tags, usually <% %> or <? ?>.

These documents are stored in a filesystem like any other document that a web user might request, but the server is configured to handle them with special instructions based on their file extensions. Before these documents are returned to the remote user, the web server runs them through a "hypertext prepro-cessor" that processes the document linearly and executes any of the bits of code within it.

So the following fragment might be used to conditionally display an administrative link section to a page based on whether a variable has been set:

```
<? if (user_is_admin) { ?>
<ul class="link_section">
  <li><a href="adduser.php">Add User</a></li>
  <li><a href="resetpassword.php">Reset Password</a></li>
</ul>
<? } ?>
```

Or a list of comments for a blog entry might be shown as follows:

```
<? foreach ($comments as $comment) { ?>
    <div class="comment">
      <h1><?= $comment->title ?></h1>
      <p><?= $comment->contents ?></p>
    </div>
<? } ?>
```

Using the document-first style, web developers can work in their native environment of HTML while still writing the code needed to control decision-making and load data. It preserves the document feeling while still allowing dynamic behavior. The document is its own output — nowhere, as the developer, do you need to state that a particular portion of text is headed to the remote user. As long as the control code embedded within the document does not prevent a particular region of HTML from being parsed over, it will be appended to the output.

This style of coding is also more web-designer friendly than the code-first style. Despite the presence of embedded code, HTML is the dominant structure, so web designers can work around the control statements and make edits to regions of HTML without having to change any code. Document-first files can be referenced for inclusion to other files, so the heavy bits of programming can be roped off into library files and simply included near the beginning of a page. File-inclusion also allows web designers to avoid repetition, breaking often-used idioms into their own file for reuse across the site. Although the document-first approach presents a much easier way to dynamically build HTML documents, it is not without its own problems from a web *application* perspective:

- ❑ **Every file is parsed as potential output.** Document-first programming presents a developer-friendly way to craft HTML output but does so at the cost of providing a straightforward way to write the portions of your application that are pure code. Model objects that encapsulate data in the database and libraries with helper functions must be written inside files that are included at run-time during the preprocessing step, which means that they are parsed as potential contributors to the application's output. You therefore must be on guard against accidentally including any strings in those files that will be appended to the output because such strings might prematurely begin the server's response to the client (before cookies are sent or before a redirect decision is made, for example).

- ❑ **Managing the decomposition of documents can be arduous.** There is no centralized entry point in document-first applications; each document that can be addressed via a URL serves as its own entry point. This means that developers must include all dependencies at the top of every web-accessible file. In practice, many of these initializations can be abstracted into a single file that may be included with one line on top of each file. But this still doesn't quite solve the problem, because developers are still left to create their own "pipeline" of operations that help fulfill the web request. It would be much nicer if the framework did not require every page to start from scratch and instead provided a single entry point that could handle details such as database connections for you.

    The decomposition problem is made more difficult by the fact that a single document type is used to store every possible construct within the project. Whether you are defining a class, writing a set of functions, performing a login operation, or outputting HTML, the setup of the file looks identical. Where should cookie and session-keeping operations go? What about database management code? Should SQL queries be allowed to occur in the middle of a page definition? How should errors be handled at various stages of the page's parsing? These types of questions are all made difficult to answer because all documents in a document-first system such as PHP are treated the same: They all are potential entry points into the application containing embedded code. Without strong guidelines from the framework about proper decomposition strategies, developers are left to find a solution on their own, and the solution will vary from developer to developer.

- ❑ **Document-first programming can result in just as much code juxtaposition as code-first programming.** Data operations such as performing a search, loading a user object, or saving a new object must occur inside code blocks embedded in HTML. Although this requirement doesn't present any technical problems for the developer, it is just as poor of a juxtaposition of concerns as concatenating HTML strings inside control flow. There is no reason that developers should have to cope with an SQL statement embedded in a PHP function embedded in an HTML file. Scale this scenario over hundreds of files, and you have a maintenance nightmare.

The document-first approach of hypertext preprocessing has many advantages over the code-first style for web application programming, but it still leaves developers with much to be desired. As long as the code embedded in document-first files directly pertains to the display of information within the document, it seems an efficient and easy-to-maintain solution. But as soon as control logic, database operations, and other such tasks are thrown into the mix, document-first files can become just as difficult to maintain as code-first files.

Emergency Room

The Web has come a long way. It started as a distributed document repository and quickly became the launching board for a new type of application. Propped on top of the original HTML+HTTP architecture, this new application platform shifted the way the architecture was used so that commands and functionality were embedded in the form data of web requests rather than in the HTTP command conveying the request. This approach enabled web requests to convey any type of data, not just document operations, but it also sent the whole industry of applications programming crashing into a medium whose semantics and programming styles were in a state of flux.

So here we are today, with web application development simultaneously revolutionizing our economy and experiencing an emergency. The revolution is occurring because the web provides such a powerful and democratizing platform on which to create applications. The emergency is occurring because web development methods are still in the process of evolving toward the structure and stability required to take on this enormous new role.

If you peered behind the curtains of many web companies during the early 2000s, I suspect you would see waters churning as a result of these two opposing forces. I worked briefly for a major online commerce site at which you've no doubt shopped, and the tension between these two forces could be seen clearly there. The web application that comprised its entire business appeared flawless to the outside web user, but inside it was chaotic. The web application code had grown organically until it reached gigabytes in size, and it contained so many memory leaks that each production server had to be rebooted at semi-random intervals. The company wanted to patch up this software, but it was too large, too intertwined, and too confusing for anyone to attempt such a feat. The result was a multiyear effort to rewrite the entire codebase from scratch. This web application is part of the revolution taking place, both in the Web's importance and in the need for better web development practices.

As the needs of developers change, certain themes that arise more frequently than others become embedded into new environments as built-in idioms to support those needs. Until recently, web application programming has largely been done with a set of keywords and metaphors developed long before the web became a popular place to program. APIs have cropped up to support web-specific features, but they are no replacement for fundamental changes in the programming environment itself. The growth of web applications requires a new type of programming designed specifically for the needs of the Web. Luckily for you, such environments are now beginning to flourish.

Emergence of the New Web

A new breed of development frameworks has appeared that reflects a true maturation of web development as a discipline all its own. With the charge being led by Ruby on Rails, these frameworks represent the idea that web applications are neither code-first nor document-first, but rather a combination of the two. The code-first approach best addresses entry points, control logic, and data operations, whereas the document-first approach best handles the creation of output to be sent to the web client. These new frameworks reflect a belief that web programming is heterogeneous in language while homogeneous in process, that a successful web framework should not be general-purpose language with a few helper libraries attached but rather a complete environment whose every design feature assumes operation over the Web. As a result, the Web is built into everything from the directory structure of a project to the tasks that no longer have to be performed by the developer.

Ruby on Rails is on the leading edge of web development techniques, both because of its own originality as a framework and its adoption of the latest technologies and ideas from the web development community. This book focuses on both. Some of the chapters cover features or innovations specific to Ruby and the Ruby on Rails framework, but some cover topics in modern web application development embraced by Rails but not monopolized by it.

This chapter outlined the history of web development to highlight not only how much it has changed over the years but also how many of the ground assumptions of the Web have stayed the same. Understanding the assumptions that created your chosen development environment will help you design web applications that integrate into the web more smoothly. And in later chapters, such as Chapter 6, you will see that in many ways, the very latest in web design is a return to the original semantics of HTTP.

There has never been a more exciting time to be a web developer. The web has broken through its adolescent years as a new medium and is now accepted from the living room to Wall Street. As the Ruby on Rails framework demonstrates, the web is no longer just an output file format but a full application development medium of its own, with its own patterns, abstractions, and vocabulary. The remainder of this book shows you how to take hold of this new application medium and use the latest design abstractions and techniques to bring your web development to the next level.

The Rails Concept

W. Web approached the picnic tables set up for breakfast cautiously, clutching the orientation binder in his hands. He waved as he saw Vik, the man he had met preaching on the street outside the hospital after being discharged. Here in the camp outside the city, all the cult members he remembered from the recruiting sessions were much more relaxed, their nervous edge gone.

Web grabbed a paper plate from the serving line and began perusing the platters, deciding what to eat.

"Excuse me; I'm new here. Do you know if there is a serving spoon for the eggs?" he asked the woman in front of him.

She turned, amused, and smiled with a quizzical brow, "Serving spoon? No, just imply to the platter that you'd like some."

"Imply to the . . I'm sorry, what?"

The woman held her empty plate out to the platter and looked expectantly at it. W. Web couldn't tell whether he had blinked while she pulled a fast one or he just hadn't noticed the eggs on her plate all along, but when she pulled the plate back, it was full.

"We always felt serving spoons were redundant, anyway," she said with a smile. "After all, what else were you going to do with them?"

Web inched his plate toward the inanimate platter, looking a bit confused. He jerked his hands back as an omelet suddenly weighed down the plate.

"There you go! A natural. If you want scrambled, try not to look so confused. And smile for sunny side up."

Web offered a timid smile back and muttered his thanks, shuffling away to clear his head. He slid past the filling picnic tables and back up the hill toward his cabin, the woman's voice wafting behind him.

"If you're headed back to your bunk, make sure you touch the door with your left hand first, otherwise the door won't unlock!" and then after a pause, "Don't worry! It will all start making sense!"

If Rails were a mixed drink, the recipe for it might read, "1 part framework, 1 part language, 2 parts mindset." Rails is as much a set of guidelines for thinking about web development as it is a framework for using web development. The two can't really be separated. Everything from the Rails project structure to the layout of your HTML files is affected by the Rails mindset, driven by one opinion of how web development should work — and understanding that design philosophy can be as important as the mechanical task of writing Ruby and HTML code.

This chapter is a concise review of these components to Rails: the framework, the language, and the mindset. Rails code looks and feels different from non-Rails code, but when you become used to its look, the code you write will be far more productive. This chapter briefly covers these aspects of Rails to review topics such as project structure and how the Rails pipeline operates. Later in the book, you will learn how to extend this architecture with plug-ins and new language-like features. After discussing Rails as a framework and a language, this chapter delves into several vignettes that describe Rails as a state of mind, a style of programming driven by beliefs about how effective and enjoyable programming should work. All these ideas affect the way in which the Rails framework operates and should motivate the design choices you make in your own code. Many of them are also the topics of later chapters in this book.

In many of the areas discussed below, the Rails concept extends past Ruby on Rails itself and to many of the other Rails-like frameworks available. Today, Rails developers can choose from a number of rein-terpretations of the basic Rails idea, or they can start from scratch and pick and choose the ideas in Rails that make sense for their own application:

- ❏ Merb for Ruby (www.merbivore.com)
- ❏ TurboGears for Python (www.turbogears.org)
- ❏ Django for Python (www.djangoproject.com)
- ❏ CodeIgniter for PHP (www.codeigniter.com)
- ❏ CakePHP for PHP (www.cakephp.org)

Each of these frameworks looks and feels different to the programmer, but are all striving toward a set of similar goals. These shared beliefs and goals are important because they represent a new branch of thought about web development. Few of the ideas in the Rails mindset are inventions of Rails. Many are broader movements in the web community or traditional programming ideas reinterpreted in the context of the Web — things such as test-driven development, REST-based design, and MVC. But Rails is unique in collecting all these ideas into a unified framework and so thoroughly and seamlessly integrating them into the brick and mortar of web development.

This chapter does not go into deep detail of how to set up a Rails application or how to use the many features the Rails libraries offer you. Several books address these concerns already, among which two of the best are *Agile Web Development with Rails*, by Dave Thomas and David Heinemeier Hansson, and *The Rails Way*, by Obie Fernandez. These books are a definite must for the bookshelf of any Rails developer and are valuable references regardless of your skill level. Coupled with one of those or a similar book, this chapter will provide you with a better understanding of the design choices that accompany the Rails framework.

One Part Framework

Rails is referred to as a "full stack" framework because it handles everything from web serving to database management right down to HTML generation. As with the JSP and ASP-style environments, the idea is that a vertically integrated web development environment can provide a better experience for the developer; the components can be more tightly coupled and the default configuration more optimized out of the box.

In such a tightly integrated environment, the developer interacts with Ruby on Rails through a series of shell scripts that generate and manage the Rails project environment. The script/ folder in the Rails project directory contains a generator to create code and database schema stubs, a Ruby-based web server so that you can test while you code, and a console for experimenting and debugging. Other tasks are handled through Rake, Ruby's equivalent of Ant. Rake handles everything from database schema migration to automated testing and code deployment.

Because the breadth of Ruby on Rails' functionality spans so much ground, it makes sense to look at the framework from a few different angles. What follows is a high-level rundown of Rails from a configuration perspective, a coding perspective, and a process perspective.

The Configuration View

Rails differs from other vertically integrated environments in its strong preference for convention over configuration. So where Tomcat and Jetty often require pages of XML configuration, Rails requires none, or perhaps only a few lines of YAML (the Ruby-preferred markup language). This extreme aversion to configuration files (or XML sit-ups, in Rails-speak) makes for a very distinctive and recognizable code structure that is the same across all Rails apps. This may annoy control freaks to no end, but it comes as a welcome relief to developers who are interested in spending time on their web application rather than their server configuration.

It comes as no surprise, then, that all Rails projects have exactly the same directory structure. The first command every Rails developer types to begin a Rails application, rails appname, creates a new directory and prepopulates it with the folders and files that comprise an empty and waiting Rails application. This directory structure is a useful template for web development projects, so if you've decided to go with another language, still consider giving it a try. Many of the Rails-style frameworks already follow this general project structure, each with its own custom variations, thereby making it an informal standard among MVC web frameworks. Here is what you get:

- ❏ **app:** The dynamic portion of your web application
  - ❏ **controllers:** The interface and business logic
  - ❏ **helpers:** Supporting code for your views
  - ❏ **models:** The model objects persisted to your DB and used in your application
  - ❏ **views:** Templates for the responses sent back to remote users
  - ❏ **layouts:** Page layout files
- ❏ **config:** Environment, database, and application configuration
  - ❏ **environments:** Environment-specific configuration
  - ❏ **initializers:** Configuring files to be parsed at server startup
- ❏ **db:** Your database schema as a set of ActiveRecord migrations
- ❏ ***doc:** Documentation for your web application
- ❏ ***lib:** Any Ruby libraries specific to your web application
  - ❏ **tasks:** Project-specific rake tasks

- ❑ **log:** Logging output
- ❑ **public:** The static portion of your web application
  - ❑ **stylesheets::** Your CSS files
  - ❑ **javascripts:** Your JavaScript files
  - ❑ **images:** Your image files
- ❑ ***script:** Shell scripts to manage your Rails project
- ❑ ***test:** All the testing code and data for your application
  - ❑ **fixtures:** Database data to be preloaded during testing
  - ❑ **functional:** Functional tests to verify correctness of your controllers
  - ❑ **integration:** Integration tests
  - ❑ **mocks:** Mock objects for testing use
  - ❑ **unit:** Unit tests to verify correctness of your models
- ❑ **tmp:** A place for Rails to store its temporary data
- ❑ **vendor:** External libraries used by your application
  - ❑ **plugins:** Rails plug-ins

This directory structure standardizes the way in which Rails applications are designed and allows Ruby's shell scripts and automated features to function correctly. In addition to the regular directory structure, file and class names are strictly regulated, which is one of the reasons that nearly every new object you create outside of the `lib/` directory is created via the `script/generate` utility.

Such a standardized environment doesn't leave much to be configured, which is the point. Preparing a web application for deployment is the exception, and no matter what your framework, deployment will likely require extensive environmental tweaking. But for development purposes, the configuration of a Rails project generally consists of three steps:

1. **The database:** Rails assumes that every web application must have a database and pre-populates the file `config/database.yml` to store its connection information. This YML-encoded file defaults to three separate database definitions: one for development, one for testing, and one for production. These definitions are preconfigured to use SQLite, a light-weight database that stores its files locally to your project directory and does not require any special configuration. The connection is global to your web application — no special initialization or connect code is needed on your part. More advanced database configurations are possible — for example, splitting data over multiple databases or replicating data.

2. **Routes:** As Chapter 4 illustrates, Ruby on Rails takes URL design seriously. Routes are templated rules that take an incoming web request and route that request to a controller and action. The driving philosophy is that the URL, not request parameters, should specify the nature of the web request, and routes are a way to accomplish this. Most other frameworks have the concept of routes (for example, in Tomcat, they are defined in `web.xml`), but Ruby on Rails provides a set of Ruby routines that make route definition simple and concise. The default routes automatically generated for all Rails applications is the following:

   ```
   map.connect ':controller/:action/:id'
   map.connect ':controller/:action/:id.:format'
   ```

These routes map any URL in the form `http://domainname.tld/a/b/c` into three separate variables: `controller`, `action`, and `id`. The `controller` and `action` variables get special treatment. They determine what code executes to form a response for that URL. All other variables (including `id`) are passed along to this executing code in a hash table called `params`.

3. **The environment:** The file `config/` directory contains several files that give the developer a chance to insert Ruby code that is executed when the Rails server starts up. It is the one-stop location to perform project-wide operations, such as including external libraries, setting logging levels, or overriding the default behavior of Rails components. Later in this book, you will see how to place code here that overrides and extends the Rails framework with custom code.

The Code View

The Rails architecture, as the developer interacts with it, is divided into three separate subsystems: ActionPack, ActiveRecord, and ActiveResource. These three are accompanied by a number of supporting libraries. ActiveResource is the newest addition to the bunch and provides support for models that wrap around remote, RESTful resources. ActionPack and ActiveRecord are the traditional Rails libraries and govern the three main components of a Rails project: the model, the view, and the controller. ActionPack handles the controller and view, and ActiveRecord handles the model. Chapter 3 is devoted entirely to the proper breakdown of these components, but for now, I'll just stick to the high-level structure, shown in Figure 2-1.

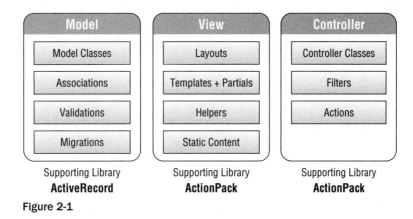

Figure 2-1

ActiveRecord supports all the various components that comprise code supporting the web application's model. The base class `ActiveRecord::Base`, from which all model classes derive, contains the functionality that handles the automatic mapping and persistence from model object to database table. It also contains a number of helper methods that manage relationships between model objects (such as `belongs_to` and `has_many`) and a subframework called *migrations* that provides versioned database schema management. (Migration-based development is covered in depth in Chapter 11.)

ActionView is a library within ActionPack that provides the basis for the view portion of a Rails site and handles the parsing of template files with embedded Ruby (the variables are initialized from within the controller). It includes its own pseudo-language, RJS, that allows Ruby developers to write Ruby that compiles into JavaScript. It also comes with numerous helper functions to manage everything from text manipulation to form generation.

Finally, `ActionController` is a class within ActionPack that provides the basis for Rails controllers. By subclassing `ActionController::Base`, developers can define the basic actions available to remote users by declaring and implementing public methods. The details of HTTP, such as request-types, response-types, and parameters, are abstracted away into a set of class-accessible variables and helper functions. ActionPack also provides a feature called *filtering*, which creates a set of aspect-oriented programming-style cut points into which developers may inject code that modifies the nature of the web request fulfillment. Filters allow cross-cutting concerns, such as authentication or character set specification, to be handled from centralized routines and then applied to a number of possible actions within the site.

The Process View

Rails provides a fixed pipeline through which incoming HTTP requests are served. Figure 2-2 depicts this process. First, an HTTP request arrives at the server and is checked for a match against static resources in the `public/` directory. If a match is found, then that file is immediately returned, just as with a regular web server; otherwise, the URL is passed to the router.

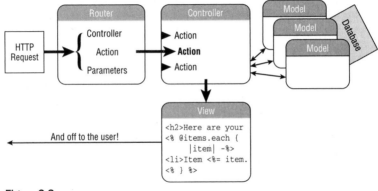

Figure 2-2

After the request hits the router, the following series of steps take place:

1. **Routing:** The router matches the HTTP request against its known routes, using the first match it finds. It uses the route definition to interpret the URL as a call into your Rails application, defined by the notional tuple {`Controller`, `Action`, `Parameters`}, where `Parameters` is a hash table.

2. **Controller instantiation:** Based on the results of the Routing step, a controller instance is instantiated. This controller derives from the base class `ApplicationController`, which is also a part of your Rails project and usually contains methods that handle session and authentication functionality.

3. **Action invocation:** Based on the routing results, an action on the instantiated controller is called. The term "action" is just Rails-speak for a public method on your controller. The action

    ❑ Uses the model classes to perform any necessary modifications in the databases

    ❑ Uses the model classes to load any database data necessary for constructing the view

❏ Specifies a view to render as a result to the user

4. **View rendering:** The view specified by the controller action is processed as an ERB document (a document-first programming-style file containing embedded Ruby). This view may use any variables set up by the controller, may render other partial views as components, and may be rendered within the context of a layout.

5. **Response:** The results of the view rendering are sent to the remote user.

This process represents one round-trip through a Rails-hosted application. Besides being straightforward to understand, this process conforms well to the MVC design pattern (discussed in Chapter 3) and works well regardless of response type. So whether you are rendering HTML pages, PDF documents, or XML, the same application flow can be used and certain elements of it even reused (discussed in Chapter 5).

One Part Language

In addition to being a framework, Ruby on Rails dons the guise of a domain-specific language (DSL). It takes advantage of Ruby's malleability as a programming language to appear as one of its own, a superset of Ruby made just for the web. Although technically this "language" is really just method calls into a cleverly designed set of base classes and mix-ins, it certainly doesn't feel that way to the programmer. So let's afford it that status, because it is far more useful to do so than to limit ourselves with the technicalities of what it means to be a programming language.

Key to the idea of Rails as a language is the importance of new abstractions in the evolution of programming. An analogy might be drawn to C. As the last mainstream language in which programmers really program a machine rather than a set of abstractions, C is very powerful when it comes to low-level tasks. But application programming has moved past the days of allocating memory and manipulating null-terminated character arrays and onto higher-level abstractions that allow us to express more complicated thoughts with greater ease. The evolution of programming languages is, in many ways, the continual layering of new abstractions upon existing ones.

New abstractions on a language usually first appear as third-party libraries. Examples are the strings and collections provided by the STL for C++, abstractions such as servlets in Java, and, to a certain extent, how Rails attaches itself onto Ruby. But the Ruby language is among a small group of peers in its great flexibility. Optional parentheses allow method calls to appear as keywords. Symbols (the colon-prefixed strings used all over Rails) provide a clean way to humanize hash keys and object names, and Ruby's extensive support for features such as closures, late binding, and self-modifying code allow a level of linguistic trickery that is a great strength in the eyes of framework developers.

The result of all this is a framework that recognizes the important role abstractions play in advancing technology and that melds these abstractions into part of a larger language. Rails makes Ruby behave as if it were a language created just for the Web. Sure, you can fetch a user's address from a database by issuing a SQL query and parsing the results, such as the following code in PHP:

```
$sql = "SELECT * FROM addresses WHERE users.id = 34 AND users.address_id =
addresses.id;"
$result = mysql_query($db, $sql) or die ("Failed query of " . $query);
$row = mysql_fetch_array($result, MYSQL_ASSOC);
if ($row) {
    $zip_code = $row["zip"];
}
```

```
else {
    // Uh oh!
}
```

but this is a task that web developers do all the time. Isn't it a lot easier to abstract it away so that we can simply state the following?

```
user = User.find(34)
zip_code = user.address.zip_code
```

In Chapter 10, you will learn how Ruby on Rails pulls off these tricks and how you can, too. For now, I'll just focus on what it does and why this is useful to developers.

This new pseudo-language is useful because it abstracts away common web development tasks that normally require low-level attention from the developer. Some of the features of this language replace concepts that would otherwise have had to be developed in Ruby, such as data validation and layout decisions. Other features abstract away the complications of other languages, such as SQL and JavaScript. These features occur throughout the Rails framework, but the three main areas that affect you, the developer, are in your model, your HTML templates, and in your options for writing JavaScript.

Models on Rails

The most unique and immediately apparent element of "Rails as a language" comes from ActiveRecord. Right from the start, ActiveRecord acts as though it knows you. It infers database table names based on the names of your model classes (don't worry, this can be overridden) and automatically generates getters and setters based on the schema that you've defined. It also provides a set of base methods that can be used in the body of the model definition to create associations with other objects and set up validations for instance data.

Altogether, these features may result in little else for you to do in terms of model writing, depending on your application. In fact, that is exactly the point — it removes the yak shaving from the model, leaving you to focus on other things, such as good model design and application-specific algorithms. Automation is half of the way Rails does this for you; the model-specific language Rails creates for you is the other half.

Yak Shaving

Yak shaving is defined on Wiktionary as "any seemingly pointless activity which is actually necessary to solve a problem which solves a problem which, several levels of recursion later, solves the real problem you're working on." Seth Godin illustrates the concept with a story actually involving a yak in a March, 2005, blog post:

Yak Shaving is the last step of a series of steps that occurs when you find something you need to do.

"I want to wax the car today."

"Oops, the hose is still broken from the winter. I'll need to buy a new one at Home Depot."

> "But Home Depot is on the other side of the Tappan Zee Bridge and getting there without my EZPass is miserable because of the tolls."
>
> "But, wait! I could borrow my neighbor's EZPass. . ."
>
> "Bob won't lend me his EZPass until I return the mooshi pillow my son borrowed, though."
>
> "And we haven't returned it because some of the stuffing fell out and we need to get some yak hair to restuff it."
>
> And the next thing you know, you're at the zoo, shaving a yak, all so you can wax your car.

Rails uses associations to state how model classes are related to other model classes. Associations sit inside the class definition, usually right near the top, and hide away the details of foreign-key relationships in the database schema. Using associations, ActiveRecord is able to perform many join, ordering, and filtering operations for you automatically, allowing you to treat data in the database as though it has never been anything other than a regular collection of Ruby objects.

As an example, the following code shows how you might join the Photo model to the User model. This book does not include a reference to associations API, so if you are unfamiliar with it, take a peek in one of the books mentioned earlier or check online at www.rubyonrails.org. What is important here is not the mechanics of the association, though, but rather the way Rails allows you do it a manner that simulates natural language.

```
def User < ActiveRecord::Base
    has_many :photos
end
```

A "User has_many :photos." From this statement, Rails makes several assumptions, all of which can be overridden with extra arguments if needed. By default, this bare-bones statement modifies the User object so that it expects a foreign key association on the field user_id of a table named Photos. The developer is then able to access a user's photos as if they were a regular collection on the User object.

ActiveRecord associations can get a lot more complex, including many-to-many relationships, join tables, conditional joins, and polymorphic associations. All these are handled in a similar fashion, starting with a simple assertion in the model definition and possibly expanded with refinements to the default assumptions that come packaged with that feature.

Validations on data are performed in a similarly language-native way. As are associations, they are inserted into the body of a model class definition; they then expand themselves behind the scenes into code that monitors your instance data as you load and save it. Again, read the following code with an eye for how the Rails framework attempts to enable code that reads like a sentence:

```
def User < ActiveRecord::Base
    validates_presence_of :user_name, :password
    validates_confirmation_of :password
    validates_uniqueness_of :user_name, :on => :create
end
```

The unique innovation in each of these scenarios is the manner in which the Rails framework presents this functionality to the user. Rails does not use configuration files stored elsewhere, or require users to create their own object-to-database mappings; instead, the Rails framework provides a mixture of automation and helper functions that appear to create a model-specific language built on top of Ruby. The end result is a programming language that understands the high-level concepts important to database work as well as it understands simple data types such as integers and strings, making you more productive as a developer and making your application more understandable as a code artifact.

Web-Specific Tasks

The Rails language extends to the view portion of your site, where Rails provides several libraries called "helpers" that semi-automate common tasks in HTML development. These functions do more than just replace HTML; they provide a buffer layer between implementation decisions on the server side and design choices on the client side. They also blur the existence of multiple languages working together: A single call to a Rails helper might result in HTML, JavaScript, and Ruby code being generated behind the scenes.

The `routes.rb` file, for instance, does more than just set up routes to match incoming requests to controllers and actions. It also sets up methods that return URLs referencing your resources and named routes. These methods can be used throughout the web application in place of hard-coded URLs to guard you against changes that may occur in these URLs. The following route definition, for example, sets up both a series of URL paths for account objects and also creates helper methods that generate URLs conforming to those paths.

```
map.resources :accounts
```

In addition to establishing several REST-based routes, this command creates methods such as `accounts_url`, `accounts_path`, `new_account_url`, and `edit_account_url` that can be used throughout the application to encode links to various account features without your ever having to worry if the physical location that idea resides at changes. (You'll learn all about REST, resources, and `map.resources` in Chapter 6.)

```
link_to 'New Account', new_account_url
```

Within the RHTML template of a particular page, helpers such as `link_to` and `form_for` provide a standard method of creating HTML structures throughout the site. The components that make a web page are often very modularized, even if we tend to think of them as long, continuous HTML documents. These helper methods hide the complexity of the HTML beneath, instead replacing it with a Ruby-based pseudo language for describing page elements.

Despite the extra processing cost (helper methods are some of the first to go when optimizing a high-traffic Rails site), using the HTML surrogate Rails provides can be a very clean way to construct your pages. The reason is that web sites are really composed of concepts, not HTML. Objects such as search results, navigation links, articles, forms, and even links, are the concept-level abstractions that our minds prefer to design with, rather than tags and attributes. The true value of these abstractions is the idea they represent rather than the HTML structure that makes the idea appear in the browser. Abstracting the HTML into a series of helpers is a way to move past the HTML and begin describing your site in terms of these concepts instead of just writing HTML. Then, when the implementation for a particular concept changes, you don't have much work to do.

The `link_to` method, for example, results in a normal `<a href="#"> link </a>` by default, but what if you needed to change the implementation beneath the concept of a link? Perhaps you are implementing an advertising system for your blog. It is essential to record which ads users click on so that you know how to bill your advertisers. In this case, the `link_to` function could be overridden so that it detects off-site URLs and links instead to a local redirector for statistic-keeping purposes, such as `/ad_redirect?adurl=urlhere`. If you used the `link_to` helper throughout your site, implementing this change is a snap and can be done without changing any of the actual links as you originally wrote them.

Other helper abstractions standardize interaction patterns between client and server. In a framework that stresses convention over configuration, such consistency is necessary to receive many of the automation benefits. The `form_for` helper is a good example. Web developers know the monotony of implementing forms; that's why so many form generators utilities are available on the web. We need to manage field labels and IDs, handle the server-side ID-to-variable mapping, prefill the form in the event of error, and highlight erroneous fields where errors occurred. Except for visual styling, all these tasks are yak shaving: auxiliary work that needs to be done to meet our real goal of acquiring some piece of data. The `form_for` helper automates much of this work:

```
<% form_for @user do |form| %>
   First name: <%= form.text_field :first_name %>
   Last name: <%= form.text_field :last_name %>
   Email: <%= form.text_field :email %>
   <%= submit_tag 'Submit' %>
<% end %>
```

This block of code results in the type of HTML code most of us would write anyway, but it automates much of the mundane tasks that we would otherwise need to implement, such as prepopulating fields with any data belonging to the `@user` object.

JavaScript

Advanced developers are unlikely to want to abstract away JavaScript entirely, but for quick and simple JavaScript tasks, Rails provides a meta-programming language called RJS that allows developers to code in Ruby and have that code translated at run-time into JavaScript. RJS lets developers treat the remote web page and its elements as if they were regular Ruby objects and provides access to any of the variables and helpers that a regular RHTML view gets.

By default, RJS hooks into the Prototype and Script.aculo.us libraries bundled with the Rails framework, but, in theory, it could be overridden to use any JavaScript framework. This shields the developer from the particulars of the JavaScript framework being used and the browser interpreting it, providing a unified, platform- and framework-agnostic JavaScript front.

Let's say you are coding a shopping list application that allows users to store lists online so that they can add to them whenever they remember a new item. The list might look something like this, with an AJAX-based form beneath it to add new items:

```
<ul id="shopping_list">
   <li>Tomatoes</li>
   <li>Garlic</li>
   <li>Mozzarella</li>
</ul>
```

If you choose to implement the AJAX request for adding a new item with the Puppet Style pattern (described in Chapter 7), the response will be a block of JavaScript for execution instead of an HTML fragment. This is exactly the type of scenario in which RJS steps in to help. RJS "templates" are a special kind of view that describes how an existing HTML document should change. For example, an RJS template that instructs the existing view to add the new shopping item to the list would be as follows:

```
page.insert_html 'bottom', 'shopping_list', content_tag('li', @new_item)
```

Say you also wanted to create a nice notification that said "Item Added" and to highlight all notifications currently on the page:

```
page[:header].insert_html :bottom, content_tag('div', "Item Added", :class =>
'notification')
page.insert_html('bottom', 'header', content_tag('div', '<p>Item Added!</p>',
:class => 'notification'))
page.select(".notification").each do |note|
  note.visual_effect :highlight
end
```

This example, along with the source code, is available from this book's companion web site at www.wrox.com or from www.artofrails.com/chapters/2/shopping_list.

Plug-Ins

To top off the Ruby on Rails framework and language, Rails provides a plug-in architecture through which to change and add to the language and framework. Rails plug-ins are different from extensions to many other frameworks in that not only is extra functionality added but also existing functionality of Rails can be completely overwritten. In Chapter 9, you will learn how to use this technique, called "monkey patching," for yourself.

Two Parts Mindset

To become a Rails developer is not just to write code that uses the Rails framework but also to enter a community of common culture and practices about web development. Learning the ground assumptions from which the technical choices by this community arise not only gives you better understanding of the community's existing code but also allows others to read and help with your code, should they need to.

In Japan, Ruby's home country, the suffix ~ *kata* is used to mean "the way of going about ~ ." Learning proper Rails-*kata* is important for two reasons: First, it will give you a better understanding of the Rails framework from a conceptual standpoint and will help you understand why certain elements of Rails have been designed as they are. Second, it will give you a set of guidelines to use when designing your own applications and Rails extensions. These guidelines will ensure that your code plays along with the Rails framework nicely, keeping the overall effort to design and code a web application to a minimum.

Web Sites Are MVC Applications

The most defining philosophical choice made in the Rails design is an abandonment of the document-centric style of web development for a strictly Model-View-Controller-based paradigm. Under the Rails view, web sites are full-blown applications, deserving of every traditional application development technique and pattern. (But as in the novel *Animal Farm*, some patterns are more equal than others, and the MVC one isn't a choice!)

The driving practice behind many (if not most) scripting language–based web applications before Rails came along was that web sites should be developed from the file system's point of view. URLs corresponded to folders in the server's file system, and the names at the end of the URLs corresponded to scripts containing code that would create the page you wanted. Rails throws this assumption away under the opinion that web sites should be developed from the developer's point of view — with abstractions and file organizations designed for the benefit of developers, not the web browser. It divorces the URL from the filesystem, instead using it to address a virtual endpoint into the application as a whole. The inner gears of the framework do the heavy lifting to ensure that the right files are still loaded at the right times.

Developing web applications with the MVC pattern has rippling effects on the way you work. It provides well-understood guidelines for how to structure your code. It enforces a breakdown of code that facilitates testing and reuse. Most of all, it brings the art of engineered design to what was once a largely free-for-all environment. In Chapters 3 and 4, you will learn more about the MVC pattern on the web and see how to design your applications around it.

Web Applications Are Ecosystems

Rails web sites are structured as ecosystems of concerns, just as operating systems are. When you dig down into the details of an operating system, you find that it is impossible to separate the code comprising the kernel from the environmental details it depends on — everything from process scheduling to memory management to file and device interaction. It can't exist on its own.

No family of operating systems demonstrates this more than the Unix lineage. The Unix family includes a large collection of operating systems, all of which implement the POSIX standards and contain roughly the same directory structure. Although these operating systems are diverse (Unix, Solaris, Linux, Mac OS X, BSD), they all implement the same ecosystem on which applications can be built and experienced. Ruby on Rails proposes such an ecosystem for web applications.

Before Rails, web application developers started from scratch with every project they built. A new PHP or Tomcat-based project would begin with an empty folder, and only the developer's ideas filled it. Many web-based utilities and web-aware methods were included in these frameworks, of course, but they were tools included by the developer in his or her file for reference. The web application was built on top of these tools, beginning with a blank slate and growing from there.

Rails applications are not built on top of Ruby on Rails; they are built within it. Ruby on Rails is a programming framework, but it is also a web-centric ecosystem for web applications. Ecosystems are different from plain-old frameworks. They are multilingual and far from agnostic. They treat problems as a heterogeneous basket of concerns ranging from functional to structural. And just as developing for the *nix ecosystem requires conformance to a particular world view of device drivers and interaction patterns, developing for the Rails ecosystem requires buying into the Rails view of development.

So a brand new and "empty" Rails project already contains 37 directories and 48 files (as of Rails 2.0.2), setting up the basic structure of the web development ecosystem and providing scripts and templates to manage it. Paying a visit to each of these different directories, one finds different types of content. Some are filled with Ruby code, some have CSS, some have schema migrations, and others have RHTML. Each cluster of tasks in the web application is implemented in the language best suited for it and kept together with its peers.

Convention over Configuration

If you look at any introduction to Rails, two overarching philosophies are always referred to: The first is MVC; the second is Convention over Configuration. One of the difficult tricks in software development, and especially framework development, is finding that sweet spot between specificity and generality. Make a framework too specific and it will never gain wide adoption, but make it too general and its users will drown under the extra work required to implement their particular task.

Web development is already a very narrowly defined task, with certain predictable characteristics and interaction patterns. Although there is some variation of the architecture from project to project (one developer may prefer HTML interfaces while another may prefer to use Flash, for instance), most characteristics of the web environment are fixed across all projects, such as:

❑   The HTTP connection separating client and server

❑   The use of a URL to reference resources within the web application

❑   Databases as a persistence layer

❑   The necessity of database schemas

❑   The presence of both static and dynamic content

❑   The use of layouts and templates

The Ruby on Rails design expresses the opinion that good web development should take advantage of the fact that the web is a predictable environment instead of erring on the side of generality. The framework should natively understand and expect the environment so that the developer doesn't need to jump through hoops wiring all the different components together every time a new component is introduced. So Ruby on Rails does not attempt to be general purpose and doesn't try to provide developers with the flexibility to create their own conventions. You must use its predefined patterns of doing things, but in return, you get a framework that automates most of your tasks for you.

A convention-based framework comes with a cost, though — you didn't design it. The use of tabs versus spaces, curly braces verses do-end blocks, `CamelCase` versus `underscore_separated`, pluralized table names and collections — means that some of the choices are bound to be outside your tastes. But a tool's primary purpose is to be useful, not pretty, and a tool well used becomes beautiful in the hands of the craftsman no matter the paint job. By standardizing the way to organize and write code, the need for custom infrastructure can be dramatically reduced, and that can be a beautiful thing. This is the gamble of convention over configuration.

A Little Assumption Goes a Long Way

A framework based on strong conventions can cut a lot of the fat out of your code, but it can go only so far. At some point, decisions need to be application specific. So although a Rails convention might be that all document templates must reside in the `app/views` directory, you still need to tell your app which of those templates to load.

That doesn't mean that the framework can't guess, though. It just won't be right all the time. For situations when a guess has a reasonable chance at being right, it makes sense to build that guess into the environment as an assumption. Without any explicit direction from the developer, the framework will assume that its guess was right and follow this default case, but the developer always has the option to override the base case with custom behavior. Call it a relaxed convention.

It turns out that our languages and frameworks have been assuming things about our intentions for a long time:

❑   White space is the default delimiter for many types of inputs.

❑   Programs return an "everything OK" exit code unless otherwise instructed.

❑   Graphical programs render their windows on the primary monitor by default in a multihead display.

❑   In Java, a class variable with no modifiers is assumed to be package private.

The list goes on and on. All these are reasonable assumptions made to reduce the amount of code developers must write, but each of them can be overridden when they don't fit. Given the fact that the Web is such a predictable place, there should be a rich new set of assumptions that can be made to speed development and add a bit of default behavior as a starting board.

When new Rails users view the famous "Creating a Weblog in 15 Minutes" screencast, the initial reaction of many is suspicion at the "magic" taking place to allow the application to be constructed so quickly. The suspicion only grows when features such as scaffolding are encountered. In reality, this magic is just a base set of assumptions that the Rails framework will make in the absence of explicit direction. Because the assumptions are correct most of the time, they can be left as implicit by the developer, but in most real-life circumstances, a bit more coding will be needed.

Following are some of the assumptions Rails makes about web development and how these translate into code:

❑   **A controller action should render a view of the same name.** A web user's request URL is translated into an action that gets called on one of your application's controllers. Nearly all web requests are met with a response, so it is assumed that the action will render the view located at `app/views/{controller}/{action}.rhtml` if it exists. If that file does not exist, or if you want the action to render some other file, you must manually call the `render` function from within your action.

❑   **A controller renders views with a layout of the same name.** When rendering a view, Rails looks for the file `app/views/layouts/{controller}.rhtml`. If it finds it, then it applies that layout to whatever RHTML template is being rendered unless it is explicitly told not to.

❑   **Database tables represent objects, and their fields represent object properties.** Active-Record assumes that database tables in a web application generally represent an object that the program is interested in. Fields on this table (such as `first_name` and `last_name` for a table about people) then represent the interesting things we might want to store about that object. As a result, ActiveRecord automatically generates getters and setters for all fields on a table that is associated with a model object in Rails. You can override these functions, of course, but they are there for you automatically as a base condition.

These are just three of the ways in which Rails assumes things to reduce the amount of code that needs to be written. In many ways, it is the 80/20 approach to framework development: Satisfy the needs of 80 percent of the users while acknowledging that the other 20 percent may need to put in a bit of extra work. But in this case, the extra work put in by that other 20 percent isn't any more than they would have had to do anyway with a generalized framework that assumes nothing about you.

Aesthetics Matter

A co-worker once told me that whenever he came into my office, I was always grimacing at the computer screen. I replied that coding in Java made me feel like a participant in *American Gladiator*, always dodging one surprise from the JRE after the next. But his comment got me thinking. We developers spend so much of our day in front of computers — it can't be good to always be frowning at them. So, strange as it may sound, I resolved from that day on to smile at my computer whenever I remembered, and especially when under attack from the JRE. But a programming language shouldn't frustrate us in the first place — instead, it should be a pleasure to use.

In an interview for *Professional Rich Internet Applications: AJAX and Beyond* (Wrox), David Heinemeier Hansson describes Ruby as follows:

> Ruby is a language for writing beautiful code. Beautiful code is code that makes the developer happy, and when a developer is happy, they are more productive. Ruby is unique in the way it lets you express something briefly, succinctly, and beautifully.

Developers can quickly see that many of the design decisions in the Rails framework were made as much for aesthetic reasons as for technical ones. This aesthetic is reflected throughout the Rails community, which has drawn to it individuals across the Web who share a belief in its importance. As a result, the Rails community is known for being particularly obsessive about issues that have nothing to do with the run-time workings of an application but everything to do with the developer experience.

The debate over pluralization is one of the most well-known examples of such issues. From its start, the Rails framework has included a pluralization engine so that its pseudo-language can enforce proper pluralization of the English language. You might state that a `User` object `has_one :address` but that it `has_many :photos`. The model name for a user in your application will probably be `User`, but Rails will pluralize this and expect the database table to be named `users`. Heinemeier Hansson discusses the debate in an interview with technologist Scott Hanselman:

> We actually had a very interesting debate at one point on how to pluralize "octopus." We actually have that now — there is a special rule just for Octopus and Octopi. [So if I have an octopus model] it will look for an Octopi table.

> People say, wouldn't it just be easier if you have "person" and "person?" There wouldn't be any translation, there wouldn't be this big scheme for pluralization. . .but we made a point that we prefer those aesthetics. My collections are plural, so my tables should be plural, too. So we went through all this effort just to make the point that aesthetics matter.

Of course, aesthetics are subjective, and this is where critics of the Rails framework have the loudest complaints. It might not be for you, but if it is, take time to understand the attention paid to developer experience in the design of the Rails language and try to incorporate this into your code. Although your web site may ultimately end up functioning the same as it would have otherwise, your code-base will have you smiling the whole way.

Restraint Can Be Liberating

As you've seen already, the Rails framework forces a lot of opinions upon its users. Rails developers have no choice but to participate in MVC-guided design, use certain predefined naming conventions, and place their code in pre-prescribed folders. Convention is the overarching belief driving this dictatorial environment, but a more subtle driving attitude is the value of restraint. Convention attempts to relieve the developers of having to perform the same type of work over and over again. Restraints combat the need to spend your time worrying about issues that probably don't matter anyway. (And those issues that do matter are outsourced as decisions to third-parties such as the Rails Core team to think about as a full-time job.)

Getting Things Done: The Art of Stress-Free Productivity, by David Allen, has become something of a cult classic in the web developer world. The book promises to teach readers how to manage the torrent of tasks and concerns of the modern lifestyle in a stress-free way. One of the primary revelations of this book is the immense toll that ''having things on one's mind'' takes on our ability to think. When we are constantly trying to remember who we are meeting tomorrow for lunch, when and where, and what needs to be done to finish our project proposal, our brains are unable to devote their full attention to any one particular task. The result is stress and a cluttered mind. Part of Allen's solution is to keep a trusted location where we dump our mental to-do lists without fail so that we can let go of them inside our heads and clear our mind to focus on only what is in front of us. Proponents of meditation might give a nod of recognition to this sentiment.

Restraining the process of web development to one fixed way of doing things is certainly extreme, but it allows us to forget all the structural details of web development and focus on only our application. So the many Rails restraints, such as having one fixed directory structure, one pattern of code organization, one fixed request/response pipeline, and one method of accessing database data, are all tools to remove an unexpected burden from the developer: *choice*. In an ideal world, the only choices left for the web developer would be the application-specific ones, because those are the important and exciting ones, anyway. Everything else is left to the worries of the framework designers.

As a non-Rails example of how restraint can be harnessed as a tool, read Google's MapReduce paper, available at `http://labs.google.com/papers/mapreduce.html`. Google employees Jeffrey Dean and Sanjay Ghemawat realized one day that many of the processes governing Google's calculations seemed to follow a similar basic pattern, which they dubbed the ''Map-Reduce'' pattern, consisting of two basic operations:

❑   `map(key1, value1) - > list(key2, value2)`
❑   `reduce(key2, list(value2)) - > list(value2)`

By creating an entire distributed computing architecture around this pattern, they reasoned, employees could focus on the particular details of their problem and completely forget about the details of the distributed architecture on which Google runs. Maybe 70 percent of the code could be ported to the Map and Reduce steps without any change, and the other 30 percent of the programmers would just need to be a little more creative to make it work, the thinking went.

The plan worked. The two internally released the distributed MapReduce architecture and a set of APIs that allowed employees to use it. Compared to the anything-goes freedom of normal programming that we are all used to, MapReduce is amazingly restrictive. All problems must be described as a series of Map and Reduce steps (with a few extra possibilities). But the restraints of this framework created an environment in which development could thrive. It exported the task of managing and processing data to a team dedicated to just that task, and it freed developers to spend more time thinking about their application-specific problems and less time about how to implement them. The result, as Dean and Ghemawat write, was that:

> The indexing code is simpler, smaller, and easier to understand, because the code that deals with fault tolerance, distribution, and parallelization is hidden within the MapReduce library. For example, the size of one phase of the computation dropped from approximately 3800 lines of C++ code to approximately 700 lines when expressed using MapReduce.
>
> . . .We have learned several things from this work. First, restricting the programming model makes it easy to parallelize and distribute computations and to make such computations fault-tolerant.

When properly applied, restraint is a valuable development tool. At the sacrifice of choice, it provides fixed structures on which to lean and depend and the prospect of a highly-predictable process that can be maintained and optimized by a dedicated third party. Most of all, it provides a grounding stability that permits the web developer to spend his or her time making important design choices about web applications rather than design choices about the development environment.

You Repeat Yourself Too Much

We all know the feeling of "I've already typed something like this before. . .I should put a note here to refactor it out when I have time." Often, the refactoring never happens, and our code ends up full of statements like the following:

```
// TODO: Can we pull this routine out into some separate class?
```

Code repetition is plain-and-simple bad programming, and it should be avoided whenever possible. It hinders the ability to maintain consistency in large programs and hurts your chances of being able to change your program without great effort. Two scenarios frequently cause code repetition:

❑   Some entity must occur in several different places, but it isn't easy to abstract this idea into a class of its own.

❑   A small fragment of functionality, useless by itself, must be applied to many different objects and situations. This situation is one of the primary motivations for aspect-oriented programming (AOP), a style of programming in which the implementation of cross-cutting concerns can be separated from the locations to which they are applied.

Rails provides solutions for both situations in the places where they most often occur in web development.

Repeated Objects

Repeated objects are addressed both with Rails' model design and view design. ActiveRecord models generated by the script/generate command eliminate the need for SQL from within your web application. SQL statements are a particularly sneaky form of code duplication in web applications because inline SQL is so accepted in interpreted frameworks. In reality, using SQL is dangerous because every SQL statement you make encodes assumptions about your database schema, which may change. By using ActiveRecord model objects to access and save your data, and by extending them to encapsulate any advanced functionality you need, you avoid the need to repeat assumptions about your schema structure throughout your application.

When implementing view code, developers are encouraged to split up different components of a view into partials, small fragments of preprocessed code that atomically express a single concept, such as a form or a list item. Although partials are not objects in the "object oriented" sense of the word, they go a long way toward preventing copy-and-paste style coding within your HTML. Think of them as the Rails equivalent of light-weight UI widgets.

Code duplication is also battled in the view front with helpers, the small libraries that define methods such as link_to to assist view code to concisely express itself. In addition to the many helpers provided by Rails, you can add your own in the app/helpers directory. Consider this popular method of creating rounded corners around a div element. This technique has many variations; the one that follows is the popular "Nifty Corners" by Alessandro Fulciniti:

```
<div>
    <b class="rtop">
        <b class="r1"></b><b class="r2"></b>
        <b class="r3"></b><b class="r4"></b>
    </b>
        <!--content goes here -->
    <b class="rbottom">
        <b class="r4"></b><b class="r3"></b>
        <b class="r2"></b><b class="r1"></b>
    </b>
</div>
```

Combined with a bit of CSS styling, this HTML structure creates nice, image-free curves for your UI. But manually coding this HTML fragment every time you want rounded corners would lock your site into this particular style and implementation. Instead, use a helper:

```
def rounded_corners(&proc)
    raise ArgumentError, "Missing block" unless block_given?
    opening = '<div><b class="rtop"><b class="r1"></b><b class="r2"></b>'
    opening << '<b class="r3"></b><b class="r4"></b></b>'
    concat(opening, proc.binding)
    yield
    closing = '<b class="rbottom"><b class="r4"></b><b class="r3"></b>'
    closing << '<b class="r2"></b><b class="r1"></b></b></div>'
    concat (closing, proc.binding)
end
```

Then, each time you need a rounded box, simply use the following:

```
<% rounded_corners do %>
<h1>Great Scott!</h1>
<p>This is a box with rounded corners!</p>
<% end %>
```

Repeated Behaviors and Processes

Rails also provides AOP-style hooks in which to connect cross-cutting functionality that may apply to several points in a program. Filters are bits of code that can be applied before, after, or around a controller's execution to change the way in which it occurs. Many controllers and actions, for example, need to verify that a user is logged in before they can perform their function, both for security reasons and for the sake of user-specific content. These operations can be defined in a private method on the ApplicationController, the base class for all other controllers in your application, and then applied as filters to any particular controllers that need them.

The cross-cutting concern of validating that a user is logged in, for example, might be implemented as follows:

```
def check_authentication
   unless session[:user]
      session[:requested_uri] = request.env["REQUEST_URI"]
      redirect_to signin_url
   else
      @me = User.find(session(:user))
   end
end
```

This code will check for a session variable called user that contains the signed-in user's ID. If it finds it, then it loads the corresponding user object in the database into the variable @me. If it doesn't find it, then it records the URL of the attempted page and redirects the user to the sign-in page.

This functionality may be applied to any controller as a filter with the before_filter command, resulting in code that looks like this:

```
class AssetController < ApplicationController
  before_filter :check_authorization
end
```

In this way, the authorization behavior is kept as a separate concern, relieving the need to copy and paste it throughout the project and keeping the code in your controllers free of housekeeping code auxiliary to their main purpose.

Testing Isn't a Choice

Testing isn't a very common practice in the web development world, but Ruby on Rails presents the argument that it should be. The Rails team feels so strongly about the testing issue that you aren't even given the choice of whether to write tests. Each time you generate a model or controller, a test class for that object is automatically generated for you. You may choose not to implement anything within that test container, but it is there for you.

The rarity of automated testing in the web development world is not surprising given the way most web application architectures are organized. The document-first model of programming leaves the different concerns of a web application so intertwined that it is difficult to isolate any one of them and evaluate its performance. A single file may contain authorization code, a form processing routine, SQL statements to insert new data into the database, and HTML to display the various possible outcomes of the form processing.

On top of the intertwining of concerns, testers must deal with the pesky issue of HTTP. Web applications are experienced over an HTTP connection, not directly, so a proper test must take this connection into account. The level of effort required quickly expands here. The remote connection isn't just an issue of HTTP but also one of sessions. Some tests may be possible only as the interactions occur over time between multiple users on a site. Each test user must have its own data in the database and authenticated sessions during testing, so the tester must build sample data and session support into the framework. All these characteristics unequivocally lead to the conclusion that testing a web app is a hard, hard thing to do.

Despite the seeming impossibility of testing web applications, there is no environment in which testing is more crucial. The web is an interpreted programming environment to the extreme. Not only are many of the popular web development languages interpreted, late-bound, and dynamically typed, but the output of these languages is just input to yet another interpreter — the web browser! Although your PHP or Ruby environment is controlled and predictable, the web browser interpreting your data isn't, and many web developers have bonded over the shared experiences of trying to manage the quirks and eccentricities of each particular browser.

Using such a language, a developer has no way to verify whether a piece of code will function correctly other than by trying it. Testing is nothing more than automating the trial process. Because it is the only miner's canary available to you by dynamic languages such as PHP and Ruby, you cannot afford not to make extensive use of it.

The Ruby on Rails framework contains a mature testing library that addresses the complications of testing web applications and hides as many of them as possible from the test writer. This library manages everything from seed data (called fixtures) to session handling within tests, and the Model-View-Controller division of Rails code paves the way for componentized testing. With this library, test developers are able to concentrate on the content of their tests rather than on the complications of testing over an HTTP connection. Chapter 12 covers a type of test-based development called Behavior-Driven Development that provides a novel way to frame both the testing and development activities for a Rails project.

The Web Is a Set of Resources, Not Services

Two predominant styles of web services exist in the wild today: Web Services and RESTful Services. Web Services, with a capital W and S, often refers to the WS-* series of specifications working their way through the W3C and sponsored by the big names in business such as Microsoft, Hewlett Packard, and IBM. This is where you find SOAP and WSDL, two very capable albeit heavy-handed technologies that work together to provide language-independent remote objects. REST, or Representational State Transfer, represents the other end of the spectrum. Born out of a doctoral dissertation in 2000 by Roy Fielding, REST in practical use refers to a style of design organized around the viewing and editing remote resources rather than calling remote services. REST services do not attempt to provide remote objects, but rather manage the transfer of object state over HTTP.

Both the WS-* collection of Web Services specifications and REST style of services provide a powerful ability to decouple components of an application across the network. However, although these two schools sit alongside each other as complementary implementation strategies, they belong to fundamentally different views of the direction in which web development should head, as illustrated in Figure 2-3.

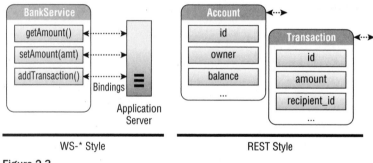

WS-* Style   REST Style

Figure 2-3

The WS-* family of technologies tends to represent a world in which servers host *capabilities*, such as purchasing a book, sending an e-mail, or performing a credit check. Each of these capabilities has certain data type requirements, which are highly specified, and if these are met, then that service can perform whatever it was you needed accomplished. Throughout the process, the client interacts with a remote address that represents the service.

The REST view of the web represents the web as a set of *resources*. This view preserves the momentum of the initial vision of the web as a collection of interlinked documents, except it expands the definition of documents to include any structured resource. So a bookstore provides books, an ISP publishes e-mail accounts and e-mail messages, and a bank provides transactions, credits, and debits. The key difference is that REST is a world consisting almost entirely of nouns, but Web Services are full of verbs.

REST isn't the end-all of design patterns, but it can be a particularly useful one for web applications. Chapter 6 takes a closer look at RESTful web development and how to use this pattern in your designs.

Summary

So, there you have it: one part framework, one part language, and two parts state of mind. At first glance, Rails is a development framework. It contains a set of scripts to create and manage web application projects and a routing pipeline to handle requests and responses from the application you create. Three separate frameworks provide well-integrated support for all the tasks common to web development, from parsing request parameters to managing database schemas and applying layouts.

At a closer look, Rails appears as its own domain-specific programming language, too. It uses several capabilities of the Ruby programming language to expose its APIs as if they were native language keywords, and it uses the names of your objects and files to assume things about your intentions and automate common tasks.

Finally, as your experience with Rails grows, you will see that Rails is also a collection of beliefs about web development and the way web applications should be designed. Not all these beliefs are unique to the Rails community, but nowhere do they all intersect and materialize into code as they do in Ruby on Rails. In this light, Ruby on Rails is an excellent framework to master to learn about the cutting edge of web design in general.

No Silver Bullet

In 1986, Frederick Brooks published his now-famous essay, "Essence and Accidents of Software Engineering." In it, he argues that there will never be a single innovation that suddenly removes the work and risk from programming. It opens as follows:

> Of all the monsters that fill the nightmares of our folklore, none terrify more than werewolves, because they transform unexpectedly from the familiar into horrors. For these, one seeks bullets of silver that can magically lay them to rest. . . .
>
> So we hear desperate cries for a silver bullet — something to make software costs drop as rapidly as computer hardware costs do. But, as we look to the horizon of a decade hence, we see no silver bullet. There is no single development, in either technology or in management technique, that by itself promises even one order-of-magnitude improvement in productivity, in reliability, in simplicity.
>
> Skepticism is not pessimism, however. Although we see no startling break-throughs — and indeed, I believe such to be inconsistent with the nature of software — many encouraging innovations are under way. A disciplined, consistent effort to develop, propagate, and exploit these innovations should indeed yield an order-of-magnitude improvement. There is no royal road, but there is a road.

Rails is no royal road, but it is a good road, with a highly evolved philosophy on web application design. This is why, as a developer, learning which parts of the Rails philosophy work well and why they work is just as important to your long-term success as learning the details of writing Rails-based sites in the near term. As the Web changes, so will the abstractions needed to program for it. The long-term lessons that Rails teaches us are not exclusive to Ruby on Rails, and they are portable to whatever great framework comes next.

Optimize Your Coding Before You Optimize Your Code

As you read the rest of this book and practice its ideas, stay focused on optimizing the way you write code, not the performance of the code itself. In other words, in this new era of web applications, good design is far more important than good performance. CPU cycles get cheaper by the day, but, as Frederick Brooks observes, the task of programming will always be one of time and effort. Our goals in choosing a language and designing abstractions, therefore, should aim to improve our experience and effectiveness as programmers.

With a good framework and well-designed abstractions, developer output soars. You can write a minimal amount of code to express even complex concepts. You aren't burdened by build issues and configuration problems, and, it is hoped, your environment is aesthetically pleasing, driving you to strive for good aesthetics in your own designs and to make your code stand the test of time. If all these conditions are present, odds are high that you will create a well-designed application that can easily be changed and improved over time to achieve your goals.

If you run into performance problems, take it as a sign of success — it means that there is a growing demand for your application. You'll need to work to keep up with that success, of course, but you will have already won the hardest battle, and that battle is won with quality design. Dealing with success on the Web only builds on the application that you've already designed:

❑ **You can always optimize the little stuff.** Identify the parts of your application that impose the highest performance penalty, whether because they are computationally intensive or because they occur many times. Rework these parts to run more efficiently by writing them in a lower-level language or reconfiguring the way they are executed.

❑ **You can always parallelize the big stuff.** The web architecture is the ultimate parallelizable environment, and a whole industry of specialized hardware exists to take the elements of a web site and distribute its work across clusters. Ruby on Rails even has growing built-in support for these types of setups, so when you are ready to scale, Rails is ready to scale with you.

The rest of this book will help you gain a deeper understanding of all three of Rails' faces: a framework, a language, and a way to think about application design. Some of the topics addressed are Rails specific; others are relevant to anyone writing a web application. Some are about modifying the Rails framework itself, whereas others are strictly about the code that goes into your web pages. In all topics, try to understand how you can optimize your design and coding practices to get the most out of the code that you write.

The Server as an Application

W. Web boarded a bus heading into the city from the Rails compound. It had been a long orientation week. He wasn't sure whether he was ready to shave his head as the rest of them had, but he liked a lot of what he had heard.

Web was on his first trip for the group — a rally down in the Big City. It would be interesting, for sure. He squeezed through the crowd to find a seat near the middle, right next to a tall man with a buzz cut who happened to be named Rick.

Rick was riding the bus home from work. He had the reverse commute, living in the city but working out in the country. It was an unusually crowded day for a Tuesday — people of all destinations packed together, muffled music seeping from earphones, blank stares emanating from tired faces. Rick inched sideways to create more room as a man wearing a papier-mâché globe around his body struggled to fit into the center-facing seat next to him.

As the bus pulled away from its next stop on the city's edge, one last passenger, dirty and tattered, pushed his way onto the bus.

"Move it!" he shouted gruffly as he pushed a small boy and his mother out of the way, the smell of liquor on his breath.

Rick had just received his black belt in Karate and was not about to watch this man bully a child and his mom. To be honest, he was a little excited at the chance to put his hard-earned skills to use. Rick rose from his seat, chest out like a Marine's, and moved swiftly down the bus toward the offender. His every move signaled confrontation.

"Hey!" a voice rang out toward the disheveled man.

But the voice was not Rick's. It was that of an old woman observing the situation from the rear of the bus. The old woman smiled warmly, leaning at an angle to see through the crowd.

Chapter 3: The Server as an Application

"Young man, I have a seat for you right here!" she shouted up to the front of the bus, patting an empty seat next to her.

The man paused, his eyes darting back and forth, and then he made up his mind. He tromped his way unsteadily past Rick to the back of the bus and sat down next to the old woman. "Aren't you glad spring is finally here?" the elder asked with excitement in her voice. "I'm on the way home to garden with my husband. You should see how happy he is when he gardens, and the hydrangeas are just about to bloom!"

The man wrinkled his face, blinking, and his lips began to quiver. Within seconds, a tear had broken free and began to roll slowly down his cheek.

"I was a husband once, and my wife gardened with me every spring," he managed to stammer. "I lost my job last year, and then lost everything."

The old woman patted his shoulder, a small gesture to acknowledge his grief. And as the two talked and the story unfolded, the rest of the bus silently listened in, faces softening with compassion.

At the next stop, W. Web watched curiously as Rick stepped off the bus. Five minutes and two miles ago, the stranger sitting next to him had been ready for a fight, but the man getting off the bus was different, with all the look of someone contemplating the hard blows life can deliver.

   — Story adapted from Steve Hagen

Whoa. W. Web's adventures are getting a bit heavy for a technical book, and this is only Chapter 3. But his bus ride brings up an important point: Our assumptions and expectations play a powerful role in how we think about and experience the world and the ways in which our plans for action unfold. Two men on the bus experienced the same event with two different ground assumptions about the world. The situations that manifested for the two were entirely different as a result.

Software design and development follow this same pattern. At the beginning of a development project, before any design is laid down on paper, we have already made several important choices even if we don't realize we have made them. These choices — that is, our assumptions about the way that software should be developed — shape the direction of the design and development process.

When programmers make these choices deliberately, we call them abstractions. Many people think of programming abstractions as class definitions that encapsulate some piece of functionality, but classes and objects are just the actors in your play. Abstractions also determine the rules of the game, all the way from turning voltage into binary logic to allowing memory allocation and database access. Abstractions encompass every environmental detail we have constructed to help us write computer programs.

It isn't surprising, then, that choosing the right programming abstractions is perhaps the most important and influential step in the software development process. It should always be done intentionally instead of left to our unconscious assumptions. Good developers don't write more code than poor ones; they paint better abstractions so that each line of code they write is more meaningful.

This chapter examines the basic abstraction that defines Ruby on Rails more than any other: that a web site is actually a Model-View-Controller (MVC) application.

This choice seems innocuous at first, but as any script-turned-Rails developer will tell you, it has far-reaching effects on the way you design and develop your code. This chapter takes a quick, light-weight look at what the Model-View-Controller paradigm is and why it aligns with the Web so well. I also cover some project design and refactoring strategies to help you on your way toward MVC-grounded design.

Model-View-Controller: The Abbreviated Version

The Model-View-Controller pattern is one of the most well-known and broadly applied design patterns in software engineering. This pattern is used in applications that are information and usercentric. These applications store bits of information that users want, and they provide users with access to that information through a user interface. The MVC pattern guides the way this type of application's functionality is organized based on the observation that all such applications are composed of three fundamental parts:

- ❏ **The Model:** The objects that represent and encapsulate the fundamental "things" that your application is all about
- ❏ **The View:** The code that your application uses to interact with the user
- ❏ **The Controller:** The code that performs operations on the model, such as finding particular model instances or changing a piece of data

Inherent in this organization of a piece of software is the dependency graph of these components. Keeping the components free from bad dependence on each other is just as important as knowing which parts of your program's functionality to place in each. Figure 3-1 shows the idealized dependency graph.

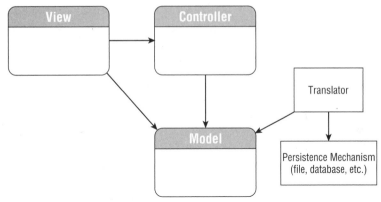

Figure 3-1

This graph states:

- ❏ The model depends on nothing else in your application.
- ❏ Persistence is accomplished with a translator that understands both the model and the persistence mechanism.
- ❏ The controller and view depend on and use the model.
- ❏ The view depends on the controller, makes calls into it, and displays the results.

In practice, especially in the web world, it is a bit harder to determine exactly what depends on what. The model standing on its own without any dependency on the view or controller is the one part of this design that generally remains true in any MVC implementation. The relationship between the view and controller is a bit more complex and largely depends on the way you choose to write your application and the environment it is built in.

Although MVC isn't the only way to organize a program, it is a proven and consistent methodology that makes software easier to write and safer to maintain. Users of J2EE and Java Swing, for example, will be right at home with these benefits, because Sun has been a strong supporter of the pattern in its technologies. Designing software components on top of the MVC abstraction leads to a natural modularity that makes future programming tasks fall into place with little effort:

❑　Do want to support saving and loading application data to and from a file? Just implement a translator for your model layer that writes to files.

❑　Do you need to implement a command-line interface? Just reuse the model and controller without the view.

❑　Do you want to create a demo for a trade show? Use the view and controller with a mock model behind it.

❑　Need to turn your application into a networked service? Replace the view with service bindings.

These scenarios are all straightforward decisions when software has been split along the three boundaries of model, view, and controller.

In addition to providing abstractions on which to build your software, the MVC division of labor also encourages developer specialization within a multideveloper project. The types and styles of programming used to perform UI tasks, data tasks, and business logic tasks can be very different. In the Java world, it might be the difference between specializing in the Swing framework or learning to be an expert in Hibernate. In web programming, these different tasks even use different languages. An MVC approach to software design makes it easy to determine which developers are right for implementing which pieces of code because it aligns with the programming specialties that already exist.

As with many good ideas in life, the code concept of MVC is short and sweet: a breakdown of roles that describes a broad range of applications very well. The next step is to understand why the MVC idea is such a great fit for the Web and how you can use it effectively in your web application designs.

MVC and the Web

The MVC programming abstraction that Ruby on Rails employs fits particularly well into the Web because the physical architecture of the Web is already MVC in everything but name. Regardless of whether you are implementing Code-First applications out of the /cgi-bin directory or Document-First applications with files such as index.php, you are working on top of a fundamentally MVC-biased architecture without even knowing it.

Here's why: Web applications, by definition, are separated into client and server. The client browser requests and displays pages of information to the user (the view) and turns the user's actions into requests back to the server. On the server side, some piece of code receives the web request and decides what to do (the controller). This almost always involves performing database operations (the model) and then generating a web page to send back to the user (the view again). In light of the physical architecture on which web applications operate, it seems almost inevitable that MVC-style programming would find its way to the Web. The two are a star-crossed match. These three components of every web application — the database, the client, and the server — present a division of concerns that tracks almost exactly to the Model-View-Controller paradigm.

Also unique to programming for the Web is its multilingual nature, which aligns nicely with the division of MVC components. In traditional desktop graphical user interface (GUI) applications, MVC is just a way to organize code; all the components usually still use the same programming language. On the Web, the Model, View, and Controller each use a mix of domain-specific languages to achieve their goals. The result is more languages for developers to learn, but much less clutter and effort required to express oneself when developing, because each component is written in a language designed specifically for that purpose.

The following table shows the Model-View-Controller architecture breakdown as applied to the Web.

	Model	View	Controller
What	The objects representing the domain of the web application. These objects encapsulate tables in a database.	The set of HTML templates, CSS styles, and JavaScript code that creates the user experience on a web site.	The code that accepts web requests, manipulates the model, and renders a view to send back to the user.
Example	User Post Comment Auction Photo	A user's profile page A blog article An "add comment" form An auction detail page A photo thumbnail	An account controller to manage sign-ups, sign-ins, and lost passwords.
Language	Ruby/PHP/Java/etc. for object representation SQL for object persistence	HTML, CSS, JavaScript	Ruby/PHP/Java/etc.

This breakdown shows all the components necessary for a complete application, from data to display. The fact that it is distributed across many machines and implemented over a client-server architecture is largely an unimportant detail that you don't need to focus on until you're ready to make the transition from development to deployment.

Notice, too, the difference between thinking of a web application as consisting of "pages" and as consisting of "views." Views are not just pages. More accurately, they represent the rendering of a particular concept within your application. The bits of code stored in each view object could be as small as an image thumbnail or as large as a full web page. (When the view is small and meant only to be composed into larger views, we call it a *partial*.) Page-sized views wrap around one or more smaller object-level views (partials) and contain the scaffolding necessary to apply the right style sheets and load the right JavaScript files.

There is another difference between MVC views and the documents that make up the view of document-first code. Although the contents of your Rails views are implemented in document-first fashion, having the ability to contain embedded Ruby code, the informal contract is that this code is allowed to make decisions related only to display. No model operations, disk access, authorization decisions, or session management should be done from within the view. Technically, any operation possible in the Ruby language can be performed embedded in a view, but write this out of your mind as a possibility. Views exist only to display information and solicit input.

The argument for MVC-guided design on the Web is largely the observation that it seems to fit the underlying architecture of the Web very well. Developing with this underlying MVC architecture in mind is the hybrid approach that is beginning to change the way web applications are designed and written. So, how do you design such an application?

The MVC Design Process

You've got an idea, a blank piece of paper, and a pencil, and you are ready to begin designing your web application. (You do design before you code, right?) No two people agree about the best order or strategy for finding and identifying the right M, V, and C. In reality, the different components of a design emerge in parallel in your subconscious and float up to the surface somewhat randomly. With that admission, here is a design-time workflow that many use and find effective.

1. **Pregame warm-up.** Sit back, clear your mind, and think about the goals of your application. Then visualize yourself in the shoes of one of your users. Run through a few tasks with your application. Encounter a problem. Add some new data. This will get you into the mindset of thinking about the components that need to fall into place to make your application run.

2. **The model.** Identify the fundamental "things" that your application will deal with. These are your model objects. These do not need to correspond directly to tables in a database, but they likely will. Also, don't worry about the properties on these objects just yet, although do start thinking about the relationships between them.

3. **The static HTML prototype.** After you've found the muse driving you to create this application and thought about it enough to identify the fundamental model objects that comprise its functionality, take a step back to the user's perspective and plan specifically how the user's needs drive him or her to interact with those objects. Develop a series of static, CSS-backed HTML pages that could be used in a pinch to show the site concept to another person. This prototype will inspire and drive the rest of your server-side development.

4. **The controllers.** Using the static HTML prototype as a guide, think about the main feature areas of your application. Each one of these areas becomes a controller, containing all the entry points and business logic necessary to address that area.

5. **The actions.** For each controller, think about the actions that users will need to perform. In Ruby on Rails, each action corresponds to a public method on the controller. Some actions correspond to web pages, but others simply perform a function and redirect a user to some other page based on the result. In general, actions that don't create or modify data should have associated RHTML files, and actions that do create or modify data should just redirect or render the views of other actions. This rule of thumb helps minimize code duplication and the overall amount of HTML code that needs to be written.

6. **The icing.** Not every page on your site is dynamic or interactive. These static pages, usually with names like "About" or "Contact," or even your main index page, can get left behind by the preceding development steps. Fill in the gaps in your views by listing all the pages that don't correspond to actions on a controller.

Follow these steps and you will create a blueprint to guide your coding. This design step can be done completely independently of your HTML design and development because it concerns the organization of your web application code rather than the details of its presentation.

The View Is Your Spec

In traditional application programming, the coding usually begins by creating Unified Modeling Language (UML) diagrams, designing class interfaces, or by creating the data model. Web programming offers a somewhat different possibility, though, that seems backward from the standpoint of traditional application development but can be used with great success: Build your application interface to completion before you start coding.

As domain-specific languages, HTML and CSS are amazingly efficient at what they do. A good web developer should know how to create complex pages with HTML and CSS manually, and when you gain proficiency in them it can be a lot of fun, too. So why spend time writing stuffy documents about how your application should work when you can simply define it functionally in the very same languages that will be used to implement your application?

When your specification comes in the form of the actual HTML interface to your application, there is little ambiguity as to what needs to be implemented on the server side to support the interface. Each server-side development task should be directed at enabling the dynamic functionality of one element of your static HTML spec. Piece by piece, the spec will come alive in your real application.

Using your view as the specification in traditional application development is difficult because it requires the developer to write stubs and mock objects to stand in for the controllers and models that provide the necessary flow to make the view possible. At the level of the HTML page, the web application is divorced from these concerns, and this can become a great benefit for these purposes. What would have been mock controllers and model-provided data are just plain strings in the HTML page, meaning that view development can take place entirely without having to worry about coding stand-ins for these objects. When it comes time to integrate the sample view with the real code, just replace the dummy data with calls into the variables and methods of the running model objects as though you were doing a fill-in-the-blanks exercise.

Another reason that the HTML-first approach can be a good one is that web applications are the ultimate in user-focused development. Until you have an interface to expose them, few of your coding accomplishments matter. When developers start coding with the models and controllers, they have a tendency to begin redesigning and optimizing the application before they even have an interface for it. Starting up front with the interface emphasizes this fact and prevents you from falling into the common trap of cyclically tweaking your design without making real progress that the user can see.

Example: Social Networking for Cooks

Consider the example of a social networking site for cooking enthusiasts, something akin to OpenSource-Food.com. In this example, the goal is to allow users to share and discuss their recipes and food photos, as well as to record their favorite chefs and interests on the site.

Here is how the five MVC-guided design steps described previously might be applied, starting with Step 1 — the warm-up.

Visualizing a Run-Through

Ah, your new Shrimp Scaloppini recipe. How would you add it? You'd want others to be able to search for recipes including shrimp, which means it might be a good idea to line-item the ingredients. And users should definitely be able to rate and add comments to your recipe, so you need to have a facility for that. Each recipe should also have a picture that makes everyone's stomach growl, of course. Okay, enough visualizing — time for the design.

The Model

What are the "things" needed to make this application work? User objects, definitely, and recipes, of course. The instances of these two primary objects will also own a number of other objects: photos, ratings, and so on. The following table lists some of these model objects.

Model Object	Purpose
User	Contains basic information about the user.
Profile	Contains a user's interests, favorite cuisines, and thoughts on cooking.
Favorite	Stores bookmarks to a user's favorite recipes and chefs on the site.
Recipe	Owned by a user. Contains the instructions for preparing a dish.
Ingredient	Owned by a recipe. Contains one ingredient and the amount for that recipe.
Photo	Owned by a recipe. Contains a photo with a caption for that recipe.
Rating	Stores a user's rating for a particular recipe.
Comment	Stores a comment about a recipe.

Each of these model objects is created with the `script/generate model` command, which creates both the model and an empty schema migration for you to fill in (more about these in Chapter 11, "How I Learned to Stop Worrying and Love the Schema"). `ActiveRecord` (the library that handles your model objects) will take care of all the SQL details as long as you write down the required fields in the migration and the relationships and validations for each in the model.

Most of the objects in this example are tangible, but it is important to remember that the model also contains "relationship objects" that record the existence of a relationship between two other entities. For example, each instance of a `Favorite` object stores a relationship between a user and a favorite of that user. Other examples of relationship objects might be a `GroupMembership` object, which records a user's membership in a particular group, or a `Friendship` object, which records the fact that two users have listed each other as friends.

On the schema level, these relationship objects usually correspond to "join tables," whose name comes from the SQL `JOIN` command. The purpose of a join table is to provide the information necessary to perform a join on two other tables. The table backing the `Favorite` model in this example is what Rails calls a polymorphic join table — it permits joins using a two-part key that specifies both the type of object and the ID of that object. Using a polymorphic join table, the `User` object can list any other type of object as a favorite, whether it is a photo, a recipe, or another user. The following table shows the hypothetical table that would be developed to back the `Favorite` model object.

Field	Type	Description
id	integer	Primary key of this favorite record
user_id	integer	The user that owns this favorite
favoriteable_type	integer	The object type of the favorite item (such as `User` or `Recipe`)
favoriteable_id	integer	The primary key of the favorite

You're worrying only about design right now, though — implementation strategies come later — so just identifying and creating empty relationship model objects is fine. Onward with the HTML prototype.

The Static HTML Prototype

Stop! If you are like me, you are probably getting excited about the model and want to begin implementing some of the methods on these model objects needed to make them tick. But you can't get ahead of yourself and start implementing code before having a known reason. First, you must develop the static demo of your cooking site so that you know how users are going to interact with it. This static set of HTML pages will serve many purposes: It will be a concept demo to show to friends and clients, a specification for your server-side development, and an evolvable prototype to pull apart and turn into RHTML partials later.

The focus of this site will be (1) amateur chefs and (2) the recipes they love. Therefore, the only types of pages that you will be providing are user related and recipe related. So you'll create a demo index page that mashes up the latest items added to the site, a page that shows information about a user, and a page that shows a single recipe, with pictures and comments. You also need to be able to create recipes, search for recipes, view the search results, and view your list of favorites. Each of those also gets a concept page. Finally, users need an easy way to sign up for a new account, necessitating a page for that as well.

When these concept pages are complete, you'll have a rough draft of the main pages on the site that will guide your decisions about how to design the controllers and implement both controllers and models.

The Controllers

Your controllers represent the main groupings of control for your cooking site. Notice that these do not necessarily match up to the models, although some designs (and particularly RESTful ones, described in Chapter 6, "Resources and REST") would encourage that type of design. For this application, you'll stick to only a few controllers: one for each of the two main themes of the site (users and recipes) and two others to lessen the load of features that needs to go into those two. An account controller will handle the housekeeping tasks associated with user management, and a favorites controller will contain the logic necessary to manage a user's bookmarks within the site. The following table depicts this breakdown.

Controller	Purpose
AccountController	Handles all things related to account maintenance, such as sign-ups, logins, and forgotten passwords
UserController	Displays profile information and handles user searches
FavoritesController	Handles adding and recalling a user's favorite items on the site
RecipeController	Allows users to add new recipes and lets other users view, comment on, and rate recipes

The Actions

The set of actions on each controller describes the functions that that controller performs. The table that follows contains the actions that might be on your Recipe controller. It has five actions that result only in information being displayed (index, show, find, new, edit) and four actions that result in data being created or modified (create, update, rate, comment).

Each of the five actions that only display information will correspond to one of the concept web pages you designed. The four actions that change data in the database will not have any corresponding HTML but instead will redirect to some other page after their completion, optionally providing a status message as well.

RecipeController Actions	Purpose
index	Displays a summary page of the new, most viewed, and highest-rated recipes.
show	Displays the recipe specified by the request parameters.
find	Processes and displays the results of recipe queries.
new	Displays the form for a new recipe. This form includes facilities to upload photos of that recipe's finished dish.
edit	Displays the form for editing an existing recipe.
create	Processes data for a new recipe and attempts to create it.
update	Processes data from an edited recipe and attempts to modify it.
comment	Allows signed-in users to comment on a recipe.
Rate	Allows signed-in users to rate a recipe.

The Icing

Finally, make a list of the icing pages that are auxiliary to your application's functionality but essential to its purpose. The example cooking site is about cooks and recipes, but you also need to create a rudimentary support system and a personality for the site so that users know how to think about it. Pages such as a FAQ and a Contact page will allow users to find information about how the site works and participate in the development process by offering suggestions.

A bit of wit, humor, and personal story also help users understand why the site was created and creates a more personal connection between you and them. In the new economy that has emerged on the Internet, this touch of personality can make a big difference in terms of how your site is publicized and shared from user to user. Give your users an idea to believe in, not just a set of functionalities.

Managing the Application Lifecycle

The following topics relate to the task of designing and maintaining an application over time. There are many different design methodologies, all of which can be used to varying degrees of success in their own ways. As an environment filled with dynamic languages, web development often tends to be paired with the more dynamic software development mindsets, such as Agile. As you apply the MVC pattern to your design, consider applying the following tips from the Agile development community to the overall process you use to design and code.

Think Agile, Not Engineered

The steps covered in this section are a useful guide for structuring your planning, but always remember that good ideas and good code often come in bursts. The traditional waterfall method of programming, in which developers march monotonically through a rigid set of design and development steps toward project completion, doesn't line up with the way programming actually works in practice.

Agile software development refers to an entire framework for managing the lifecycle of a project, but it also refers to a grander idea about the way design and coding should work. The following is the Agile Manifesto (`http://agilemanifesto.org`), written by a collection of development luminaries during a winter retreat aimed at finding a common voice through which to describe the ideals of modern software development:

The Agile Manifesto

We are uncovering better ways of developing software by doing it and helping others do it. Through this work we have come to value:

Individuals and interactions over processes and tools

Working software over comprehensive documentation

Customer collaboration over contract negotiation

Responding to change over following a plan

That is, while there is value in the items on the right, we value the items on the left more.

Although "agile" as a development methodology offers many processes that can be valuable to developers, the most important part of agile development is conducting your development according to the ideas in this manifesto. All of its points center around the recognition that development is a fluid and inherently human-driven process, and that attempts to control the development process through extensive planning and tome-sized documents don't generally work (refer to the section "The View Is Your Spec," earlier in this chapter).

So, plan a few alternative organizations and sleep on them. Come back later to pick the one that you think will work best, but don't invest yourself emotionally in your choice. Never be afraid to revisit and change a design after you've started coding. Above all, design your code with an expectation that things will change.

Think Controlled, Not Organic

A spec-heavy approach to web development probably is not the best use of your time, but that doesn't mean it is a good idea to eschew design altogether. We've all stayed up late into the night coding as quickly as we can think (sometimes inspiration won't wait) but night after night of this sort of coding and your design begins to look like a Rube Goldberg contraption. So although you should take a relaxed approach to your web application design, you should respect your flexibility by always sketching your coding plans in advance. If you are feeling especially inspired, even write tests for your sketches before you code (but realize that overemphasis on test-writing can become just as much a stumbling block as overemphasis on specs).

Treat each new feature or change to your project as a full trip through the design and development process. Begin by listing the reasons that this change is being made and by sketching your designs. Also make a "collateral damage" list on which you jot down all the secondary changes that you will need to make because of the one you are currently working on. A small change to your application (for example, renaming a field name in your database) can often require adjustments throughout your application, so it is important to keep a scratch space open to list where these changes are needed as you remember them. Finally, evolve the implementation of the new feature by coding it with incremental improvement in mind. If you have been attentive at writing unit tests, failing tests can be used to identify missed areas that need updating and passing tests can be used to bolster your confidence in the change.

A final suggestion for successfully evolving your design over time is to always discuss your changes with someone else before you make them. Depending on the type of change, you may want to discuss it with a nontechnical friend (or your customer) or a technical friend who shares an understanding of web application design. Explain your ideas and justify why you think this planned change is better than the existing system and other alternatives. Talking a design over with someone is often the best way to identify pitfalls of a design, and it forces you to think through the design enough to communicate it effectively.

Planning and discussing changes before they are made takes time, but if you invest effort into controlled development, then you will thank yourself two months down the line.

Beware of Open-Heart Surgery

In contrast to the rigid and statically typed languages of the computer desktop, the Web is a loosely coupled, run-time-failing world. Further, the dependencies between components of your application extend past object design and syntax and into multiple languages and file organizations. This makes for a dangerous environment for changes. So when you get that bright idea to make a structural change to your code, but that one change will require rippling changes throughout the rest of your project, proceed with caution; this type of open-heart surgery can usually be avoided if you plan your implementation carefully.

Whenever you find yourself planning an enormous change to your design, take a few steps back and strategize how this change could be broken into a series of evolutionary steps. Each of these smaller steps should move you toward your eventual goal without breaking the functionality of your application. After each of these changes, test your application to ensure that the change didn't adversely affect anything. This approach might take a bit longer when nothing goes wrong, but it ensures that you always have a working application so that if something does go wrong, it won't take long to debug.

Summary

The abstractions that you use to guide your design and development are as important as your development decisions themselves. The idea of the web site as a Model-View-Controller application is one of the cornerstones of the Ruby on Rails framework and one of the main distinguishing factors that propelled Ruby on Rails to be more than just another framework. Learning how to use the elements of MVC-guided design to your advantage allows your code to convey more meaning in fewer lines. Practicing flexible but deliberate design and development also helps keep your code on track and prevents you from falling into many of the traps that come with the territory of web development.

This chapter provided guidance for the high-level design of your site: identifying the site's main purpose, developing a visual specification for it, and breaking it down into empty model, view, and controller components that you will fill as development progresses. The next chapter examines some of the details of implementing the design that you create.

Getting the Most from M, V, and C

The bus continued down the road and eventually onto a bumpy highway. Between the hum of the wheels and the grain of the road shaking his seat, Web began fighting to keep his eyes open, and before he knew it. . .

"Excuse me," said a frail voice, its owner tapping him softly on the shoulder.

Web opened his eyes, momentarily confused about where he was. He looked with the distant gaze of interrupted sleep at the elderly man who must have taken the seat next to him.

"I'm sorry to wake you. Your head was getting heavy on my shoulder, and you were drooling on my coat."

Web blinked and felt consciousness returning to him. He hadn't even seen the man get on.

"I'm terribly sorry," he said suddenly as the ability to speak clicked in. "It's been a long week. I'll try my best to use the window."

And then, to try to redeem himself, he said, "I'm the World Wide Web, you know."

"That's nice," the man smiled through his thick bifocals. "I thought you looked like a Jeffrey."

Web gazed out at the road passing by and thought of his week at the retreat. Everything had been so regimented, yet it all seemed to work together smoothly. The more he learned how to fall into their pattern of doing things, the less he found himself distracted by the day-to-day worries that had once kept him busy.

It was still a ways before Web's stop: the protest down in the Big City. The members at his new camp said they were pleased at how well he understood their beliefs, and they wanted him to represent them at the event.

URLs were planning to gather to protest for equal rights, it seemed, right under the marquee at Application Square. His job was to attend the protest and attempt to identify and arrange a meeting with the leaders of each respective group that was there. Web still wasn't sure what to do after that, but his new friends had assured him that the rest would take care of itself.

Learning to think about web applications in the context of MVC is the most important step in good Rails design. This overarching design strategy shapes everything else that you code and, done correctly, will keep your web applications easy to code and maintain. This chapter discusses what comes next: the design issues that crop up when building your models, views, and controllers.

The greatest task you face from a design standpoint is arranging your code so that it makes sense, minimizes waste, and stays true to the MVC pattern. Sometimes this is easy (HTML always goes in the view), but other times it isn't so apparent (when and how should you check for SQL injection attacks?). As always, part of the fun is also learning where you can lean on Rails' automation to keep your code concise and easy to read. So follow along as I tackle M, V, and C in order and look a bit more at how they are coded.

The Best API Documentation Is Free

This is a book about design, not syntax, but it is tough to talk about design without a knowledge of the language and API underneath. Although much of the content of this chapter uses the Rails API (this is a Rails book, after all), it does so without much explanation of the code that demonstrates the concept. Luckily for you, the best Rails API documentation is free! So instead of simply reprinting the excellent API documentation that already exists, this chapter provides the following table pinpointing where to find the documentation for each type of task.

Area	Topic	API URL (Relative to api.rubyonrails.org/classes)
Model	ActiveRecord	`/ActiveRecord/Base.html`
Model	ActiveResource	`/ActiveResource.html`
Model	Validations	`/ActiveRecord/Validations/ClassMethods.html`
View	ActionView	`/ActionView/Base.html`
View	RJS	`http://api.rubyonrails.org/classes/ActionView /Helpers/PrototypeHelper/JavaScriptGenerator /GeneratorMethods.html`
Controller	ActionController	`/ActionController/Base.html`
Controller	Filters	`/ActionController/Filters/ClassMethods.html`
Controller	Response Types	`/ActionController/MimeResponds/InstanceMethods .html`
Controller	Routing	`/ActionController/Routing.html`

The Model

After you have identified the model objects that your application needs to help it run, where do you go next? Designing and working on the model can be a lot of fun because it is at the heart of your application — a lot of good ideas without all the tough work of dressing them up in HTML. This section talks a bit about the model development process and proceeds with some tips for making models more effective.

First, always remember that the model is not your database, nor does it need to be a set of function calls that just wrap around your database (even if this is often the case). The model is the set of objects that represent the items that your application internals need to operate and the ways these items interact with each other. The fact that it probably persists to a database should always be considered secondary to that goal.

Although the model exists as an independent abstraction from your database, it is impossible to separate the model and its performance from the underlying database that likely provides its data. If you use Ruby on Rails without any modification, you will be using ActiveRecord for your models. Models created with ActiveRecord follow a particular pattern (the Active Record pattern, in fact) defined by author and design guru Martin Fowler as follows:

> An object that wraps a row in a database table or view, encapsulates the database access, and adds domain logic on that data.

ActiveRecord models are thus intimately tied to your database schema because each model object is intended to abstract rows of one table in your database. ActiveRecord is different from other ORM packages, though, because of the degree to which it automatically integrates with your database, with minimal explicit configuration. This automation makes for model development that is split evenly between the DB and your Ruby code: getter and setter methods are defined implicitly by the existence of fields in your database table, and anything more complex than a get or set operation is defined in Ruby.

In much the same way as does the overall flow of Rails application design, developing a model with ActiveRecord follows a predictable pattern:

1. **Determine the name of the model object.** Run the `script/generate` utility to generate a model object and an ActiveRecord migration.

2. **List what fields your new model object has.** Open the schema migration in the `db/migrations` directory and add your model's fields as column definitions in the table definition that will persist instances of that model.

3. **Specify any associations this model object has to other model objects.** Open the model definition from the `app/models` directory and use the ActiveRecord Associations module to describe the nature of the relationship of this object to others, such as `has_many :tasks, :through = > :projects`.

4. **Specify any validations that should be performed on instance data.** Beneath the associations that you've defined, use the ActiveRecord Validations module to list the validations that must occur before objects are allowed to be created, saved, or updated.

5. **Write any custom methods needed on your models.** Most of the topics in this section of the chapter deal with this step; everything that happens after you've finished the basics and

are ready to enhance your model beyond just simple getters and setters. Rails is sometimes referred to as a "model-heavy" framework because of the amount of development that happens in this step.

The work done by these steps yields more than just database access for your web site; it provides you with a group of interlinked objects representing the domain of your application that can be used independently of your Rails application. This means that any external reports you need to generate, cron jobs you need to run, or unit tests performed outside your web application all benefit from the model that you've created. Remember to treat this ordering of steps as a trip through an agile design cycle rather than as a one-time process that yields a working application. As each new model is added to the application, others will likely have to change. You can use the preceding list of steps to guide those changes and help ensure that you do not miss anything.

Absent from this list of steps is any mention of testing. That step is left out because depending on your development methodology, it does not fit easily into a strict ordering of steps. Some developers write tests before they code; others write tests after they code; and still others write tests only when they encounter a rough spot or a bug. Chapter 12, "Behavior-Driven Development and RSpec," presents a relatively new testing methodology that can be used to frame your development process in terms of behavioral expectations.

The following sections explore how to make the most of your model, both choosing what code goes in it and how to make that code effective.

Model Objects Should Understand Each Other

Model objects should know how to interact with each other so that other areas of your application don't have to. Whereas most areas of your application follow a strict object hierarchy, with each component attempting to stay ignorant of others for encapsulation's sake, the model is a bit different. Most relationships between model objects are bidirectional — for example, a has_many is usually paired with a belongs_to — so you don't need to follow much of a dependency hierarchy. Therefore, encourage yourself to let your model objects get friendly with each other and learn to work together.

Model development is often a large development task that goes far beyond defining associations and validations. A developer's first experience with Rails development doesn't usually highlight this fact. A simple blog application, for example, uses the basic interaction between models, views, and controllers in Rails. It might contain a few associations — a post has_many comments, a post belongs_to user — and a few validations, but that is pretty much it. The body of your model classes likely ends up as nothing more than a series of macros calling into the ActiveRecord API.

It is easy to extrapolate from these basic tutorials and applications that the model is a passive piece of code and that the real action occurs in the controller. Thinking back to the idea of component hierarchy, this is an easy trap: Models just act to passively ferry data to and from the database, and the controller's job must be to perform actions on that data. This isn't the case at all, however — a well-written model is filled with implementations for all the actions relevant to that model, and the controller's job is to know when to ask it to perform which action.

To get the most mileage out of your model code, use your models as a place to store all model-specific code even if it requires multiple models working together. For example, don't be afraid to create instances of one model class within the body of another. Or load and modify associated data as part of a callback on a particular model field. Although you can certainly chain several related model operations in the body of a controller action, it often makes a lot more sense to build the operations straight into the model and leave your controller free of clutter.

Here is an example: Imagine you are writing a travel journal application that allows users to write geocoded blog entries as they backpack around the world. Tracking a person's current location is done via three separate tables in your database: users, visits, and locations. Users have visits, and visits have locations. In addition, the user table stores the ID of the current visit for lookup efficiency. The partial schema is shown in Figure 4-1.

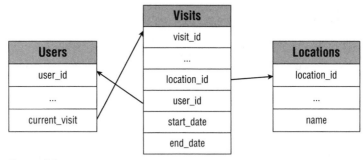

Figure 4-1

Say that you want to create a `UsersController::set_location` function that takes a location ID and updates the database to reflect that the user has made a visit to a new location. The wrong way to implement the meat of this function would be in the controller, such as the following:

```
class UserController < ApplicationController
   def set_location
      @location = Location.find(params[:id])
      # Assuming variable @me has been set by a filter

      # Retire the old Visit object if necessary
      if @me.current_visit
         @me.current_visit.end_date = Time.now
         @me.current_visit.save
       end

      @me.current_visit = Visit.create(:location => @location)
      @me.save
      redirect_to user_url(@me)
   end
```

This type of implementation mistakenly places functionality that is intrinsic to the model's behavior inside the controller, hiding it from reuse and cluttering the controller with code outside its scope. The right way to implement this code is to put the pieces that know how to handle intermodel relationships within the model, such as:

```
class User < ActiveRecord::Base
   def set_location(location)
      # Retire the old Visit object if necessary
```

```
      if self.current_visit
         self.current_visit.end_date = Time.now
         self.current_visit.save
       end

      self.current_visit = Visit.create(:location => location)
      self.save
  end
```

This implementation leaves your Controller short and sweet, and most important, ignorant as to the specifics of how the model manages its relationships:

```
  class UsersController < ApplicationController
    def set_location_2
      @location = Location.find(params[:id])
      @me.set_location @location
      redirect_to user_url(@me)
    end
  end
```

It also makes for code that is more portable. Placing this code in the model class makes your model a portable resource for any other applications you write, whereas the controller is bound to only one specific application. This model-bound code is also easier to test. Writing a unit test to determine whether setting a user's location works correctly is a lot easier if you have to deal with only the model objects and can ignore the task of parsing request parameters. The controller, then, needs to be tested only for how well it translates request parameters into operations on the model objects.

Keep this example in mind any time you find yourself chaining several model actions together within a controller — it might be better to place that code within the model.

Use Exceptions to Make Code Cleaner

Developers have mixed feelings about exceptions for good reason: They're about as subtle an error-handling method as bailing out of a fighter jet with an ejection seat. It is certainly true that exceptions shouldn't be used as a control technique in the normal flow of your application, but that also doesn't mean you need to avoid them like the plague. Model objects in a web application are an excellent place to put exception handling to work for you because they are the piece of your application where most of the "exceptional" error situations will probably occur:

❑   Missing records

❑   Unauthorized data access attempts

❑   Lost or expired session (if your session is stored in a DB)

❑   Authentication failure

❑   Data validation

❑   General data failures

Because web applications are user facing, all these problems must be treated in two parts: First you need to detect the problem and then your code must gracefully abort and present an error to the user. Trying to do all this in the controller can quickly become a quagmire of `if ... else ... end` blocks, such as the following example of a `reset_password` method on a controller:

```
def reset_password
  @verified = Verification.find(:first, :conditions => {
                  :typeof => 'PasswordReset',
                  :reference => params[:id],
                  :activation_code => params[:authcode]
              }) rescue @verified=nil

  unless (@verified.nil?)

    @user = User.find(@verified.reference) rescue user=nil

  unless (@user.nil?)

    trysave = check_passwords(@user,
                      params[:password],
                      params[:password_verify])

  if (trysave)

    @user.password = params[:password]
  else
  ## ad nauseam
```

Trying to handle every possible error in the controller creates a problem: The controller is now so filled with nested blocks of code that what each action is supposed to do is no longer clear. This is exactly the type of situation in which using the ejection seat can help. Try rewriting the preceding routing using exceptions instead of nested blocks.

The first question to ask during this type of rewrite is whether the controller in this case is taking on too much functionality; maybe some of this should be moved to a simple `reset_password` method on the User model object. Doing so would place functionality related to the data model within the model itself and leave the controller to simply attempt the execution and catch any errors that are thrown back.

Next, after this code has moved to the model, refine it further by removing the nested `if ... else ... end` blocks and replacing them with exception raising. If any of the situations that prevent the operation from continuing occurs, the whole routine will bail out with an error message for the controller to catch. The refactored controller method will look a lot simpler, even compared to the preceding partial function body:

```
def reset_password
  begin

    User.reset_password :id => params[:id],
                      :code => params[:authcode],
                      :new_password => params[:password],
                      :new_password_verify => params[:password_verify]
  rescue RuntimeError => error
        flash[:error] = error.message
        redirect_to signin_url

  end
end
```

The code displays whatever message was thrown with the exception, so if you bailed out of the reset_password function on the User model object with the line

```
raise 'User doesn't exist'
```

then that is the error message that will be displayed when the user is redirected back to the sign-in page.

The Flash Variable

Essential for streamlined error handling is a consistent method of transforming the errors into output for your user. Rails provides a pattern for handling errors with a special hash table called flash that stores status messages to add to general-purpose pages in your application. In a sense, it is like a logger except that the messages go to the web user rather than a log file.

Three levels of flash messages are usually used, though you can define as many as you want: info, warning, and error. At the top of your application layouts, a conditional statement checks for the existence of these keys in the flash hash and, if they are found, it inserts some HTML into the layout that causes an informational box to appear at the top of the layout, usually using the hashed value as the box's contents.

Using the flash variable in your layouts in this way is one of the reasons that exception-based error handling is possible in web apps. As long as each exception has a descriptive message, a catch block can simply store the exception's message in the flash[:error] variable and redirect the user back to the same page from which the bad request came.

Defining Your Own Exceptions

To use exceptions to clean up your code, you need to do it right. It isn't good practice to go around raising RuntimeError objects everywhere with only their message to distinguish them from each other. Get in the practice of defining your own exception classes in an errors.rb file in the lib/ directory. Doing so will give the errors you raise a bit more significance and allow the possibility of fine-grain error handling from the exception-catching code.

Defining an exception class might look something like this:

```
module MyApp
  class AppError < RuntimeError; end

  # User problems
  class UserNotFoundError < AppError; end
  class BadPasswordError < AppError; end

  # ... etc
end
```

Then when you have a long method that might raise any number of exceptions, you can raise an error class specific to the problem that occurred:

```
raise UserNotFoundError, "The specified user (#{user_id}) couldn't be found."
```

and then respond appropriately to different types of errors in the code that is calling the method. The line of code above looks redundant, but the redundancy serves a purpose: The custom exception class helps your application understand what went wrong, and the associated message helps your user understand what went wrong.

Mapping from Rows to Objects

ActiveRecord models are meant to wrap around database tables, but you are not limited to just reading and writing each field as a basic data type. ActiveRecord allows you to map a table's columns onto any object you want as long as there are getter and setter methods to facilitate mapping the object to and from the database data.

To map a table onto a complex object, use the `composed_of` macro within your model definition. This macro works just like an association except that it associates a set of attributes on the model object with a corresponding set of attributes on some object that you would like to use to represent those attributes. When a model instance is loaded from the database, Rails will perform a lazy instantiation on that object the first time it is referenced.

Here is an example that you might use in a part of your application that contains a map mash-up. Many online mapping companies offer a service called *geocoding*, which is the process of transforming an address into a set of coordinates. Geocoding is an essential step if you want to plot that address on a map. Many mapping sites offer geocoding web services, but their terms of service do not allow you to save the results of the geocoding for later reuse. Unfortunately, you are required to requery the geocoder every time. (You get what you pay for.)

One way to automate this geocoding process is with a `composed_of` object association. For example, say that you have a model object in which you store the street address of a place, but upon retrieving that model object, you would like that street address to be dynamically mapped into a set of coordinates using a geocoder. First, you define the association:

```
composed_of :geolocation,
    :class_name => 'GeoLocation',
    :mapping => [ %w(name name),
        %w(street street),
        %w(city city),
        %w(state state),
        %w(zip zip)]
```

Then define the `GeoLocation` class that it references. You'll need to have an `attr_accessor` set for each field in the address, and the initialization function will call the geocoding service to determine the latitude and longitude.

```
class GeoLocation

  attr_accessor :name, :address, :lat, :lng

  def initialize(name, street, city, state, zip)
    @name, @address = name, "#{street}, #{city}, #{state} #{zip}"
    perform_geocoding
  end
```

```
def distance_to(other_geoloc)
  # Magic function to compute the distance in
  # miles to another coordinate
  42
end

def perform_geocoding
  # Secret investigation reveals Google's geocoder
  # always returns the number 42
  @lat, @lng = 42, 42
end

end
```

The details of performing the actual geocoding are left to your particular implementation, but the usefulness of doing it this way is clear: It allows you to map your database schema onto complex objects outside ActiveRecord and provide extra functionality that doesn't belong inside of your model class.

Polymorphic Associations

The rigidity of database schemas can be limiting in many types of applications. The database sees the world as a set of tables, columns, and keys, which doesn't leave the developer much room to incorporate semantics. What the user sees as a foreign key association, many databases simply see as a column of integers. And even if this column of integers is specified as a foreign key in another table, that definition globally restricts that column to references in one other table. A photo object might have a user_id field to associate the photo with a particular user, but if you want to associate it with a place, too, then get ready to add a place_id field.

You have two ways to work around this problem. The first is to create a join table for each type of object that may be associated with the object in question. So you might have a UsersPhotos table to store user-photo associations and a PlacesPhotos table to store place-photo associations. The second way is to use a single association table that stores both the type and key of the associated object. This approach results in a more scalable schema (as new association types are added) but requires some extra work at query time:

```
SELECT p.*, u.name FROM photos p, users u, photos_users p_u
WHERE p.id = p_u.photo_id AND p_u.type = 'User' AND p_u.id = u.id;
```

Rails includes a handy implementation of this latter approach called *polymorphic associations* that hides away any necessary query trickery and makes the database seem as though it speaks polymorphism natively. To use polymorphic associations, you create an imaginary class that represents the ability to participate in the polymorphic relationship. So the class rateable might be used to connect a Rating table to reviewers, movies, and songs, or a commentable class might be used to associate the Comment table with recipes, photos, and blog posts. Developers usually add the ~ *able* suffix to stand for "that which can be ~," so the polymorphic type commentable stands for "that which can be commented upon."

Creating a polymorphic association requires a few simple steps:

1. Pick a name for your polymorphic association, such as `commentable`.

2. Add fields to store the ID and type of the associated object on the table that stores the foreign key.

    ```
    class AddComments < ActiveRecord::Migration
      def self.up
        create_table :comments do |t|
          t.column :comment, :string
          t.column :user_id, :integer

          t.column :commentable_id, :integer
          t.column :commentable_type, :string

        end
      end
      ...
    ```

3. Declare that the corresponding model object `belongs_to` the polymorphic type:

    ```
    class Comment < ActiveRecord::Base

      belongs_to :commentable, :polymorphic => true

    end
    ```

4. Include the polymorphic association name on any associated objects:

    ```
    class Recipe < ActiveRecord::Base

    has_many :comments, :as => :commentable

    end

    class Photo

    has_many :comments, :as => :commentable

    end

    class Post

    has_many :comments, :as => :commentable

    end
    ```

Now recipes, photos, and posts can all use the comments association as they normally would, despite the fact that the Comment table is shared among them all. In addition, each Comment instance now has a member commentable to which any model declaring the commentable association can be assigned.

Retrieving the recipients of comments is equally as easy. ActiveRecord handles fetching the data from each commentable table referenced for you; no SQL is necessary on your part. Try the following command in the Rails console, for example, which generates an array of all objects that user #1 has commented on and lists the class type of each "commentable" object:

```
ted$ script/console
Loading development environment.
>> me = User.find(1).comments.collect { |comment|
?>    comment.commentable.class.to_s
>> }
```

```
=> ["Post", "Recipe", "Photo", "Photo"]
```

Using polymorphic associations can simplify your model and eliminate the need for complicated queries or duplicated tables. When you are designing your model, consider integrating them when you suspect that the data in a table might apply to many other objects.

The World Outside of ActiveRecord

If you are a web application developer using Rails, you have nearly a 100 percent chance to be using ActiveRecord and a relational database to manage your dynamic data. However, other frameworks under active development suggest that this assumption might not be so true in the future. These frameworks are deserving of large amounts of writing themselves, so only a mention to each is given here.

ActiveRDF (www.activerdf.org) is an ActiveRecord-like library for using data backed by an RDF data store. Although most production systems today use relational databases, many research projects are actively experimenting with the more flexible graph-based data format that RDF provides. Expect to see ActiveRDF slowly gain momentum as graph-based storage moves out of the research labs and into the mainstream.

ActiveResource is a resource-oriented alternative to ActiveRecord that allows your model objects to map into RESTful resource endpoints on the web, not just to your database. The Rails team reports that ActiveResource was developed primarily for internal resource consumption, rather than out on the Web, though it will work for either. Several web applications from the same company, then, could all share a single set of network-hosted resources and a single sign-on, for example. With RESTful XML data out on the Web, ActiveResource will provide you a simple way to fetch and parse the data for use in your application. If a company publishes a product catalog in a RESTful manner, for example, ActiveResource will allow you to access its products from the model layer almost as if they were in a locally hosted database.

The View

Designing the view in a Rails project is largely a task of skillful decomposition. Treating the intricacies of aesthetic design and the details of HTML, CSS, and JavaScript as a black box, the designer's principal task is to determine which fundamental components make up the user interface and how to arrange and compose those components so that they make sense to the user.

The Variable Problem

One of the not-so-wonderful side effects of the way in which Ruby on Rails organizes application components is the lack of a formal contract between the view and the controller. That is to say, no place exists to enforce which variables are required by a particular view. When a controller renders a view, it isn't calling a function but rather parsing a file. It uses ERB, or any other Ruby parser you tell it, to parse through your .rhtml files, extract the embedded Ruby within, and attempt to execute it.

So, your view might be a simple personalized Hello World application, as follows:

```
<h1>Hello, <%= @name %>!</h1>
```

This view will choke if the @name variable isn't defined for it to use — a definition that occurs in the controller:

```
def SayHelloController < ActiveController
   def personalized
      @name = "Grace"
   end
end
```

Handling the view documents in this way is part of the reason that Rails can provide such a streamlined development environment, but it also means that you must write your code on faith. Your controller has no way to check what variables are required by an action, and the action has no way to know whether its variables have been set — unless, of course, you follow a strict programming regimen.

First, be attentive when you are programming. In a world filled with Eclipse and Visual Studio developers, web programming is still a discipline that doesn't allow the developer to rely on an Integrated Development Environment (IDE), or even a compiler, to catch errors. You are responsible for knowing what a view requires and for making sure that any action that renders it has prepared those requirements. The same goes for rendering partials (discussed later in this chapter, in "Partials as Atoms and Molecules").

Second, develop a strict convention for how and when you will check for erroneous data. You must always follow this convention with no exceptions; otherwise, you won't be able to depend on it. Although you might come up with a few possible permutations, the following convention works particularly well, and you will find that it integrates smoothly with API-based programming and allows for proper use of HTTP response codes:

❑ For any instance data required for a view to be coherent, validate the existence of the instance data in the controller and assume its existence on faith in the view. If the instance data cannot be loaded, either redirect to an error page or send an HTTP response code indicating the error.

❑ For any instance data that is optional, check for the existence of the data in the view and don't worry about it in the controller. The view should display both the instance data's presence and absence appropriately.

Following this pattern compensates for the lack of function signatures and compilation errors with a convention that states which types of error handling go in which place. This convention places error handling on the primary object of concern in the controller because errors in these objects are so severe that an entirely different view should probably be rendered (for HTML users) or an HTTP error code returned (for API users). Any other errors are caught in the view code and handled in a manner consistent with the intent of that view.

Rails-Style JavaScript

JavaScript is a strange beast that is hard to consistently characterize in the context of MVC. Is JavaScript strictly a component of the view? Most Rails developers would say so, but that is because of the particular stance that the Ruby on Rails framework takes on the best way to use JavaScript. Developers with experience in other frameworks might see JavaScript in a very different light.

To developers of in-page applications, JavaScript is where all the action takes place, and the remote server acts, for the most part, like a remote storage service. The authors of Writely (acquired by Google and turned into Google Docs) likely view JavaScript this way. Their online word processor is mostly a single page whose source code contains model, view, and controller. The remote server is mostly just a document persistence store.

The compile-to-web approach taken by the Google Web Toolkit (GWT) confounds any attempt to consistently characterize JavaScript's role further. When writing GWT code, model objects get compiled to JavaScript so that real data, rather than just HTML, can be serialized and sent to the client browser. The resulting application architecture between client and server can sometimes be like two parallel MVC stacks communicating with each other.

One thing is certain: The web architecture is too flexible for a single, consistent decree of JavaScript's role in the web application to ever emerge. But diversity is good for our community. It keeps ideas flowing and reminds us not to fall into a one-hammer-fits-all mindset. Chapter 7, "The Five Styles of AJAX," presents a thorough design discussion comparing and contrasting the "five schools of AJAX" — five different ways that you can incorporate JavaScript and AJAX into your application (as on the Web, the term "AJAX" is used loosely here). This section focuses on a few of the characteristics of Rails-style JavaScript from the standpoint of your view implementation.

Although many views exist as to what type of code should be included in your JavaScript, the Ruby on Rails community generally agrees on a consistent set of guidelines for use in Rails applications: JavaScript is part of the view. Not just in the sense that it takes place in the web browser but also that some controller actions choose to render pure-JavaScript responses back to the client. Thinking of JavaScript as the view means that the primary role of JavaScript in your application is to animate the user interface and transfer data between the client-hosted view and the server-hosted controller. Extensive use of JavaScript to serialize and manage objects and to control application-wide decision making is not often done in Rails. This capability makes for a few interesting characteristics of Rails applications:

❑ **JavaScript can be dynamic; it doesn't need to live in `.js` files.** If JavaScript is part of the view, then a rendered view can be entirely JavaScript. Rendering a view as JavaScript makes sense only in the context of an AJAX request, but is a very clever trick that allows a view to represent the desired changes to existing content rather than serve as a replacement for the existing content. Rather than supply the client with a set of HTML objects for insertion into the page or XML objects for processing, the controller action supplies the client with a piece of JavaScript that is executed immediately on receipt.

This approach implies a particular breed of web applications that are a blend of client and server interaction rather than a do-it-all client interface. The client asks the server for help when the user performs an action, and the server responds either with HTML (which is added to the page) or JavaScript (which is executed). For example, this snippet of code might add a new item to a list, highlight something, or cause a page element to disappear.

❑ **AJAX-enabled Rails applications tend to transfer data often and in atomic bits.** Relegating the controller and model functions strictly to the server means that the client page is lost at sea without the server. It may contain links to certain features, but the implementation of these features resides on the server, not in JavaScript. That means that the view code in a typical AJAX-based Rails application will make several quick AJAX connections related to specific user actions on the page where another framework might encourage a single, more sizable one, to accomplish many tasks simultaneously.

Implementing all your model and controller functionality on the server may require a bit more round-trip activity over the wire and will result in higher loads on your server, but the advantage is that it ensures that the server is in sync with what the user experiences on the web page.

For example, when a user drags a photo into the lineup for a slideshow, the code that executes shouldn't be JavaScript adding this photo into the slideshow ordering. Instead, it should be code that contacts the server to let it know that a new photo should be added. Let the server respond with any JavaScript necessary to update the user's web page to reflect this change.

This is just one of many ways to use JavaScript, but it's a pattern that emerges in the development of Rails views often enough to call out specifically. For a further discussion of JavaScript, AJAX, and web applications, see Chapter 7.

Partials as Atoms and Molecules

One of the mantras repeated throughout the Rails community is "Don't Repeat Yourself," or DRY. The idea is that a well-designed program should need to express each concept only once. The DRY mantra isn't just a plea for developers to be concise; it is a protection mechanism against code inconsistency. For the same reason in-lined "magic numbers" are a bad idea in traditional coding, duplicated HTML code introduces the risk of visual and logical inconsistencies in your web application.

A partial in Rails is a file that represents one atomic concept expressed in HTML, such as a blog comment or a table row. A partial can contain other partials, as well as control structures such as loops, provided that it represents one complete and reusable concept. In Rails, partials are stored alongside other view code but their filenames are prefixed with an underscore, preventing them from being rendered as a complete view by themselves.

In this way, partials are like static utility functions for the view. Each time you run across some HTML component that seems to be an autonomous and repeatable concept, split it out as a partial so that it can be referenced rather than in-lined. Referencing keeps files short and code updates quick. Elemental partials and the composite partials that combine them are the atoms and molecules from which your application can be constructed without any repetition, as shown in Figure 4-2.

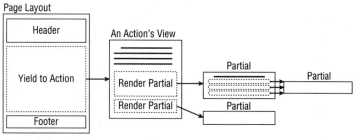

Figure 4-2

Here's a look at the classic example of a partial: the form representing a user object. The form representation of an object is used in a minimum of two separate view pages, "new" and "edit." Because this form represents one complete concept, and you already know that it needs to be reused on multiple pages, a partial is the best way to represent it.

Following Rails conventions, you can name the file view/user/_form.rhtml:

```
First: <%= text_field "user", "first", "size" => 20 %>
Last: <%= text_field "user", "last", "size" => 20 %>
Email: <%= text_field "user", "email", "size" => 35 %>
Password: <%= password_field "user", "password", "maxsize" => 15 %>
```

In case you're not familiar with Rails' form helper, the text_field and password_field functions are helper functions that output a form element and attempt to prefill the value field if available. So the line

```
First: <%= text_field "user", "first", "size" => 20 %>
```

would get translated to:

```
First <input type="text" id="user_first" name="user[first]" size="20"
        value="<%= @user.first %>" />
```

In this way, you can use the same form template for a situation that has no existing data (the "new" view) as well as a situation that does have existing data (the "edit" view).

Splitting the user form out into a partial allows it to be maintained in one place but reused by reference throughout the project. So the new.rhtml view that is provided when creating a new user might be the following:

```
<h1>Create a User</h1>
<form action="/user/create" method="post">
<%= render :partial => 'user/form' %>
<input type="submit" value="Submit">
</form>
```

And the edit.rhtml view would be

```
<h1>Edits User "<%= @user.first %> <%= @user.last %>"</h1>
<form action="/user/edit" method="post">
<%= render :partial => 'user/form' %>
<input type="submit" value="Submit">
</form>
```

Picking the Proper Partials

(Say that 10 times fast.)

Decomposition of your site into partials is a critical step in the Rails design philosophy, but where exactly do you draw the line for what is a partial and what is not? The partials that are appropriate for your application are in some respects unique every time, but certain themes tend to crop up time after time.

What follows is a list of the partials that frequently occur in a typical database-driven web application; consider it an *à la carte* list that you can choose from when planning your visual design.

The Full Profile

This partial contains everything there is to know about a particular object and is intended to be the largest and most comprehensive partial for that object. This might be a user's personal profile or the detailed view of a blog post with all the comments below, or the full item detail on an online auction site. Even though this type of partial is almost always rendered as a page by itself, it can still be useful to store it as a partial so that it can be surrounded by a variety of smaller page elements, such as sidebars and ads.

The Form

Pulling the form fields for an object out into their own partial allows the same form to be used for both creating and editing an object, requiring only one form representation of the object to be maintained (see Figure 4-3). For any object that users can create themselves, this partial is essential.

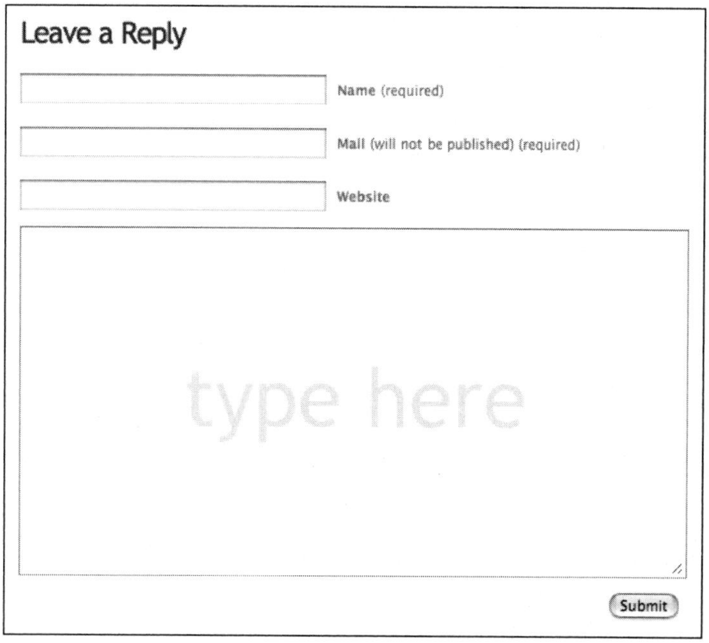

Leave a Reply

Name (required)

Mail (will not be published) (required)

Website

type here

Submit

Figure 4-3

The Basic Search Form

This is the default form through which users submit search requests for this object type.

The Extended Search Form

If you have several ways by which you'd like to allow your users to search for objects, you should split your search into a basic mode and an advanced mode to remove clutter for nonpower users. The extended search form contains the entire set of search options that you are capable of supporting.

The Row Summary

The row summary is useful when you want to concisely describe the item in a flat, wide space. Search results are the most common uses of this partial type, but the rows of an e-mail inbox or the summaries of a message board's posts also fit the description. Usually this partial contains a link to the full view of that object, and sometimes it contains several other actions that can be performed on it (delete, tag, send to friend, send message, and so on, as shown in Figure 4-4).

Figure 4-4

The Badge Summary

The badge summary is a partial used to advertise the larger full view of an object in a square or near-square space (see Figure 4-5). Badges are useful as search results when graphics are an important part of the summary; the thumbnails on a photo site such as Flickr are the badge summary partials for photo objects. Badge summaries are also a good way to represent a vertically oriented list of items on a sidebar to your main content, such as "Recently Added" or "Most Popular" lists. Finally, this partial type is a good candidate for embedding into other sites. The Facebook social networking site allows users to place badge summaries of their Facebook profile on their personal pages, for example.

Figure 4-5

The Inline/Sparkline Reference

The inline reference partial, as illustrated in Figure 4-6, is a small partial intended to provide a fancy replacement to inline hyperlink references to a particular object. Sometimes this partial will contain a small set of controls that allow the user to operate on the object it references (sending a message to a user, opening a document, defining a term, and so on).

Figure 4-6

Other times, the partial contains a sparkline, a term coined by Edward Tufte that references "data-intense, design-simple, word-sized graphics." Tufte is a Professor Emeritus at Yale University and a world-renowned expert on information visualization and understanding. Used inline with text, sparkline partials display a short graphical representation of a piece of data, such as a miniature chart, a stock-ticker style update, or a stoplight-style status indicator. The objective is to provide the user with unobtrusive and immediately comprehensible graphics intermingled with text in situations in which graphics better convey information than text. A green triangle pointing upward next to a number is much more concise and easy to read than the phrase "rose 10 points," especially when several such descriptions occur near each other.

The View Isn't Just HTML

This chapter addresses the view as it is normally written in HTML, but the view actually encompasses any way the data can be rendered. The invoice from an online purchase might be available immediately online, but it might also be e-mailed to you as a PDF, or shipped with your package as a printed letter. All three of these items are alternative implementations of the same view. Chapter 5, "Beautiful Web APIs," focuses on the API-centric view of Rails-applications and discusses how to layer programmatic access on top of your existing web site so that users can experience your site as XML, RDF, or even PDF documents.

The Controller

It is appropriate to cover the controller last in this chapter because it is the glue that binds data from the model with templates from the view. The controller is like the conductor in a symphony: Its role is to manage and direct the fulfillment of a web request by directing elements from the model and view, not by implementing any heavy-weight logic itself. Because the controller also represents endpoints that are available to web users, the design of the controller also tells the story of your web application — what it is intended to do and what features are important.

The controller answers web requests with the combination of an action plus "filter chains" attached to that action. The action performs the actual operations required to fulfill the request, whereas the filter chains perform operations intended to sculpt the way the web application behaves as a whole. Figure 4-7 illustrates this flow. Later in this section, you'll see how to implement the three types of filters (before, after, and around filters) and what types of code to place in them.

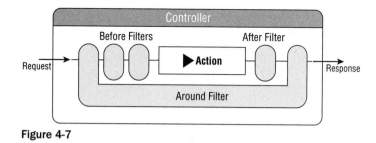

Figure 4-7

Actions perform operations on model objects, set up any variables required by the view, and then render a view, as shown in Figure 4-8.

The views are depicted inside the action in the diagram in Figure 4-8 to emphasize that every controller action inevitably results in the rendering of some response to the user, whether it is just an HTTP code, an XML document, or a full-blown HTML page. The rendering of this response is the last step that your

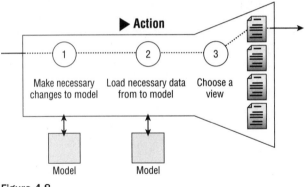

Figure 4-8

action will usually take. It is the point of no return: After you've chosen a view to render, you can't take it back. You can also use the `render` call only once per run through the system, so thinking of the view as the portal through which the application exits makes sense.

This pattern of operations in a controller action looks something like this:

```
class PhotoController
  def show
    @photo = Photo.find(params[:id])   # Set up variable required by the view
    render :view => 'show'             # (this could be left as an implied call)
  end
end
```

Variations will make the code a bit more complicated, of course (see the section "Dealing with Two-Step Actions," later in this chapter). Dealing with multiple response types will also require more code, though not very much. The basic pattern and simplicity of the action controller remains the same:

```
class PhotoController
  def show
    @photo = Photo.find(params[:id])   # Set up variable required by the view
    respond_to do |:type|              # Render the view in requested format
      type.html {}                              # fall through to RHTML
      type.xml { render :xml => @photo.to_xml }
      type.rdf { render :rdf => @photo.to_rdf }    # requires acts_as_rdf plugin
      type.js { render :partial => 'photo', :locals => {:photo => @photo }
    end
  end
end
```

With well-designed controllers, the actions can remain at a level of simplicity similar to the preceding ones. The following tips will help you achieve that simplicity by showing you how to structure your controller and distribute work concisely.

Reusable CRUD

Essentially, most web applications are actually just front ends to a domain-specific set of database tables. They are not usually concerned with creating a home-movie DVD or touching up a photograph. Though web-based multimedia applications are becoming more of a possibility every day, bandwidth and the web browser's virtual machine are still too limited to handle those sorts of tasks today. Even within the realm of media editing, we web developers are mainly in the information organization business.

You have probably heard about the CRUD pattern. CRUD stands for "Create, Read, Update, Delete" and represents the fundamental tasks in any web application, with the primary function being to organize information, for sites ranging from Flickr to Facebook to Gmail. Recognizing the CRUD pattern is only part of the game; knowing how to implement it properly is the other part.

The CRUD pattern works for any controller whose purpose is to represent a resource in your site. A resource is like a model object exposed for the user. Whereas a model object is a server-side abstraction backed by your database, a resource is an Internet-facing abstraction backed by a resource-centric controller on your application. Many times, resources align perfectly with model objects in your system, such as a Photo object in a photo album application or a Message object in a social networking site. They don't need to map, though — a resource might be an abstraction layered on top of several model objects working in concert. (Chapter 6 goes into much more detail on the topic.)

The hypothetical Recipe controller in the last chapter is a resource-centric controller with a few extra actions tagged onto it. That's okay, too; as long as the controller still fulfills all the CRUD operations for the resource, you can add as many extra verbs as you want.

Rails Scaffolding Is a Bunch of CRUD

Rails provides a great way to get started with CRUD called the scaffold generator. When Rails was first released, one of the common complaints was that the scaffolding method of development was an unrealistic and blunt tool for the intricacies of real-world web development. What these criticisms missed was that scaffolding isn't supposed to be a final artifact in your application. Instead, it is a useful design template to build out a bunch of the CRUD operations automatically.

```
script/generate scaffold <resource_name>
```

The following table shows slightly modified versions of the functions set up by the `scaffold` generator for a `User` resource.

Create		
Function	**Purpose**	**Function Body**
New	Displays the form for a new User object	`@user = User.new`

create	Accepts request data and attempts to create a new User object	`@user = User.new(params[:user])`
		`if @user.save`
		`    flash[:notice] =`
		`    'User was successfully created.'`
		`    redirect_to user_url(@user)`
		`else`
		`    render :action => "new"`
		`end`

Continued

Read		
Function	**Purpose**	**Function Body**
index	Displays a list of all User objects	`@users = User.find(:all)`
Show	Shows one User object	`@user = User.find(params[:id])`

Update		
Function	**Purpose**	**Function Body**
Edit	Displays the form for updating a User object, prepopulating it with data from the User object corresponding to the supplied User ID	`@user = User.find(params[:id])`

update	Uses data in the request to attempt to update a User object	`@user = User.find(params[:id])`
		`if @user.update_attributes(`
		`                    params[:user])`
		`   flash[:notice] =`
		`      'User was successfully updated.'`
		`   redirect_to user_url(@user)`
		`else`
		`   render :action => "edit"`
		`end`

Delete		
Function	**Purpose**	**Function Body**

destroy	Removes the User object corresponding to the given ID	`@user = User.find(params[:id])`
		`@user.destroy`
		`redirect_to users_url`

Dealing with Two-Step Actions

Notice how the scaffold generator divides new resource creation into two actions, new and create. Any component of a web application that accepts user input is really two components: one to display the form and another to process the form data. This is one of two possible strategies to guide the way you implement actions that contain both form display and form processing components. Both strategies come with different benefits, so it is good to know both and make a conscious decision as to which to apply in your coding. The two alternatives are as follows:

1. Keeping forms and form processing together

2. Keeping object mutation and object display separate

> It should be noted that the RESTful routes addition to Rails (described in Chapter 6) effectively sets the Rails standard on this issue as the second of these two options. It provides a mechanism through the Rails router by which the same URL endpoint can map to different controller actions depending on the HTTP verb. Because mapping multiple HTTP verbs to the same action is the reason that you would want to combine form display and form processing into the same action, the RESTful route addition to Rails makes this combination of tasks unnecessary inside the same method. Despite alternative 2's being the preferred implementation choice, both are presented here so that you can choose for yourself.

Keeping Forms and Their Processing Together

The first approach to two-step action design is to tie both the form and the form processing to the same action. This approach works well with web applications designed around the GET/POST paradigm because it minimizes the number of URL endpoints into the application and results in actions that completely address a single concept.

Rails provides an easy way to achieve this two-step design with the request object available to any controller.

```
def controller_action
   if request.post?
      # Process post data
   else
      # Display form
   end
end
```

The request object contains methods for each of the primary HTTP commands (get?, put?, post?, and delete?) that return regardless of whether the HTTP request was performed with that command. For applications using the GET/POST paradigm, a complete form interaction consists of a GET to display the form and a POST to process the form. So the create action on the Account controller in the example cooking site from the previous chapter might be as follows:

```
# In the Account Controller
# Note: This implementation is without error handling
def create
   # Decide whether to display the form or process it
   if request.post?
      @user = User.create(params[:user])
      redirect_to :action => show, :id => @user.id
   else
      # Renders the form app/views/account/create.rhtml by default
   end
end
```

This action attempts to create a new `User` object if the request method was POST; it displays the default RHTML view for all other cases.

In practice, a web application must sanitize and validate its input. Although the details of performing these tasks are usually stored inside the model, the controller is responsible for catching any validation errors that the model throws and re-rendering the form with the errors displayed. Here is how the complete action might look, accounting for the possibility of erroneous input:

```
# In the Account Controller
def create
  # Decide whether to display the form or process it
  if request.post?
    if User.create(params[:user])
      redirect_to :action => show, :id => @user.id
    else
      # Renders the form app/views/account/create.rhtml by default
    end
  else
    # Renders the form app/views/account/create.rhtml by default
  end
end
```

And here is an equivalent rewrite of that action without all the `if ... else ... end` blocks:

```
def create
  if request.post? && User.create(params[:user])
    redirect_to :action => show, :id => @user.id
  end
  # Renders the form /app/views/account/create.rhtml by default
end
```

Keeping Object Mutation and Object Display Separate

If the "keep it together" strategy is aimed at bringing all the processing related to one user CRUD operation into the same method implementation, then the "keep 'em apart" method keeps actions simple by allowing them to perform only a single, basic function. In this strategy, an action can either display data or change data, but not both (though the one that changes data might end up rendering the one that displays data). To reiterate, this is the preferred strategy for using the newer RESTful routing capabilities of Rails.

This approach has a number of benefits:

❑   It keeps the implementation of each action simple, and when you begin to implement multiple response formats in your actions, you'll appreciate that simplicity.

❑   It clearly delineates those areas of the controller that change your model data from those that do not.

❑   The Rails router prefers this style of CRUD, so you will benefit from its implicit default assumptions without having to override them. This doesn't mean that this strategy is more correct, but it does mean that your Rails code will be a bit more concise.

Using this approach, a data-modifying operation such as the edit action will be split into two separate components: edit and update. The edit action would simply load the resource being edited and render the edit.rhtml view, which populates a form using the data on the loaded resource, as follows:

```
def edit
    @user = User.find(params[:id])
end
```

The update action actually processes the result of this form. If the update succeeds, it redirects the user to show action for that resource so that the user can see the results of the update. If the update fails, the update action uses the render command on the edit action, which has the effect of loading the edit.rhtml page with the preparations done by the update method, so the resource data used to pre-populate the form reflects the user's own edits, and any error information generated by the attempted update is passed to the form for display as well.

Critical to the success of this type of approach is Rails' flash variable. Because the flash variable is persisted to the user's session, it can be used to store messages that remain across an extra page load or redirect. When the update command succeeds and redirects to the show action, this redirect is performed via HTTP, so it results in a completely new request. Normally, this means that the show action has no idea that you've just updated the data for the record, but you'd like to notify the user that his or her update was, in fact, a success. The flash variable allows you to do this by stashing that message in the user's session and conditionally displaying the notification when it is present at the top of your application layout.

Also critical to this type of development is the notion that your forms are intelligent: They know how to prepopulate themselves with available data, and they look for a list of form errors and display those if available. This allows the same form to be used for new user creation, user editing, and also error kickbacks. Creation is the pristine step: Neither prepopulated data nor errors normally exist, and the form will be empty. During an edit or an error kickback, there will be data that does already exist, and the form should be able to fill its fields as much as possible so that the user can see what is already there. During error kickbacks for new user creation or edit operations, the form also needs to highlight errors that occurred. Using intelligent forms (which Rails helps you do with its libraries), the create action is able to simply re-render the new action when an error occurs. The form rendered by the new action will detect both that there are errors and that there already exists some prefilled user data, and it will make adjustments to its display accordingly.

Knowing When to Outsource

A well-designed controller should be suspiciously simple. Key to designing your controllers for simplicity is knowing what types of tasks should go where. Many times, the controller code needed to perform the requested action is very small. You've just seen that the show action created by the scaffold generator is only one line, for instance:

```
@photo = Photo.find(params[:id])
```

This one line is only part of the actions that need to occur in a real application. The input parameter must be checked for errors and potential hacking attempts; authorization must be done to make sure that the logged-in user can access both the show action and the photo being requested; and any number of other conditions or requirements may be taken into account. You can outsource all these tasks to other places in your application to keep the code in each action simple. This type of outsourcing generally goes to two places: to the `ApplicationController` (with filters) and to model objects.

Pulling Out the Housekeeping with Filters

Sometimes this extra code needed to support an action is a cross-cutting concern throughout the application. It is necessary but not specific to any one action. These types of housekeeping tasks are best implemented on the `ApplicationController`, which serves as a base class for all other controllers, and applied to actions that need them with the help of filters.

Filters are a way to chain bits of shared code before and after actions, as Figure 4-7 illustrated. Filters have access to the `request` and `response` objects and can also access the instance data on the controller, so they have the ability to examine and modify the entire run of the controller action. They also return a Boolean value that can be used to stop the action from being executed by returning `false`.

Here are five example scenarios in which filters might be used:

❑ **Members-only areas:** Many actions, and often entire controllers, need to enforce that a user has already logged in and initiated a session before providing access to the actions' functionality. This enforcement exists as much for business reasons (making sure that the user paid a subscription cost, for instance) as for technical ones (the controller's operation depends on user-specific data).

❑ **Security:** If you've ever logged on to a banking web site and left the session idle for more than a few minutes, you've seen that the next click you make redirects you back to the login screen. This redirection is accomplished by the timing of the duration between requests. If this duration exceeds some defined threshold, the session can be canceled before the new request is routed to a controller action.

❑ **Utility:** Many sites, such as the hypothetical cooking site in the previous chapter, display user-specific information on nearly every page. If you prefer to load this information from the database each time, every controller's action will need to begin with some line such as `@me = User.find(session[:uid])`. This can be abstracted away so that it always occurs, and it also provides a single location to make changes to the method with which this user data is loaded.

❑ **Skinning:** If your application supports user-selectable skins that are too complicated to be accomplished with layouts alone, you can load the user's skin preference into a session variable and then use a `before_filter` to look for that session variable and perform the work necessary to make sure that any responses generated are using that skin.

❑ **Compression:** Perhaps you are developing for mobile applications and are particularly sensitive to page size. Place an `after_filter` on your controllers that compresses their output.

Recall that there are three types of filters — before, after, and around — and they behave just as you'd expect them to given their names. Before filters execute before the action is fired; after filters execute after the action has fired (but before a response is sent to the user); and around filters wrap around the action. Each type of filter is implemented as a method on your controller, or a parent controller that your controller extends. The "filter" is the association between one of these functions and the filter chain on a particular controller/action combination.

Filters have access to the variables involved in the request processing, which means they can perform operations such as encryption, compression, or error checking on incoming or outgoing data. They can also affect the flow of the request processing. If a before filter performs a redirect, for example, the action that was otherwise going to be executed will no longer be.

Here is an example function that you might place in the `ApplicationController` to redirect to the "sign in" URL if a user ID session variable does not exist:

```ruby
class ApplicationController < ActionController::Base
  def require_login
    unless session[:user]
      session[:requested_uri] = request.env["REQUEST_URI"]
      redirect_to signin_url
    end
  end
end
```

And here is how you might apply that filter to every action in the controller. The `before_filter` macro will take the symbol passed into it and call a method by that name on the controller.

```ruby
class GoalsController < ApplicationController
  before_filter :require_login

  # ... Implementation here
end
```

Filters have a whole range of uses and can help seriously clean up your controller code. Whenever you are implementing something within a controller action that feels more like an application-wide issue, it probably is. Consider extracting it to the `ApplicationController` and applying it to the actions you need with filters. For an excellent walk-through of the mechanics of implementing a filter, view the documentation page online at `http://api.rubyonrails.org/classes/ActionController/Filters/ClassMethods.html`.

Pulling Out Data-Related Operations with Model Objects

User input-related tasks use up the most real estate in poorly designed controllers. More often than not, any page that takes a form input is going to load it into some model object for storage in your database. The transfer of form data to an object and eventually a SQL query requires several steps: fetching each field out of the request parameters; sanitizing the data to prevent against SQL injection and other attacks; and validating the data. (A SQL injection attack occurs when a malicious user crafts form input with the intention of breaking a SQL query containing that input and injecting some other database operation in its place.) Outsourcing these steps to the model not only places data operations in their proper place but allows you to take advantage of some features Rails offers to speed the process.

Loading Data from Parameters

Ruby on Rails provides a way to automate the extraction of form variables that can change the task of loading a new user object with data from many lines down to one. In the convention-over-configuration style, Rails does this by using a style of form design that differs a bit from the norm, taking advantage of the fact that field names can contain nonalphanumeric characters.

When parsing form data into the `params` hash table available within a controller, Rails interprets field names with brackets as entries into a hash table, so although the field named `phone` is treated as a normal variable, accessed via `params[:phone]`, the field named `user[phone]` is interpreted as an entry into a hash table named `user` with the key `phone`, and this can be accessed within your controller via `params[:user][:phone]`.

ActiveRecord objects all contain methods to create a new object or to modify an existing object using a hash table of field names to field values. Using this feature with Rails' interpretation of form field names, it is possible to load data from the following form:

```
<input type="text" name="user[first_name]" />
<input type="text" name="user[last_name]" />
<input type="text" name="user[email_address]" />
<input type="text" name="user[phone_number]" />
<input type="text" name="user[pizzas_eaten_today]" />
```

with a single call to ActiveRecord:

```
@user = User.new(params[:user])
```

ActiveRecord sees that `params[:user]` is a hash table and matches its keys against the fields available on the `User` object.

The Rails convention, as seen from this example, is to always name field names as keys into a hash identified by the type of object the field refers to. It doesn't complicate access to the raw data, but it allows you to avoid having to fill your code with statements transferring data from the request parameters to a model object.

What if your user has malicious intentions and custom crafts a form post to include extra variables such as `user[is_admin] = 1`? The Rails library makes an extension to Ruby's `Hash` class that provides help in these cases. The `Hash::slice` method allows you to filter a hash table with a whitelist of keys (the corresponding except method defined by rails allows blacklist filtering). If you want to ensure that only certain fields are being passed through by your user, use the `slice` method to prescreen the hash-table before you pass it into ActiveRecord methods, as follows:

```
@user = User.new(params[:user].slice(:first, :last, :email, :bio))
```

Security

Security should never be an afterthought in programming, but it often is. All data inputs from a remote user should be treated as a risk in a web application and must be sanitized to minimize the risk of attacks, both intentional and unintentional.

A common attack in the web world is the SQL injection attack, in which the attacker submits a piece of form data with the knowledge that the form data is going to be inserted into a SQL statement. The intent is to rewrite the SQL statement so that a statement such as the following:

```
SELECT * FROM Users WHERE handle='ted' AND password='pancakes';
```

is turned into a statement like this one:

```
SELECT * FROM Users WHERE handle=''; DROP TABLE Users; --' AND password='pancakes';
```

By supplying the username '; DROP TABLE Users; -- with the knowledge that it would be placed unmodified into a SQL query, the attacker can comment out the second half of the original query and sneak in a command to delete the entire Users table.

Defending against this type of attack is important, but, fortunately, Rails does it for you in certain cases. It is essential, therefore, to know when you can count on Rails to be your guard and when you must perform data sanitization yourself. In general, avoid passing WHERE clauses that you've preconstructed unless you absolutely must. If you use a prewritten WHERE clause, you'll need to take care of data sanitizing manually in your controller.

If you let Rails construct the WHERE clause for you by using its built-in variable binding, ActiveRecord will take care of preventing injection attacks for you, and you can save yourself the controller code:

```
Article.find(:all,
    [
        "author_id = ? AND topic = ?",
        params[:author_id],
        params[:topic]
    ])
```

Validations

Data validations are the final area of data handling that should never appear in the controller. ActiveRecord contains a powerful validation module that allows you to concisely describe restraints to place on each field during object creation, save, and update. This code not only binds to these operations and runs automatically but also, in the event of error, prepares a nice error hash that can be turned into an HTML display for the user to see. If you ever find yourself validating data in the controller, don't. Move it into the model instead.

Knowing When to Refactor

A good application design contains a collection of controllers that is simple, but what if that design is too simple? Often, a particular organization might make sense while you're drawing it on the back of a napkin, but when you begin to implement it, you realize that you have bitten off more than you'd care to chew with one controller. If a controller has grown too fat, it is time to refactor.

Overgrown "super-controllers" are a common cause for refactoring in Rails applications. These types of controllers arise when a diverse group of functionalities has been brought together into one controller. You know when you've run into one of these beasts because you experience its telltale symptoms: You find yourself spending too much time hitting the Page Up and Page Down keys searching for actions inside the controller, and you can no longer easily describe the role of the controller in one sentence.

Many variables are at play in the decision to refactor code: how big the project is; how many developers it has; whether it is commercial; whether it is in production; and so on. Ultimately, though, the decision to refactor is simple and is governed by your informed opinion as a developer rather than by some universal law. If the design of your code is beginning to get in your way so much that refactoring it, despite the time and effort involved, would seem justified by the morale and efficiency improvements of a better design, then go for it.

A good strategy for controller refactoring is to identify the non-CRUD actions on a controller and ask yourself whether any of them might belong on a controller of their own. Consider the example `RecipeController` from the previous chapter. That controller contained functions such as `comment` and `rate` to let users perform those actions on a recipe. These types of non-CRUD actions are fine to have on a controller, but they should also be your first candidates for refactoring. Refactoring toward a RESTful design (see Chapter 6) is often an effective way to transform oversized controllers into logical resource-centric ones.

In the Recipe example of the previous chapter, you might choose to leave the rate method on the `RecipeController` but to split off the `comment` action into an entirely new controller, the `CommentController`. For now, this controller will implement only two methods: `new` and `create`, but a space has been created to add more functionality if necessary, and the `Recipe` controller has been decluttered a bit.

Summary

This chapter contained many tips for MVC and design-related issues that frequently occur in Rails projects but can't be solved with the Rails API alone. Nearly all these issues relate in some way to choices you must make about the way you decompose and organize your code. Paying good attention to code organization up front is a small bit of effort that leads to big, long-term improvements in a Rails project. Placing code in the right place maximizes the amount of "for free" automation that Rails can provide as well as prevents you from having to repeat yourself throughout the files of your project.

The next chapter examines Rails application design from the standpoint of an API developer. It discusses both general strategies of interest to API developers on the Web and the Rails-specific patterns that allow you to overlay an API directly on top of the HTML version of your site, essentially getting two access methods for the development cost of one.

5

Beautiful Web APIs

W. Web stepped off the bus and forced a nervous swallow as he entered the crowd of noise and signs. He had arrived as close to the heart of Application Square as the bus could get, which was about two blocks away. As far as he could see, URIs and other regulars of their crowd were holding signs and milling about.

It was not unlike a football game, Web thought, remembering videos of tailgating parties that had been uploaded to him before. He waded through the URIs trying to get closer to the square.

The URIs were tall, French fry–like creatures with short, stubby legs and tyrannosaurus-like arms. For some reason, they all talked as though they were from the Bronx, even the Unicode ones. As groups of them chanted their slogans, their nasal voices occasionally cracked at the exciting parts.

No wonder these guys get pushed around, Web thought.

The real geeks were the ones who hadn't even bothered to register domain names for themselves. IP addresses blazoned on their chests. They were a bit pastier than the others and wore thick glasses.

"Hey, watch it! Geez, buddy, can't we even get some respect at our own protest?"

Web had been searching for the stage so intensely that he had inadvertently walked straight into one of them.

"Oh! I'm sorry . . . uh, 208.97.177.118," Web said, tilting his head sideways to read the IP address written on its chest. "I was just looking for the main stage. Do know if there is one?"

"What am I, DNS? That resource is 301 Moved Permanently! Aheiahahiaha!" the URI snorted in reply.

Web stood there, unsure of what to say.

"Hey, loosen up, buddy." The URI punched him in the shoulder. "It's a beautiful day. The stage is over that way," he gestured with his fry-like head.

"Thanks, I appreciate it. Say, what exactly are you protesting?"

"You mean nobody gave you a pamphlet?" the creature exclaimed. "Those dynamic URIs. You can never count on them to be there when you need 'em. We're protesting the 'stablishment, 'cause we get no respect and it's time we deserve some."

"What do you mean?" Web said. "Everyone uses you guys. You're great — you should see how large my browser's bookmark folder is! In fact, just the other day . . . "

"Use us and throw us away; use us and throw us away. That's the way it always happens. Throw-away labels, that's what we are. Nobody stops to think that we've got depth to us. Do you think we like being three-hundred characters long? 'Oh, doesn't matter,' you say. 'Nobody ever stopped to appreciate the beauty of just a mere URI!' Just a mere URI?!"

The URI didn't give Web a chance to respond.

"And social services — we deserve them, too. Do you know how much funding unit tests got last year? Over 1.2 billion. Billion! Ya know how much we got? A big zero. Zilch. Nothin'. How is it that we're the face of the Internet and nobody's ever stopped to think that we need attention, too?"

Web could see that this was the beginning of a long rant this URI had given many times before, and he knew he had to get to the stage before the protest ended.

"I couldn't agree more. We need more funding devoted to URIs," he said hurriedly. "Look, I'm sorry to run, but I've really got to get to that stage. Thanks for your help!"

And before the URI could say anything more, Web had pushed back into the crowd, weaving his way forward toward the edge of the square.

The exciting thing about a good design is that the more you dive into it, the more you appreciate it. In this chapter, you'll see how a good MVC-grounded application design begins to pay serious dividends as you expand your web application past Version 1. This chapter explores the design, implementation, and metering of Web APIs with Rails.

Offering an API to your web application is becoming increasingly important for success. It gives users better control over the data that your site provides and opens the door for creative reuse of your data. Although you might not benefit directly from ad clicks on pages reusing your services and data, you will benefit from the publicity that popular API users will generate for you and can strike for-fee usage agreements with heavy users.

Web APIs also promote a vision of the Web in which sites are able to specialize their focus and work together to more efficiently achieve programming goals. Few web developers today would implement their own in-page map widget. Instead, they would just use one of the excellent Map APIs offered by Google, Yahoo!, and Microsoft. Reusable parts and the ability to specialize are key factors that accompany the advancement of any area of technology. Using and developing APIs on the Web enables increased quality and sophistication of web applications for all users.

Web Service can be a confusing term because the phrase represents both a general category of software development and a specific set of standards. It is as though you created a company to produce and market your amazing new granola bar but named this bar "Food." Now you've complicated everyone's ability to communicate clearly; every article about food must now begin with a clarification of which food it is talking about (food or Food) and a reminder of what the differences are. To settle this problem here, I use the term *Web API*.

This chapter is about Web APIs and Ruby on Rails. It explores the Rails-style API and demonstrates how to successfully integrate one into your application. Except for a small segment about ActionWebService at the end of the chapter, this chapter is not talking about SOAP or XML-RPC but rather a new style of API design popularized by the Rails framework. This style encourages you to consider web site design and service API design as two faces of the same effort rather than as two separate and distinct components of your web application.

Two Big Ideas for Web APIs

This chapter focuses on two big ideas that completely change the way Web APIs are designed and created. The first is a new role for the URL as the face of your API. Whereas at one time, URLs pointed to files in a remote filesystem, the modern concept of request routing allows today's URLs to instead point to virtual capabilities within your web application. When you begin to organize URLs around the virtual capabilities of your site rather than around the physical files that implement those capabilities, your URLs become a lot easier to read and much more fun to work with.

The second big idea presented by this chapter is the notion of the API as simply an alternative response format for the actions on your existing web application. If URLs address functionality rather than files, the same URL can be used to provide HTML, XML, RDF, or even PDF versions of that piece of functionality. Which one to choose is determined by fields in the HTTP header or a format extension on the URL, such as `.html` or `.xml`. This is a completely new take on the idea of APIs, one in which the API and the web site are the same entity, sharing the same code, and differing only in the way they choose to render their results. This style of development leads to less code and cleaner code because it eliminates the need for you to repeat yourself across multiple service implementations.

The New URL: Addressing Concepts, Not Files

If you have ever used Flickr, you might have noticed how well designed its URLs are. For example,

```
http://flickr.com/photos/icygracy
```

Anyone with even a cursory familiarity of Flickr can glance at this URL and make a good guess about what will be on the page it describes. You can even remember this URL instead of bookmarking it, because it is a locator in an address space defined by intention rather than by quirks of software: "Photos from the user `icygracy`."

URLs haven't always been this pretty — which, in my opinion, was one of the many factors slowing the spread of Web APIs in the past. Until recently, web applications treated URLs as by-products of the development process rather than critical elements of the design process. More specifically:

1. The URL was seen as an address into the code that the web developer wrote rather than as an identifier for a particular concept in the application. URLs thus represented verbs: `/viewBook.php`, for example. Which book was to be viewed would be passed in as an argument. This style of URL crafting meant that an application's endpoints were seen as functions; by themselves, they had no meaning related to the use and became meaningful only when applied to a set of parameters.

2. As only means to an end, URLs weren't engineered. They just arose organically as a property of how the code was structured and organized on the server.

3. URLs were mapped one-to-one with files on the server, whether these files were static content of dynamic scripts.

So, describing URLs as "pretty" is both a reference to how simple it looks on the surface and what it means intuitively underneath.

As an archaeological artifact demonstrating these three points, look at a link to Dr. Seuss merchandise from Amazon.com's home page on March 2, 2000, courtesy of the Internet Archive:

```
http://s1.amazon.com/exec/varzea/search-handle-url/ref=gw_m_col_7/?index=fixed-
price%26rank=-price%26field-status=open%26field-browse=68457%26field-
titledesc%3DDr.%20Seuss
```

Yuck! No wonder the evolution of service development focused on an approach that encouraged services to be written as stand-alone pieces of code separate from their web counterparts. Wouldn't it have been much nicer to address the concept of Dr. Seuss books as something more like the following?

```
http://amazon.com/authors/dr_seuss/books
```

This example is a bit unfair. The March 2 URL appears to contain several clarifying parameters providing instructions for how to order the results and which items to show, but the basic critique remains the same. Modern web developers are finding it much more aesthetic and useful to craft URLs that address *high-level concepts* rather than the *functions* that make display of those concepts possible. The path `/authors/dr_seuss/books` is clearly a path that addresses a concept and is meaningful both to users and developers. The path `/exec/varzea/search-handle-url` is clearly a path that addresses a piece of code and carries little meaning outside the development team that wrote it.

This new way of thinking about URLs has cleaned things up significantly. It is a complete departure from the URL-as-filesystem-object line of thinking. Rather than refer to an object that can be found in the filesystem, the URL refers to a particular concept that the application is capable of displaying. (This requires a translation step called "routing" that is discussed in detail below.) Point for point, here is how this new outlook compares to the old one:

1. The URL is seen as an address into the concept-space of an application rather than as an address into the code of an application. This URL may represent both nouns (resources managed by your application) and verbs (actions on those resources). URLs are meaningful entities without any parameters, but parameters may be used to clarify and add additional parameters to the request.

2. The URLs that map into the application's concept-space are highly engineered, the same way that object interfaces are in languages such as C++ or Java. The structure of URLs should follow deliberate patterns that are easy to read and understand. These patterns are written down and enforced as part of the web application.

3. Disregarding static content, there is no set connection between URLs and files on the web server. The URL addresses locations in concept-space, in the file system. A step called "routing" occurs when a web request is received that takes this conceptual address and decides what piece of application code to use to answer the request.

The big trick isn't that files necessarily needed to be organized differently (after all, there is no directory path on Flickr's hard drive called `photos/icygracy/`). Rather, a new layer of abstraction has been added on top of your web application and is being used as the addressable space. Previously, URLs operated at the layer of abstraction provided by your physical file system — files and directories — but now they operate within a hierarchically arranged set of concepts that you choose. Although your application code and structure is meaningful to *you* as the developer, it has no meaning to your users. This new layer of abstraction means that your URLs can be "pretty" and meaningful to your users as well.

This idea is not unique to Ruby on Rails. Many web servers such as Tomcat allow developers to create multiple contexts and handlers that can interpret the URL quite flexibly. But whereas they require hundreds of lines of XML to be configured, Rails requires only one or two with a new way of handling URLs called *routing*. And in the typical Rails fashion, routing is not optional but rather is the required mechanism by which all web requests are fulfilled. Because Rails makes routing both required and easy, development of simple, intuitive URLs can realistically become an important part of your web application's design process.

The Application Is the API

The second big idea is that your application *is* the Web API, and it always was. Every time a page in your site loads, that page is the response to an API request. The fact that a web page is rendered in HTML is just because of the response type of that API request. The information represented by that web page could just have well been represented in a text file, XML, RDF, or any other format you choose.

If you follow the first big idea — that URLs should represent concepts rather than files — you have already achieved the first big hurdle in making your web site and your Web API one and the same. By crafting your web pages around a set of concept-based URIs, you have already defined the "interface" for the API, the set of concepts that your web site makes available to its users. Now you just have to implement a back-end that is able to respond to non-HTML requests at those same URL endpoints.

The code that results forms a web application that can provide the output of each web request in a variety of different formats. A site designed in such a way is an enormous convenience to the developer. If suddenly you need to support CSV dumps of your data, all you need to do is describe what a CSV dump looks like and add that output format as another option on your controllers. This is the type of decoupling that MVC-based design aspires to enable.

The following sections show you how to implement your controller actions to address the requested actions first and decide on an appropriate format for response second. Then, when people ask whether you're planning to add an API to your site, you can smile and say, "It was an API from day one."

Routing

Routing is the key enabler that makes this new breed of Web APIs possible. Routing is a process by which an incoming HTTP request is matched to a particular piece of code (in Rails' case, a controller action) that should respond to that request. To do this, Rails scans incoming request URLs against a series of routes specified in the `config/routes.rb` file in your project. This routing step is what transforms the URL from an old-school file reference into a new-school conceptual identifier. The URL is input to the router, an address in conceptual space rather than an address on your file system.

Here's how the routing process works: When a new request arrives at your server, the web server first checks to see whether a static file with the given path is available in the public/ directory. If it is, the URL is interpreted as a location of a file in the web application's local filesystem and the contents of that file are simply returned to the user, effectively making routing backward compatible with the traditional way of using URLs. If the URL path does not match a file in the public/ directory, the request is handed off to Rails, which attempts to match the request path with a known route.

The routing process uses a series of route definitions that you provide to define the URL endpoints that your web application will respond to. Each route is a pattern to be filled in — like a Mad Libs game for URLs. Routes are examined in the order in which they appear in the routes.rb file, and the first one that matches the requested path is the one that determines the ultimate destiny of how that request will be handled.

Conceptually, these Route Libs look something like what is shown in Figure 5-1.

Route Libs URI Edition

'/blog/:**year**/:**month**/:**day**/:**title**.:**format**', :controller => 'blog', :action => 'view'

'/blog/ **2007** / **12** / **3** / **hello** . **xml**

Resulting Parameters Hash

controller	action	year	month	day	title	format
blog	view	2007	12	3	hello	xml

Figure 5-1

This picking-apart of the URL is not possible in a world that views web applications as directory hierarchies containing active files. In these document-centric worlds, the URL is just a path relative to the "webroot." With the router way of thinking, the URL is a template mapping into the concepts and actions on those concepts that your web application provides.

The actual route definition has three parts in the code:

1. The name
2. The template
3. Hash of defaults and validations

These three pieces are strung together into code that looks something like this:

```
map.connect 'photos/:user_handle/:photoset',
    :controller => 'photos',
    :action => 'list'
```

The *name* of the route is defined by the method that you call on the map object. So, if you call map.user to create your route, that route is associated with the name user, giving you such methods to use in your code as user_url and path_for_user. The route map.recipe would create a route called recipe. If you don't want to name a route (and sometimes you have no reason to), map.connect is the default method that will wire up a nameless one for you, as in the preceding example.

The next piece in a route definition is the route template. The route template is shown as `photos/:user_handle/:photoset` in the preceding example. Any path segment beginning with a colon represents a variable to be filled in — the fill-in-the-blanks of the Mad Libs. Anything else in the route is a required segment of the path that must appear verbatim. So, a path of `my/super/secret/page` defines a route with no variability; the URL path must appear exactly like that for the route to match. A route of `secret/:code` will match many different URLs, though — any two-segment path that begins with `secret/` and ends in some other characters. What comes after the segment `secret/` will become the contents of the `params[:code]` variable available within the controller.

In Rails fashion, a few of the variables are reserved for special purposes, and some are even required. The `:controller` variable must be defined in each route, either as a templated variable in the path definition or in the options hash (described below) that follows it. The `:action` variable is also special because it defines which action on the controller should be called to answer the request. If this variable is not provided as part of the route definition, Rails will assume that you want its value to be `index`. (If no `index` action is present on the controller, you'll receive an error. Finally, the optional `:format` variable provides a way to specify the desired response format. This variable provides a way other than MIME for clients to specify what response format they prefer. The ability to incorporate desired response types so easily into the route is one of the cornerstones that makes API building so easy.

The third component in a route definition is the options hash, which contains additional settings for the route, such as default values and validations. This hash might be default values for variables that may or may not be in the path template. The preceding code example sets the `:controller` variable to `photos`, for example. It also might contain regex-style restrictions on the format of data passed into a template variable from a URL segment. This additional regular expression allows you to place additional restrictions required for the route to match, letting you reduce the need for error checking later on. Requiring that all IDs must be numeric is one example of this that would alleviate the need to sanity-check IDs in your model or controller code.

All together, your `routes.rb` file ends up being a nice, easy-to-read URL design file that looks like this:

```
# Maps URLs such as '/dinner/12' to the Recipe::Feature action, setting the
# dinner_feature_id parameter
map.connect 'dinner/:dinner_feature_id',
    :controller => 'recipe',
    :action => 'feature'

# Maps to a user's calendar, defaulting to the current day, month, and year
map.connect 'user/:user_id/calendar/:year/:month/:day',
    :controller => 'calendar',
    :action => 'view',
    :year => Time.now.year,
    :month => Time.now.month,
    :day => Time.now.day

# Defaults any URL in the form of /A/B/C to the A::B action, with parameter ID=C
map.connect ':controller/:action/:id'
```

Because the `routes.rb` file is the link between all nonstatic web requests and your application code, it is clear that URL design is a very engineered and explicit step in Rails application development. Even the most artsy of web pages has a URL that has been consciously defined with a route. These routes represent the public interface of an API, even if that API returns only HTML pages. In an API, the protected and private methods that accomplish the low-level work are completely hidden from the API user.

Similarly, in a Web API with routes, the actual file structure of the web application performing the work is completely hidden from the user — a complete separation between the files that make your web application work and the URL patterns that provide access to that functionality.

With the freedom to design URL templates for your web application however you want, remember to make them predictable and simple. Avoid creating extremely long routes with a lot of parameters; with them, your URLs are no better looking than those of the late 1990s. The key is simplicity: Reduce your application to the fundamental concepts that your users are interested in and the actions that you might want to perform on those concepts. Those are your route definitions. Anything else — clarifying information such as sort order, referral codes, or result offsets — should be kept as URL-encoded parameters that come after the URL. This way, the URL path always represents a clear concept and the parameters just provide additional (and optional) fine-tuning for the way in which a request is processed. Chapter 6, "Resources and REST," will provide significant guidance on this matter because much of it deals with the decomposition of your public API into concepts called resources.

Anatomy of the Web API Call

URL routing opens the doors to user-friendly HTTP-based APIs and allows URLs to represent virtual endpoints within an application's functionality. These endpoints aren't enough to fully specify the Web API call, though. Altogether, a Web API call has four distinct components.

These four components, described in the following table, look a lot like the components of a traditional method call, with a few exceptions: The function caller gets to request a return type, and an HTTP command is provided alongside the method call as a bit of data to guide the execution of the method.

Component	Provided By	Purpose
Controller and Action	Route definition	Picks a particular controller class and method on that class to execute in response to the web request
Response Format	HTTP headers or route definition (the :format variable)	Specifies what format the response from the action should be provided in
Request Parameters	Form data or URL-encoded parameters	Provides additional parameters used to fulfill the basic request
HTTP Command	HTTP request	Asserts the basic nature of the request — whether it intends to fetch data, modify data, add data, or delete data

When you define your routes, this is the larger context into which they fit. Your web site is a collection of endpoints, each defined and accessed using the four components in the preceding table. Usually, these endpoints are served in HTML, but because the client can request other response formats, these endpoints also act as your programmatic API. In the next section, you'll see how to handle multiple response formats within the same action.

> ### Colliding (and Sometimes Incompatible) Worldviews
>
> Revisit this section of Chapter 5 after you learn about REST-based design in Chapter 6. The ideas about Web API design presented here differ slightly from those that you will encounter in the next chapter. Neither of the two approaches is categorically superior; each has pros and cons, and each lends itself to a different vibe of design.

Overlaying the API

After you've designed the URL patterns that represent the concepts and actions of your web application, it is time to overlay the non-HTML response formats alongside the HTML ones that you've probably already developed. Overlaying the API is just like coming up with the view of your web site, except that these new, alternative views are probably dynamically generated rather than stored in a collection of ERB files as their RHTML counterparts are. Overlaying the API takes two steps: First, you must multiplex each action's response based on the response formats you offer; second, you need to ensure that you can generate an appropriate response for each action in each format.

The respond_to Method

The `ActionController` framework provides your controllers with a very clever method called `respond_to` that makes serving up multiple formats from the same action easy. The method yields an object that you can use to specify code that executes only if the request asks for a particular format.

Using the `respond_to` method makes it easy to keep the implementation of the action and the implementation of the response relatively separate within the body of the action. The cleanest way to arrange both is to perform whatever work needs to be done for the action first and then finish the action's implementation with a `respond_to` block defining the different ways the results of that work can be expressed. The following code shows a template of this strategy:

```
class SomeController
  def action

      # ---------------------------------------
      # Perform the work of the action here
      # ---------------------------------------

    # Once that's done, provide the results of the work in a variety of formats

    respond_to do |:type|
      type.html { # Usually an empty body }
      type.xml  { # Usually a .to_xml call }
      type.rdf  { # Usually a .to_rdf call }
```

```
            type.js   { # Usually an RHTML partial or RJS template }
        end
      end
  end
```

This template works well to consolidate the behavior of each possible response format around a single implementation of the action above the respond_to block. Here is how the template looks when applied to a real controller action; in this case, it's one for viewing a photo:

```
class PhotoController
  def show

    @photo = Photo.find(params[:id])   # Set up variable required by the view

    respond_to do |:type|              # Render the view in requested format
      type.html {}                            # fall through to RHTML
      type.xml { render :xml => @photo.to_xml }
      type.rdf { render :rdf => @photo.to_rdf }   # requires acts_as_rdf plugin
      type.js  { render :partial => 'photo', :locals => {:photo => @photo }

    end
  end
end
```

The only operation this action takes is to find the photo; displaying the photo is handled by the view code that the action yields to. If the method of finding the photo were to change (perhaps the ID should instead be relative to a particular user's photo stream), the implementation need be changed only once across all response formats.

Sometimes the operation that an action causes is more complex than simply loading a photo. You'll need to be prepared to catch any errors that might happen and respond to the user with an error message in an appropriate format. Handling errors poses a problem in our neat and tidy respond_to world: How do we keep the response format details from getting tangled up with the implementation of the action body if we might need to bail out with an error at seven points in the middle of an action? Luckily, this problem has a solution.

Recall from the previous chapter the design technique of embedding most of your heavy functionality inside the model layer and using custom exceptions to report any errors. If you follow this error-handling strategy and use custom exceptions with clear messages, exceptions can be the solution that keeps your action implementations simple.

Rather than fill your action code with layer after layer of nested conditionals to check for errors after they occur, write your model objects so that they raise exceptions as soon as errors occur. This way, you can be sure that as long as the script is still flowing, nothing that you've planned for has gone wrong, and you are free to plow ahead as if no error checking is necessary. Meanwhile, behind the scenes, you know that an exception will be raised if something does go wrong during the execution flow. To handle these exceptions if they are raised, surround your action with a rescue block that will gracefully handle the error and report it to the user in a number of formats.

Here is the template of a multiformat action that performs error handling. Notice how it looks just like the previous template except the response format fan-out occurs twice — once for a successful response and once for an erroneous one:

```
class SomeController
  def action

    # -------------------------------------
    # Perform the work of the action here
    # -------------------------------------

    # Once that's done, provide the results of the work in a variety of formats

    respond_to do |:type|
      type.html { # Usually an empty body }
      type.xml  { # Usually a .to_xml call }
      type.js   { # Usually an RHTML partial or RJS template }
    end

  rescue => err

    # Oh, no! An error occurred. Respond with the error.

    respond_to do |:type|
      type.html { # Usually a redirect with a flash message }
      type.xml  { # Usually an error structure or HTTP error }
      type.js   { # Usually an action-specific safe response with a
                  #   JavaScript-based flash message }
    end
  end
end
```

As with any pattern, this template isn't a panacea for handling all possible errors. Situations may still arise that require finer-grained attention within your controller actions in order to attempt recovery or change the action's behavior. But this basic template will give you a solid starting point within which to fill your own code.

Using the `respond_to` block, the routes that once defined endpoints into your web site have now become programmatic endpoints into a web application. If you've designed your web site well, little work is needed to extend your existing actions so that they work with programmatic formats such as XML. The action implementations are already there, so the only work left is to define the way in which the result of the action is translated into each possible response format.

Writing a Non-HTML Result

Creating the output for a non-HTML result is often easier than creating it for HTML because unless you're writing to a visual medium such as PDF, you are likely interested in only the raw data. Where this process becomes more complicated than HTML is in your ability to change the way you express your data after you've already released an API. Though you can change the look of your HTML output anytime without serious side effect, changing the structure of XML output, for example, can be a traumatic event if you have many API users. So design with care when you construct outputs in languages such as XML and RDF, because it might not be that easy to change your mind after you've deployed the service.

This section describes three data formats that you may want to use for an API and how to get started with each: XML, RSS, and RDF.

Grouping XML, RSS, and RDF

Purists will note that grouping XML, RSS, and RDF is a bit like grouping apples and oranges: XML is a data-representation syntax, RDF is a conceptual model for graph-based data that can be transcribed in XML, and RSS is a syndication standard that can also be transcribed in XML. But despite their different natures, their grouping makes sense because as far as APIs are concerned, these three are the most important data formats on the Web today.

XML

If you don't mind your XML documents matching your database schema exactly, writing XML output from a Rails application is just a one liner. Every ActiveRecord object has a to_xml method that will scan the fields of the model object and write them as though they were XML tags, so a respond_to block that looks like this:

```
@user = User.find(params[:id])
respond_to do |:type|
    type.xml  { render :xml => @user.to_xml }
end
```

could produce the following XML:

```
<user>
   <first_name>Ted</first_name>
   <last_name>Benson</last_name>
   <address>...</address>
</user>
```

The to_xml function also supports an options hash that can both limit which fields are included in the XML and extend the serialization to associated model objects. For example, passing the hash :include = > [:association1, :association2] will cause the XML writer to recurse into those ActiveRecord associations and include them in the XML serialization.

The easiest way to customize the XML output for a particular action past what ActiveRecord generates for you automatically is to use RXML templates. These files are similar to RHTML files and live in the same place in your project structure, but they use a framework called Builder rather than ActionView.

RXML files are regular Ruby files that are passed a Builder instance named xml that you use to construct your XML document. Don't let the file extension fool you: these are Code-First files, not Document-First.

Whereas the output of an RHTML file is anything that is rendered outside the `< % ... % >` tags, the output of an RXML document is the result of calls to the `xml` variable in your RXML document. In other words, RHTML files are document-first style, but RXML files are code-first style.

To create a tag, simply call the tag name as a method on the `Builder` object. This method call doesn't exist, of course, but gets passed to the `method_missing` routine on the object, which the builder interprets as an instruction to create a new tag. (You will learn how to develop with `method_missing` in Chapter 10, "Code That Writes Code (That Writes Code).") How this tag looks depends on how you make the method call:

❑   Given no arguments, the builder will create an empty tag. So `xml.br` will yield `< br / >`

❑   Given an argument, the builder will create a tag that contains a literal. So `xml.h1("Hi!")` will yield `< h1 > Hi! < /h1 >`. Attributes are added as a hash passed in as the last argument to any method call that creates a tag. So creating a hyperlink with the builder would look like the following:

```
xml.a "Art of Rails", :href => "http://www.artofrails.com"
```

❑   Given a block, the builder will create a tag that contains any tags created inside that block. So the command

```
xml.people {
  xml.person {
    xml.first_name("Ted")
  }
}
```

will yield the XML

```
<people>
  <person>
    <first_name>Ted</first_name>
  </person>
</people>
```

Put these three basic behaviors together, and you have all the building blocks for an XML document of any complexity. There's a bit more to learn (such as declaring the document type, XML comments, and so on), and the best place to do so is in the documentation for the `Builder` class at `http://builder.rubyforge.org/`.

RSS

RSS feeds have become an important way to allow users to maintain loose ties to your site. Often, a user does not want to check your blog or a particular feature of your application (for example, whether the user has new friend requests in a social network) every day, but the user is still interested in responding to those items when they do occur. Using an RSS reader, users can automate the task of checking to see whether something has changed and be alerted by a preview of the change so that they can decide whether they want to visit your site.

Creating an RSS feed for your Rails application is a great exercise in learning RXML because RXML is exactly how you do it. To get started, here is a template of what a one-article RSS 2.0 feed for a blog might look like:

```
<?xml version="1.0"?>
<rss version="2.0">
    <channel>
        <title>Art of Rails Blog</title>
        <link>http://www.artofrails.com/</link>
        <description>In search of artful bits of programming goodness.</description>
        <pubDate>Sat, 07 Dec 2007 00:00:01 GMT</pubDate>
        <item>
            <title>Welcome to the Blog</title>
            <link>http://www.artofrails.com/posts/1</link>
            <pubDate>Sat, 07 Dec 2007 00:00:01 GMT</pubDate>
            <description>This is the first blog post. Have you ever...</description>
        </item>
    </channel>
</rss>
```

The root tag is named `rss`, followed by a `channel` tag that contains the hypothetical blog's feed. After a few descriptors describing the channel, a series of `item` tags contain descriptors about the blog posts that they represent. Transforming this code into RXML is just a matter of taking each element in the example feed and turning it into a call to the XML Builder object. Following is what that resulting `rss.rxml` file might look like, contributed by Scott Raymond, author of *Ajax on Rails* (O'Reilly).

```
xml.instruct!
xml.rss "version" => "2.0", "xmlns:dc" => "http://purl.org/dc/elements/1.1/" do
    xml.channel do

        xml.title       "Feed Name"
        xml.description "Feed Description"
        xml.link        url_for :only_path => false, :controller => 'posts'
        xml.pubDate     CGI.rfc1123_date @posts.first.updated_at if @posts.any?

        @posts.each do |posts|
            xml.item do
                xml.title       post.name
                xml.link        url_for :only_path => false,
                                        :controller => 'posts',
                                            :action => 'show',
                                                :id => post.id
                xml.description post.body
                xml.pubDate     CGI.rfc1123_date post.updated_at
                xml.guid        url_for :only_path => false,
                                        :controller => 'posts',
                                            :action => 'show',
                                                :id => post.id
                xml.author      "#{post.author.email} (#{post.author.name})"
            end # End <item>
        end # End posts.each
    end # End <channel>
end #  End <rss>
```

Notice how this code depends on the existence of only one variable, `@posts`, that would have been set by the controller. Just as the URL bound to this action would have returned a web page listing all the blog posts if a web browser had asked for it, that same URL can provide the same information in RSS format when asked for by a news reader.

RDF

RDF is a web-native resource model and language for describing resources, their properties, and the relationships between them. The language views the world as a graph of nodes, representing resources, and arcs running between them. Both nodes and arcs are represented by URIs (arc targets can also be data literals), which makes RDF good at describing both abstract objects and resources on the web.

Although RDF does not enjoy nearly the popularity that free-form XML currently does as a medium for information exchange, its support is steadily growing because of RDF's ability to ease the process of merging information from multiple data sources. Graph-based information storage can be frustrating, but it is also amazingly flexible; if you gather statements about a resource from several different locations, it isn't any harder to merge that information than if you had gathered them all from the same place. As the world of web mash-ups increases in complexity, RDF should play a big role enabling that richer exchange of information.

An easy way to provide RDF as an API data format is to use the `acts_as_rdf` plug-in from www .artofrails.com. This plug-in provides your `ActiveRecord` model objects with a `to_rdf` method with similar characteristics to the `to_xml` one they already have. It also adds a `to_rdf` method to Collection objects so that you can render an entire group of model objects as RDF at the same time.

By default, `acts_as_rdf` will use your site's configured domain name and the model object's resource path as a namespace, and it will guess property names based on your database schema. These can all be overridden if necessary, and as can `to_xml`, the `to_rdf` method can be instructed to follow associations and include those objects in the serialization as well.

Adding Custom MIME Types

In order for Rails to respond to the type requested by the `Accept` header, it needs to know what that format is. By default, Rails recognizes only a few basic types of response format:

❑ HTML

❑ XML

❑ JS (Used for AJAX requests)

Rails keeps track of data formats the same way that virtually all other Internet applications and protocols do: with MIME Types. MIME stands for Multipurpose Internet Mail Extensions and was developed as a way for e-mail programs to support more complex data than just plain-text ASCII. Although much of MIME remains only in the e-mail world, its taxonomy of data formats is used across the Internet as the standard way to describe how to interpret a piece of data.

Virtually all existing data types that you would want to use over the Internet have a preexisting MIME name that you can look up and add to your Rails project configuration to support it. MIME Types are maintained by the Internet Assigned Numbers Authority (IANA) and are available on IANA's web site at `http://www.iana.org/assignments/media-types/`. There you'll find a page with nine top-level categories of types, as follows:

- application
- audio
- example
- image
- message
- model
- multipart
- text
- video

Each category is a link to the registered types that fit that category. When you find the type that describes your data, the final description to use is the category, followed by a forward slash, followed by the type name. So if you want to add JPEG images as a potential response type, after finding the `jpeg` entry under the `image` category, you would know that the proper MIME type is `image/jpeg`.

If you can't find a suitable type that describes the data format you are using, you can create your own, as you will see shortly.

Registering Types with Rails

After you know what MIME Type you want to support, registering it with Rails is easy. Open the `config/initializers/mime_types.rb` file and add a line in the form of:

```
Mime::Type.register "image/png", :png
```

This line makes Rails aware of your new type application wide so that you can reference it in your controllers just as you would the built-in types `html`, `xml`, and `js`. The first parameter to the `Mime::Type.register` function provides the description of the type according to MIME. This is what would be stored in an HTTP `Accept` header. The second argument is a symbol that you want to use throughout your Rails application to refer to that type. This symbol is also mapped into the handler that processes the `:format` variable in any routes you define.

Using the preceding type registration, a controller action that had the ability to render a user's social network as a PNG image could use `:png` as an option in the `respond_to` block:

```
respond_to do |:type|
   type.html { # fall through }
   type.png  { render_png_image }
end
```

This functionality could be invoked by the remote user either by specifying `image/png` as the first-priority `Accept` type in the request header, or by ending the request that led to this action in `.png`.

Creating Your Own MIME Type

If you are really pushing the envelope and want to create an unofficial type for that new data format you just created to describe streaming interactive holograms, you can do that, too. The general format for custom data types is to pick whatever top-level type is appropriate and combine it with the name of your creation as the subtype, prefixed by ''x-'' for experimental. Usually, unofficial MIME Types are filed under the application super-type (because everything is application specific until it becomes a standard), but you can pick any one that you feel fits. A few more naming tips:

❑   If your name has multiple words, separate them with periods. For example: `application/ x-hyper.dimensional.holography`

❑   If your data format is based on an existing syntax, such as XML, incorporate the name of the syntax into the subtype name after a plus sign. For example:

```
application/x-hyper.dimensional.holography+xml
```

API-Metering, the Rails Way

Depending on the type of API you offer, you might want to consider metering access. If your API provides alternative data formats intended for human reading, such as PDF, you might not need to meter; it is safe to expect that usage patterns of this type of API will be similar to those of the HTML version of your site. For formats that are intended to be used by a computer, however, such as XML and RDF, metering API access is an important step to protect the stability of your application.

Here's the scenario: You offer a directory of pizza parlors across the world, complete with their menus and offerings — a one-stop shop for pizza connoisseurs. You also wrote an API that allows queries to your site to be answered in XML so that other programs can easily use your data. You offer all this for free because you are, after all, dedicated to the higher cause of promoting pizza appreciation around the world.

But then a new craze catches on in Japan: After a pop star announces that she will stay in hotels only within walking distance of pizza parlors that serve mayonnaise-topped pizza, the entire country goes pizza wild. All the travel agencies begin offering web mash-ups of their hotel deals with nearby pizza outlets. Their source for this pizza information? Your API.

Your web server catches on fire from the heat generated by the heavy load on your dual Ethernet cards. Who knew XML was flammable? As you fight the fire with a garden hose and hold back your tears (you didn't make any backups), you think to yourself: Why didn't I implement API metering?!

The following sections will show you how to weave API metering into your site so that you can implement it in a few short blocks of code and apply it cleanly to any API methods that you need to protect from the mayonnaise-pizza–crazed public. All the code from this section is available for download from the book's companion web site at `www.wrox.com` or from `www.artofrails.com`.''

Authenticating the User

The first step in metering an API is authentication, because you can't meter a request unless you know who's asking. There are two broad categories of APIs when it comes to authentication: those that care about authenticating only so that they can meter usage and those that need to protect private data. Google Maps, for example, falls into the former category, and the Facebook API falls into the latter.

If you're of the first group, then the typical API key pattern will work just fine for you. If you are among the latter group and are exposing user-specific data over your API, then you should consider offering a more complex, session- or token-based API login mechanism that will provide more robust security around access to your site.

The API key pattern is one in which an API user's user name and password are rolled into a single string of characters called the API key. This string is usually long (you never actually type this key by hand; it is intended for programmatic use) and is automatically generated by the web application. Each API key serves as the unique identifier for a particular API user and is sent as a parameter on the API request for identification.

Because this form of authentication is vulnerable to attack, many sites employing this scheme will use it in combination with an IP "whitelist" that contains a list of the IP addresses that are allowed to make requests using this key. If the requesting IP is on the whitelist, the authentication succeeds. If not, it fails. Access to modifications of this whitelist is controlled more stringently through the HTML version of the web site.

Using API keys together with IP whitelists is a simple but effective way to provide authentication for a site. Following is an example of how you might do it.

First, create an `ApiUse` model class that will `belong_to` your `User` models and will contain the information necessary to track a user's API use. For now, this model has only three fields besides the implied `id` field.

ApiUse		
user_id	Api_key	allowed_domains

Next, create an authentication function on the `ApiUse` class that either returns the `ApiUse` instance object or throws an exception.

```
def self.authenticate(api_key, requesting_address)
   api_use = ApiUse.find(:first, :conditions => "api_key = '#{api_key}'")

   # Make sure the API Key refers to an existing ApiUse
   raise ArtOfRails::Chapter5::UserNotFoundError,
      "Invalid API Key." if api_user == nil || api_use.blank?

   # Make sure the requesting_address is in the whitelist
   # Assumption: the whitelist is a comma-separated list
   unless api_use.allowed_domains.split(',').include? requesting_address
      raise ArtOfRails::Chapter5::DomainNotAuthorizedError,
         "Requesting Host Not Authorized"
   end
   api_use
end
```

This function performs two checks on the data passed to it. First, it makes sure that the `ApiUse` referenced actually exists. Second, it checks to make sure that the provided requesting address is a member of a serialized array of allowed hosts stored on the `ApiUse` object. If either of these conditions is false, then it raises a custom exception defined in a module elsewhere in the project. If all goes well, then it returns the `ApiUse` object.

The Metering Algorithm

After you've authenticated the user, the next step is to ensure that the user hasn't exceeded whatever limits you've placed on him or her. The standard metering algorithm is based on the idea that users must sign up for accounts to use your API, and each user gets X number of calls to your API every T units of time, with no rollover. This algorithm can be implemented around two columns in your API use table: `last_access` and `accesses_this_period`.

ApiUse				
user_id	api_key	Allowed_domains	last_access	accesses_this_period

Let's simplify the algorithm further by saying that the "T units of time" bit is always going to be some regular calendar interval, such as an hour or a day. The example code here assumes one day to make the date math nice and easy.

The following code is one example of how you can implement a metering function. This implementation raises an exception if the user exceeds his or her limit, rather than returns a Boolean `false`. For this code to work, define the constant `DAILY_API_LIMIT` in your `config/environment.rb` file as an integer representing how many times per day any one user may use your site's API. This code should be placed as a method on your `ApiUse` model object.

```
def record_api_request
   if (self.last_access < Date.today + 1)
      # They haven't yet used the API today
      self.last_access = Date.today
      self.accesses_this_period = 1
      self.save
   elsif self.accesses_this_period >= DAILY_API_LIMIT
      # They've used the API too much!
      raise ArtOfRails::Chapter5::UsageLimitExceededError,
         "Daily Usage Limit Exceeded"
   else
      # Not the first use, but still within their limits
      self.accesses_this_period = self.accesses_this_period + 1
      self.save
   end
end
```

So on any particular `ApiUse` model instance, the `record_api_request` will attempt to increment the number of API calls that the user has made on the current day. First, it checks to see whether the last request was made on the current day. If it wasn't, then it resets the count to 1 and sets the last access to today's date. If it was, then it tries to increment the access count. If the user has already met the daily limit, then this value cannot be incremented and an exception is thrown.

Applying Metering via Filters

With both the authentication and metering functions in place, the only challenge is to apply them to your code without cluttering the implementation of your actions. Remember that Rails-style programming places a high value on code that appears neat and clean. Using filters, you'll create an implementation that can be added onto actions that serve as API endpoints outside the implementation of those actions. This approach will let you keep the code inside your actions focused on the goal of the action and not cluttered with code concerning the API policy of the web site.

Remember from Chapter 4, "Getting the Most from M, V, and C," that filters are a way to stack cross-cutting code before or after a controller action is processed. Filters get access to all the information that the action gets, and they can alter the way the request is handled, from changing the response sent to the user to canceling the execution of the action entirely. The heart of the filter is just a method on the controller.

The goal is to create a method that applies both API authentication and the metering to an incoming request. If the request is successful, then the function simply returns, and the request passes normally to the requested action. If an exception is thrown during the authentication or metering steps, however, then the method catches it and prevents the action from being called. In a real implementation, you would also want to provide some sort of error response appropriate to your application so that users know what went wrong. This code is written to be used as an `around_filter`.

```
def api_auth

    # Note: A real application should implement a better way of judging
    # the response format that will be used (see sidebar below)
    response_type =
     Mime::EXTENSION_LOOKUP[params[:format]].to_sym rescue response_type = :html

    if API_TYPES.include? response_type
        @api_use = ApiUse.authenticate(params[:api_key], request.remote_ip)
        @api_use.record_api_request
    end
    yield
rescue ArtOfRails::Chapter5::UserNotFoundError,
        ArtOfRails::Chapter5::DomainNotAuthorizedError,
        ArtOfRails::Chapter5::UsageLimitExceededError => err

    # TODO: Provide a response to the API user

    false
end
```

Add this code to the `ApplicationController` so that it is available throughout your application. An additional constant, `API_TYPES`, should be added to your `config/environment.rb` file to define the data formats that you'd like to meter as API calls. The constant definition might look like

```
API_TYPES = [ :xml, :rdf, :csv ]
```

Finally, in each controller that contains actions you'd like to meter, add a reference to this method as an `around_filter`, like so:

```
around_filter :api_auth, :only => [:action1, :action2, :action3]
```

That's a nice one liner that is easy to read and understand, and it is all you'll need going forward to protect any controllers that provide raw data. The actions that are metered will need to know how to respond properly to API requests using a `respond_to` clause, but they can now be implemented without any knowledge of metering or authentication occurring.

Spot the Security Vulnerability

Look at the following line from the `api_auth` method in the "Applying Metering via Filters" section and try to spot the concern:

```
response_type =
    Mime::EXTENSION_LOOKUP[params[:format]].to_sym rescue response_
type = :html
```

Your intention is to determine what the response format of the request will be so that you can decide whether the request needs to metered. HTML requests might not be metered, but XML requests might be, for instance.

The problem is that this line attempts to discover the response format using only the `params[:format]` variable, which is set only if the URL takes the form `/path/to/resource.format`. In reality, content-type negotiation is not that simple. Rather than use a format extension on the URL, API users might choose to send a whole list of `Accept` headers with the API request. The content type of the response will then be the result of a negotiation between the content types that your application supports and the list of acceptable types provided.

Given that, can you spot the security vulnerability in the aforementioned code? (Hint: What happens if the format is set to XML using HTTP headers rather than the URL?)

You can test this vulnerability with the command line `curl` program:

```
curl -H "Accept: text/xml" localhost:3000/your/api/call
```

The command will return the XML response from your Rails API, but the `ApiUse` object will not show an increased usage count. This is because the `params[:format]` variable will evaluate to nil (because none was provided in the URL string), causing the `api_auth` method to default it to `html` and skip API metering. When the execution reaches the action, however, Rails will correctly determine from the `HTTP Accept` header that the response format should be XML.

To implement the `api_auth` algorithm securely, you must determine the response type the same way that Rails does so that you know that your decision to meter or not to meter is the right one. To do this, look at the `ActionController::MimeResponds` module in the Rails source, and either mimic or directly call the algorithm that you find there.

What about SOAP/XML-RPC Services?

Much of the latest Rails API development concentrates on providing HTTP-based APIs that operate as alternate data formats available at the exact same endpoints as the HTML version of the site. Despite this, Web Services (the ones with a capital *W* and *S*) haven't gone away and are popular in enterprise-centric environments. This section explores briefly how to implement APIs based on SOAP and XML-RPC in Rails using the `ActionWebService` framework.

Services developed using `ActionWebService` require three definitions: service API, service implementation, and struct definition.

Service API

Whereas service APIs in normal Rails applications are defined implicitly by the routes that you set up to map URLs into your application, SOAP Web Services are a bit more strict and require an explicit document that states what is expected and offered by the service. This API definition is translated into the WSDL document that clients use to bind their code to your remote service.

Defining a SOAP-based API is much like writing a header file in a C++ program or an interface in Java. The intent is to formalize a contract that places expectations on both the client and the server. When everything works as advertised, the effect removes the need for a human to manually configure and test whether the service bindings work.

As does an `ActiveRecord` migration, Web Service API definitions in Rails take the form of a Ruby class filled with macros that define the items available on that class. Instead of fields, the API definition contains method signature definitions. Each method signature represents one method call that the service agrees to provide to remote users.

Each method signature contains two parts: `:expects` and `:returns`. These arguments map to an ordered array of values that represent information that should be provided to the method call and information that will be returned from it, respectively.

Each of the elements that can be expected or returned takes one of three forms:

❑ A symbol specifying a primitive data type (such as `:integer`, `:string`, or `:boolean`).

❑ A class that derives from a structured type, such as `ActionWebService::Struct` or `ActionWebService::Base` (see the "Creating Structs" section, later in this chapter).

❑ A single element array containing one of the previous two items. This denotes that the argument is not a single object of the specified type but an array of those objects.

These three element types provide enough flexibility to describe a wide array of method signatures. Here is an example of an API description that contains three methods. The first, `find_recipe`, takes a `RecipeQuery` object and returns an array of `Recipe` objects. The second, `rate_recipe`, takes two integers and returns nothing. The third, `add_comment`, takes an integer and a string and also returns nothing.

```
class RecipeAPI < ActionWebService::API::Base
    api_method :find_recipe, :expects => [RecipeQuery], :returns => [[Recipe]]
    api_method :rate_recipe, :expects => [:int, :int]
    api_method :add_comment, :expects => [:int, :string]
end
```

You might guess, with good chances, what the arguments on the last two methods are meant to represent, but it would help to be able to name these arguments. Rails provides a way to name these parameters by substituting each individual element with a hash that maps the parameter name to the element definition. So what once was `:string` would become `{:comment = > :string}`.

110

```
class RecipeAPI < ActionWebService::API::Base
   api_method :find_recipe, :expects => [RecipeQuery], :returns => [[Recipe]]
   api_method :rate_recipe, :expects => [{:recipe => :int}, {:rating => :int}]
   api_method :add_comment, :expects => [{:recipe => :int}, {:comment => :string}]
end
```

These service definitions live in the app/apis directory of your Rails project, a directory not automatically generated as part of an empty Rails project. The filename should match the name of the API, so class RecipeAPI would become recipe_api.rb.

Service Implementation

In contrast to the Web APIs techniques shown in the rest of this chapter, ActionWebService-based APIs cannot easily share implementations with other response data formats. Although ActionWebService allows your service implementation to exist on regular Rails controllers, the actions it uses work a bit differently from normal Rails actions. ActionWebService actions take arguments as part of their method signatures instead of through the params hash, and they do not render any results. Instead, they return the value that should be serialized as the response to the remote method invocation. So although ActionWebService methods might share the same surroundings as your web-based code, getting them to share functionality is tricky.

You have three different approaches to mapping an ActionWebService-based service onto a controller: direct, delegated, and layered. Each offers increasingly flexible management of service endpoints. I cover only the direct approach here, but more documentation is available online at the Ruby on Rails manual (http://manuals.rubyonrails.com/read/chapter/69).

Assuming that your service definition is stored following conventions in the app/apis directory, the controller by the same name (for example, RecipeController) is automatically associated with it. All you need to do is implement each method described by the API definition as a public method on the controller.

For example, the method described in the API definition by

```
api_method :find_recipe, :expects => [RecipeQuery], :returns => [[Recipe]]
```

might be implemented as

```
def find_recipe(recipe_query)
   @recipes = Recipe.find_with_query_obj(recipe_query)
   @recipes
end
```

Or the method

```
api_method :add_comment, :expects => [:int, :string]
```

might be implemented as

```
def add_comment(recipe_id, comment)
   @recipe = Recipe.find(recipe_id)
```

```
      @recipe.add_comment(comment) unless @recipe.nil?
   end
```

In short, the method must be public, must take in the :expects objects as its method parameters, and must return an object matching the :returns definition.

Creating Structs

Many times, an object required or returned by a Web Service is more complicated than a primitive data type. In these circumstances, ActionWebService provides the ability to define a class reminiscent of a C struct that specifies how a combination of primitive data types and other structs come together to form a composite object. In the API definition given above, two such objects were used — RecipeQuery and Recipe — both to make the find_recipe service call possible. Each of these can be defined with the ActionWebService::Struct superclass.

The ActionWebService::Struct base class provides macros to its children that allow them to define fields on an object in a manner similar to the service API definition you just saw. Here is an example of what the Recipe struct might look like. It contains several basic data types, an array of strings representing the genre of food the recipe falls into, an array of strings representing the URLs of photos of that recipe, and an array of Ingredient struct objects.

```
class Recipe < ActionWebService::Struct
   member : name, :string
   member :rating, :integer
   member :genre, [:string]
   member :author_name, :string
   member :author_id, :integer
   member :photo_urls, [:string]
   member :ingredients, [Ingredient]
   member :directions, :string
end
```

Using structs like these is the Web Services alternative to returning an XML document (it gets serialized to XML behind the scenes, but you don't deal with that serialization). Any client with properly generated stubs will experience the result of a Web Service call as first-class objects accessible from within the programming environment instead of as documents full of tags.

Summary

This chapter covered a lot of ground about the way your site interacts with its users. It described the new breed of HTTP-based Web APIs that the Rails community is popularizing and explained why this approach to API development can save developers a great deal of effort. The chapter touched briefly on routes — how they act as an API definition for your site and how to build them — and it discussed the respond_to mechanism in Rails controllers that allows a single action to provide its response in many formats. I also covered how to create responses in a few of the more popular formats — XML, RSS, and RDF — with pointers to more documentation online. Finally, I included a high-level run through of ActionWebService to give it its share of coverage amidst all the attention that other API techniques have been getting these days.

Two important concepts were introduced in this chapter. The first is that URLs in web applications don't have to address physical documents or scripts on your web server's file system. Instead, they can address virtual objects within your web application, such as `/users/ted/photos/12`. Routing makes this new way to use URLs possible and allows your URL route specification to serve as your API interface description.

The second important idea presented in this chapter is the belief that API development and web development do not have to be independent pursuits. This chapter showed a line of thinking quite the opposite — that your entire web application presents a single collection of functionality, and that functionality may be addressed in a number of different formats. Development of your API and development of your web site are really the same task with two different return types.

The next chapter discusses REST-based design, an architectural style that many feel to be the ultimate goal that web applications should strive toward. REST-based web sites describe themselves entirely in terms of resources that are accessed over the web via CRUD operations, and these CRUD operations are specified using HTTP commands.

6

Resources and REST

"COM! NET! ORG! We represent much more! COM! NET! ORG! We represent much more!" The chanting grew louder as Web neared the square. A stage was set up right in the center, and an empty podium waited for the gathering's speakers to begin their addresses. Web could feel the buzz that permeates the senses whenever people assemble in a herd — the echoing chants, the waving signs, motion, aspiration, all in unison.

Up near the square, the composition of the crowd was more diverse — not just URLs but protocols, interpreters, libraries — everyone gathered to support the URLs. A few technicians appeared on the stage and began tinkering with the microphone.

"Testing, testing," a skinny URL tapped on the microphone, his voice cracking. "Looks like we'll be multicasting today, ahiehaha!" he said to cheering crowds.

These guys just don't quit, Web thought to himself, shaking his head. But why am I here? Who am I supposed to meet?

And then Web caught her eye, up near the stage but off to the side where the crowd was sparse — a woman with the unmistakable look of someone who was above the fray. She held a walkie-talkie in her hand and stood with three others in deep conversation.

The woman said something and the other three turned and looked at Web.

Are you . . . ? Web mouthed from across the square, not knowing what else to say but remembering what he had been told back at the compound.

Just show up and stay alert. Everything else will take care of itself.

Yes, the woman mouthed back, nodding her head. One of the men to her left waved his arm and beckoned for Web to come over. Web began making his way across the street.

"You must be Web! We've been waiting for you!" the woman greeted him as he neared. "I'm Jen. Rusty told us to keep an eye out for you." She shook Web's hand. "And these are my colleagues, helping me keep things in order for the events today."

"It's a pleasure," Web said, "but I have to be honest; I'm not exactly sure what part I play."

"Don't you worry, everything has its place — that will soon be apparent if nothing else. I'm terribly sorry but right now I have to run. You wouldn't believe the mess that's just happened with the water truck. Someone gave the driver a private IP address to deliver to and he never made it out of the warehouse parking lot. Anyway, I'm supposed to give you this."

She handed Web a business card. On one side was his own name embossed in black ink, and on the other side was a map leading several blocks away from the main square to some place named The Underground.

"It's a restaurant," Jen continued. "We go there whenever an event is in town. Be there an hour after the crowd dissipates, and the rest of us will come meet you. It will be a much better place for talking."

"Jen! The URLs say they broke the mic! Where did you put the backups?" A man with a clipboard shouted from the corner of the stage.

"Hold on!" Jen rolled her eyes and gave Web a reluctant look, hoping to end the conversation.

"It's okay," Web said. "Go ahead. I'm looking forward to listening to the speakers, anyway."

"Thank you. I'll see you later on!" She turned, alternating shouted instructions between her walkie-talkie and the stage hand, and disappeared behind the platform.

Web stayed where he was — he preferred the sidelines where there was room to move — and watched the crowd mill about before the speaking began. He had found the people he was supposed to meet, but the question still lingered in his mind. Why am I here?

Representational State Transfer, or REST, is a design style that leads to truly "web native" applications that take advantage of the characteristics of the HTTP protocol and resource-oriented programming. RESTful development affects all aspects of your web application right from the start. At the design stage, REST provides guidelines that help you determine how to model your controllers and user-facing objects. During the implementation stage, REST allows you to take advantage of standardized resource operations provided by HTTP. And after your application is deployed, it makes you part of the REST-based web services community with little-to-no extra effort on your part.

To many web developers, REST is an architectural style for the web in the same way and with the same importance that MVC is an architectural style for application code. Both offer a systematic way to organize code, both provide a standard and predictable control flow between components, and both do so using the tools that you already have in front of you. The first half of this chapter explores the design style and implications of REST, and the second half shows how to use Rails to publish and consume RESTful resources.

A Web of Resources

RESTful design is, like the emerging Semantic Web, fundamentally grounded in the idea of resources and resource identifiers. A resource is a conceptual object, something that exists as an idea in our minds and that can be talked about — for example, your pair of ripped blue jeans, the Yahoo! search engine, chocolate cake, or the *New York Times'* front page from January 20, 2008. Resources exist only in concept-space, not in the physical world and not on disk, but there are three things you can do with them:

❑ Name a resource

❑ Talk about a resource

❑ Represent a resource

I discuss each of these three capabilities shortly, but to clarify, I offer a brief example first. Say that I created a resource to represent my old Ford Explorer — not the physical object in my driveway but the concept of that object. I can name this resource `http://edwardbenson.com/95ford` so that I can talk about it. When I tell friends that `http://edwardbenson.com/95ford` broke down, they know with certainty exactly which concept I am referring to. That resource can also be represented in several different ways in the real world. When I drive to work in the morning, I am using the physical representation of that resource. If I look at a photo of my car, I am looking at a graphical representation of that resource. When my transmission blew, the auto repair shop used their computers to pull up a repair-history representation of that resource. These are three different physical representations of the same conceptual entity, the resource. This explanation might seem a bit too philosophical for web development, but it is vital to both REST and the decentralized information system that the World Wide Web is beginning to represent.

Identifying Resources

Resources need identifiers in order for you to talk about them. A Universal Resource Identifier (URI) provides this capability. A URI looks just like a URL, but it addresses an idea in concept-space rather than a document on a physical server on the Internet. Of course, many URIs do in fact resolve to locations on the Internet, and when they do, they can also be called by the more commonplace name, Uniform Resource *Locators* (URLs).

The construction of URIs forms a global namespace that guarantees syntactic uniformity and encourages uniqueness. In the web-resolvable world of URLs, you make names in this namespace grow in specificity from left to right by separating segments of the URI using the forward-slash character. This means that anyone in the world can create an infinite number of unique resource identifiers as long as he or she acquires a prefix in the namespace to call his or her own.

The URL of the web site `http://www.artofrails.com/` can be used as such a prefix. Building off of this prefix, I can create URIs that stand for each chapter of this book:

```
http://www.artofrails.com/chapters/1
http://www.artofrails.com/chapters/2
http://www.artofrails.com/chapters/13
```

Remember that these are really URIs, so they stand for conceptual objects rather than web pages. If you try to follow these links, you will find that the first two return web pages, but the third link results in an HTTP 404 error. A web page for Chapter 13 does not exist, nor does a chapter by that number in this book, but as long as the URI exists, then so does some conceptual idea that it stands for, even if there is no available information about that idea in the resolvable world.

Talking About Resources

Because resource IDs are supposed to be unique, URIs serve as the über primary keys. The partitioning scheme for domain names in the real world helps URLs make this a reality. In a one-table, two-column database that covers the entire universe and maps primary keys to concepts, the URI is that primary key. With a primary key, you can unambiguously refer to a conceptual object in any medium and in any place: in an HREF property, in an XML file, in a letter to a friend, or in neon spray paint underneath a bridge.

In traditional CGI-oriented programming, objects and their references are kept internal to the system; they are primary keys in a database that are unavailable to the outside world. Recall from the previous chapter that the predominant style of web applications a few years ago was to use URLs to address application features and to pass object IDs in as URL-encoded parameters to those features. Resource-oriented programming inverts this style completely and uses URLs to represent the resources contained within the system — the nouns — and makes the specification of actions to be performed on those resources secondary. This inversion transforms what would be internal objects into externally available resources with URLs to name them; third-party web sites are then able to externally reference and talk about them.

Representing Resources

Though grabbing hold of the actual "stuff" of a resource is impossible because it exists in the conceptual realm, you can create representations of a resource in various formats. The resource `http://www.artofrails.com/chapters/6` might represent Chapter 6 of this book. You are reading an instance of the print representation of that particular resource right now. If you type that URI into a browser, you will get back an HTML representation that summarizes it — the HTML representation. Still further, typing that URI into a book-on-tape server might return an audio version of the chapter. Each of these representations — the print, the web page, and the audio — are independent of the URI because they are all different ways to represent the concept that the URI stands for.

Even when limiting yourself to just web development, this means that you should not treat resource URIs as web pages but rather as resolvable endpoints at which you provide various representations of the resource when asked. (From an implementation standpoint, this should be starting to sound suspiciously like an API.) A financial report may be available as a spreadsheet, a PDF, a web page, or a GIF image, but all these formats are just different representations available from the same resource URI. Which particular representation is returned when that URI is presented to the server depends on the metadata of the resource representation request. This metadata is provided just as it was for the APIs of Chapter 5 — a combination of HTTP headers and the `:format` route variable — and you can make decisions about which resource representation to use with the `respond_to` method in your controllers.

This also means that resources are not the model instances tucked away in your database. Web development is primarily database centric, so the resources you represent on your web site likely have a 1-to-1 correspondence with model instances, but this isn't always the case. Really, your database (and the model objects that represent it) just provides your MVC application the data it needs to prepare resource representations for the outside world.

Representational State Transfer

Representational State Transfer (REST) describes an application architecture based on the idea that the Web is best modeled as a large collection of resources. From the REST perspective, web applications are programs that observe and modify the states of those resources. REST provides a way to design and structure your web applications; it is an idea about how to use existing technologies instead of being a particular technology itself. Its proponents argue that its deep integration with resources, URIs, and HTTP is evidence that it represents the optimal architecture for the evolving discipline of web application development.

The term "REST" was defined in 2000 by Roy Fielding as the focus of his doctoral dissertation. Fielding was one of the creators of the HTTP protocol and a co-founder of the Apache HTTP Server, and, in many ways, REST completes and builds on his two previous accomplishments. HTTP defines a mechanism for transferring information with a remote server, and Apache implemented that mechanism to make it widely available to all. REST extends the power of these tools by defining a software architecture on top of those accomplishments that standardizes the practice of web-based application development. In the "REST and Rails" section of this chapter, you will see how Ruby on Rails provides an implementation of REST ideas that makes it easy for developers to incorporate it into their code.

Since its explosion as a buzzword, the term REST has been thrown around to mean just about anything with an HTTP-accessible API. Here is this book's attempt to boil down what REST really means as concisely as possible.

RESTful resources

❑   Are abstract notions identified by URIs

❑   Have URIs that are also URLs resolvable on the Web

❑   Can be represented in multiple content formats

RESTful applications

❑   Are defined in terms of RESTful resources

❑   Provide the same basic set of operations for all resources

❑   Communicate with the outside world in terms of resources and operations on those resources

The point of roping these features together and giving them a name is not just that it is one possible way to develop but that these characteristics result in a distributed application environment that is proven to thrive online, in scalability, in ease of development, and in interoperability.

You already have a handle on what RESTful resource requirements mean: They are just resources whose URIs also double as URLs that provide access to their web-available representations. The following sections dig into each of the characteristics of RESTful applications in more depth.

HTTP: The Resource CRUD

The first characteristic in the preceding definition of RESTful applications is that all RESTful applications provide the same basic set of operations for resources. These operations are the same operations that apply to any piece of data, and the same ones you have already seen in previous chapters: Create, Read, Update, and Delete (CRUD). Despite the fact that, deep down, you know that resources are conceptual in nature, it sometimes helps to think of them as objects on a bookshelf. The CRUD actions give you everything you need to manage that bookshelf, which means that the object representations on the shelf can remain declarative, much more similar to C `structs` than to C++ `classes`. Given this, you know that the resource itself does not perform actions but rather that actions are performed on the resource.

Back in the early days of HTTP, these CRUD operations were supported natively, because the Web was seen as a distributed document management system. Naturally, documents could be created, read, updated, or deleted, so HTTP provided commands to accomplish these operations. As HTML documents became read-only user interface (UI) specifications (form inputs do not change the web document itself, but are passed along as arguments with the next request), these commands lost their original semantic meaning and blurred, with some falling out of use and others being given new uses. RESTful development restores some of the semantic meaning to HTTP verbs by defining a universal CRUD interface. Fielding, et al., gives the verb definitions, shown in the following table, in the HTTP 1.1 specification.

HTTP Verb	Specification Excerpt
GET	Retrieves whatever information (in the form of an entity) is identified by the Request-URI
POST	Requests that the origin server accept the entity enclosed in the request as a new subordinate of the resource identified by the Request-URI
PUT	Requests that the enclosed entity be stored under the supplied Request-URI
DELETE	Requests that the origin server delete the resource identified by the Request-URI

These definitions essentially state that specifying all the CRUD operations using the HTTP command that accompanies a web request is possible, eliminating the need to have phrases such as create, edit, and show in the URL. Using special URIs to stand for each of these operations amounts to reimplementing a feature in your application that already existed at a much lower level. RESTful development suggests that developers return to using HTTP commands to specify the CRUD operation to be performed and to standardize on these commands as the common set of operations available for all resources contained within a web application.

Standardization is where REST gets tricky because the definitions in the table do not map the HTTP verbs in a 1-to-1 fashion with CRUD operations, and this is part of the reason the term REST is thrown about so loosely. (Another reason is that the PUT and DELETE commands pose a bit of a problem — more on that later in "Backward Compatibility Workaround.") The next table defines the HTTP-to-CRUD mapping that Ruby on Rails development employs. This table should not be interpreted as an official standard, but it is one widely used, and it is the default for all RESTful routing in Rails.

CRUD Operation	HTTP Verb	Endpoint	Backward Compatibility Workaround
Create	POST	Class	n/a
Read	GET	Class, Resource	n/a
Update	PUT	Resource	POST with _method = put
Delete	DELETE	Resource	POST with _method = delete

This table shows that Ruby on Rails narrows down the possible behaviors in the HTTP 1.1 specification to create an unambiguous one-to-one mapping between HTTP verbs and CRUD operations on the server. In doing this, client requests to RESTful Rails applications are no longer directed at controller actions but instead are directed at the resources themselves. The verb on the HTTP request dictates the particular CRUD operation the user wishes to perform on that resource, and the parameters and metadata that accompany the request provide the remaining information required for the operation to complete.

RESTful Endpoints

The REST mapping defined by Rails also pares down the flexibility of HTTP 1.1 in its handling of resource creation. The HTTP specification allows users to generate new resources on the server by sending data to the URI the user would like to use to represent the new resource. On seeing that the URI is unoccupied by a resource, the server creates a new resource at that endpoint. Out on the Web and in the wild, this gives the user too much control over the workings of the web application and its URL namespace, and it also complicates the ability to efficiently store data in databases using auto-generated identifiers.

As an alternative to this flexibility, Rails maintains the notion of two different endpoints for each RESTful resource:

❑ The *class-level endpoint*, or *plural endpoint*, which represents both the resource's type and the collection of all resources of that type on the server

❑ The *instance-level endpoint*, or *singular endpoint*, which represents a particular resource instance of a certain type

Class-level endpoints look like the following:

```
/users
/books
/photos
```

Instance-level endpoints append an instance-specific identifier to the end of the class-level endpoint:

```
/users/23
/books/the-art-of-rails
/photos/2
```

The semantics of the REST operation then depends on whether the endpoint being addressed is class level or instance level.

Class-level endpoints support two types of requests: POST and GET. A POST request causes a new resource to be created. After creating the resource, the web application server returns a 201 (Created) status code along with the URI of the newly created resource in the Location header. This keeps the control of URI creation within the application. When a GET request is sent to a class-level endpoint, it is interpreted as a request for the entire collection of resources of that type. This is normally interpreted as a listing of resources and their URIs at which more information can be found, so /photos might return a list of all photos on the site and their thumbnail images.

Instance-level endpoints support only Read, Update, and Delete operations, and those behave as you would expect them to.

Backward Compatibility Workaround

Because HTTP verbs lost much of their use and original meaning during a period of atrophy, some browsers do not support the creation of PUT and DELETE requests. To ensure backward compatibility of REST operations in these environments, Ruby on Rails automatically supports a workaround that you rarely need to think about because it occurs on both the client- and server-side automatically when using REST with Rails.

For both PUT and DELETE resource operations, Rails inserts client-side code to transform the request into a POST with a special variable _method that contains the name of the HTTP verb that was actually intended: either put or delete. The Rails server automatically looks for POST requests with this _method variable set and will treat the request as though it had occurred with the enclosed HTTP verb. By allowing Rails to implement this workaround behind the scenes for you, you are still able to develop RESTfully, and the workout can easily be removed in the future if PUT and DELETE return as universally supported HTTP commands.

Defining an Application in Terms of Resources

RESTful applications are defined in terms of resource operations using the universal set of CRUD commands that HTTP provides. Designing an application in this way leads to a particular flavor of web development different from those that you would design otherwise. The whole application is defined in terms of resources rather than services or API calls, placing the focus on nouns rather than verbs.

The term "resource" immediately makes most people think of model development, but, surprisingly, the primary area of resource-based application development is in your *controllers*. REST design is all about controllers because REST and resources are topics concerned with how your application looks to the outside world, whereas model objects are internal entities concerned with how your database looks to your application logic.

In previous chapters, I characterized controllers as groupings of related actions in your web application, but in RESTful applications, these actions are very specifically defined. I define the term *resource controller* to mean a controller whose purpose is to provide RESTful operations for a particular type of resource.

RESTful Routing: Mapping HTTP Commands into the Controller

Chapter 5, "Beautiful Web APIs," described the importance of URL routing to enable URLs that reference concepts rather than executable scripts. With REST, the concept-space is further constrained: As much as possible, URLs should represent nouns, the resources, rather than actions. (You will learn how to deal with non-CRUD actions in the "REST and Rails" section.) For this to be reality, the concept of routing needs to extend past the URL and into the entire HTTP request.

RESTful routing uses the combination of URL route templates plus knowledge of the HTTP command used to make the request. These two factors together determine which CRUD action the request will map to. On the controller side, the Rails CRUD actions are implemented in the same way as described in Chapter 4, "Getting the Most from M, V, and C." So a *resource controller* looks exactly the same as the CRUD controllers from Chapter 4. The big difference is the URL used to reach that controller action. More Ruby on Rails–specific discussion of RESTful routing is provided in the second half of the chapter, which addresses the Rails REST API. For now, you need only to know that this new RESTful resource interaction style is mapped automatically into CRUD controllers as you are used to seeing them.

Resources Lead to Simple Endpoints

Limiting your controller development as much as possible to only resource controllers is both a constraint and a tool. It limits you to designing the public face of your application as entirely noun based, but it also serves as a great organizational guide. API development is time consuming on any project, and the implicit API created by a Rails controller and its actions is no different. With REST-based development, controllers take on a different feel, and the pathways into your application start to look a lot simpler.

CRUD operations all collapse into just two endpoints, the class-level endpoint and the resource-level endpoint. Rather than use different URLs to differentiate between them, you use the HTTP verb, as shown in the following table.

Non-REST CRUD Endpoints	REST CRUD Endpoints
`/users/create # POST`	`/users # POST`
`/users/23/show # GET`	`/users/23 # GET`
`/users/23/update # POST`	`/users/23 # PUT`
`/users/23/destroy # POST`	`/users/23 # DELETE`

And non-CRUD operations are often refactored into resources that can be operated upon with CRUD. Rather than *close* an account, you create an *account closure*. Rather than *log in*, you create a new *session*. Rather than *log out*, you delete that *session*. By changing the way these verb-like actions are described so that they become nouns, you make them compatible with a resource-centric application design. Some example refactorings are shown in the following table.

Non REST Operations	REST Operations
`/account/23/close # POST`	`/account_closure # POST`
`/login # POST`	`/session # POST`
`/logout # POST`	`/session # DELETE`
`/recipe/44/rate # POST`	`/rating # POST`

In fact, having to decide which actions to add to a controller becomes the exception rather than the rule. Because your application strives to be defined entirely in terms of resources, and because resource controllers must all support standard CRUD operations, only the few remaining features that could not fit into the REST paradigm require that you implement an action outside the CRUD paradigm. The difficult part, then, becomes determining what resources make up your "public model" that is used to represent the functionality of your site.

One way to determine these resources is to think about the model objects that you will use to persist your data. Even though resources do not necessarily map onto your model objects, your model objects provide a good guess about the resources you will likely need.

An Example of REST-Based Refactoring

To further demonstrate how REST-based application design differs from what you might design without REST, I revisit the design of the hypothetical web site for cooking enthusiasts from Chapter 3, "The Server as an Application." That design contained the controllers and models shown in the following table.

Controller	Model
AccountController	User
UserController	Profile
FavoritesController	Recipe
RecipeController	Photo
	Ingredient
	Rating
	Comment
	Favorite

This design rolled a lot of functionality into four basic controllers that provided access to account creation and login, recipe viewing, and "favorite" management.

Revisiting this design with RESTful principles in mind, two main problems are apparent:

❏ The `AccountController` is oddly crafted from the REST standpoint because it handles new user creation, sign-in, and sign-out. The first responsibility should really be a create operation on a `User` resource. The latter two operations are verbs, which should somehow be refactored into nouns.

❏ The `User`, `Recipe`, and `Favorites` controllers appear to have too much functionality wrapped into them, because they are encapsulating operations on many different types of objects that could instead be modeled as resources.

You can tackle the `AccountController` first. You can remove the user creation responsibilities from it because they should be handled by the HTTP CRUD operations of REST. Doing so implies that you will need a `User` resource type. That leaves sign-in and sign-out. To handle that, you will remove the `AccountController` completely and replace it with a `Session` resource type that represents a user's current session with the web site. Signing into the site will be the creation of a new session, and signing out of the site will be the deletion of that session.

```
Resources so far: User, Session
```

Next, look at the `UserController`. This controller encapsulates both the user and that user's profile. At this point, you must make a decision: Either have the `User` resource represent both the account membership and the user profile, or have separate resources for user and profile. Because each user has only one profile, and because the spirit of a profile is to *represent* a user, the best decision is to include a user's profile information within the `User` resource.

```
Resources so far: User, Session (same as before)
```

Next is the `RecipeController`, which managed the interactions between several types of objects: recipes, ingredients, recipe photos, ratings, and comments. A lot of work needs to be done here:

❑   `Recipe` will become a resource type — an easy decision.

❑   The fact that you have chosen to model ingredients in a separate table in the database and associate them with recipes indicates that you may have bigger plans for recipe lookup down the road. Therefore, investing in an `Ingredient` resource now makes sense so that external users will have some way of interacting with the ingredient resources you maintain information about.

❑   Each recipe model object also contains an optional photo. Because this photo is meant only to provide an auxiliary way to view the recipe, you will include the photo with the `Recipe` resource type as a potential data format. In the HTML version of a `Recipe` object, the photo will be included with the text, and just the photo alone will be offered if the `image/gif`, `image/jpeg`, or `image/png` MIME type is requested with the recipe's URI.

❑   `Rating` will also be split off as its own resource type, and you will add extra functionality within its resource controller to include any additional summation or averaging needed.

❑   `Comment` will also become a resource type — another easy decision.

```
Resources so far: User, Session, Recipe, Ingredient, Rating, Comment
```

Finally, you refactor the `FavoritesController` that allowed users to record their favorite items on the site. This will become the `Favorite` resource type.

```
Resources so far: User, Session, Recipe, Ingredient, Rating, Comment, Favorite
```

Finishing the high-level REST refactoring, you have a much different application design on your hands. The following table is the new RESTful version of your earlier table. Instead of controllers, it shows resource types, each of which has its own resource controller to manage the CRUD operations for that resource type.

Resource Type	Model
User	User
Session	Profile
Recipe	Recipe
Ingredient	Photo
Rating	Ingredient
Comment	Rating
Favorite	Comment
	Favorite

Figure 6-1 presents this new design in a different way, showing the mapping of model objects onto resources. The model objects represent the application domain as beneficial for database modeling, and the resources represent the application domain as beneficial to the user of the application.

Resource Type	Model
Session	User
User	Profile
Recipe	Recipe
Ingredient	Photo
Rating	Ingredient
Comment	Rating
Favorite	Comment
	Favorite

Figure 6-1

In some ways, this new design results in more code; that is, for each resource type, there must be a resource controller, so the new design contains seven controllers whereas the old design contained only four. Despite requiring more code, this new design, when implemented, will be simpler, easier to maintain, and easier to understand than the prior design. Because the application is now defined entirely in terms of resources, nearly all the implementation required on each controller is limited to REST-style CRUD operations. Because REST dictates that these operations are the same across all resources, a common implementation could even be extracted into a base class if you desired (though this is not common because it obfuscates the workings of the resource controllers).

Communicating with the Client: Resources as Your API

The mandate that all RESTful resources be accessible by the same standard set of operations simplifies both API development and API use. Your web application API becomes the set of resource endpoints, and HTTP-based REST operations become the method calls into that API. Because these method calls are nearly the same across all REST-based web applications, the real API documentation becomes what resources you provide and what data fields exist on those resources.

From the standpoint of development, transforming a RESTful application into a RESTful API simply requires you to support additional response formats in your resource controllers, whether those formats be XML, RDF, CSV, or some custom format. As you will see later in this chapter when the Rails REST is explained, issues such as authentication and API metering can still be accomplished via filters on the resource controller's operations.

From the standpoint of an API user, a RESTful API offers a simple way to connect to a service and use its features without all the proxies and configuration required of SOAP web services. Because REST services are usually exposed with an XML view of the resources they support, the only tools necessary are an XML parser and an HTTP library.

Put Another Way: The Network Is the Computer

RESTful applications present resources to the outside world the same way your model objects present relational database metaphors to your MVC application. In this respect, you can think of one of the goals of REST as designing a public interface for your application's functionality that is just as disciplined and object focused as the interface that the model layer constructs around a database. RESTful applications become resource servers layered on top of the MVC application that makes resource management and display possible. For most users, the resources are served as HTML pages of content — user profiles, recipes, and so on — but increasingly, these resource servers provide yet another layer of data abstraction and specialization enabling the creation of intersite applications. Figure 6-2 illustrates this trend.

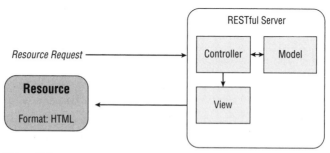

Figure 6-2

For many years, "The Network Is the Computer" was one of Sun's catch phrases. It meant that computing, and for your purposes application development, had ceased to be something that took place on a single processor and had become a distributed, heterogeneous process that spanned entire networks. The Internet is now a global ecosystem in which applications can mingle among each other and interoperate. REST-based development establishes a basic set of rules for application design and interaction in that ecosystem so that all applications can speak with each other through the exchange of resource representations.

RESTful resources and model objects both seek to provide abstractions for objects that are important to your application. Because the operations on RESTful resources look similar to the same basic operations that you would use on your model objects, REST allows you to begin replacing management of your own model objects with resources that are managed elsewhere by third parties.

This approach to management represents an entirely new type of emerging network development, depicted in Figure 6-3 — super-mash-ups, if you will. Tumblr, a host of the self-coined "tumblelog" type of blogs, provides free, reliable blogging services. Flickr will hold your photos for you. Facebook manages social networks and status updates. And Disqus hosts embeddable comment boards for use on your site. Apart, each one of these services specializes in its own particular niche of web-enabled functionality, but together they can be woven to form a blog whose every component is managed elsewhere on the web.

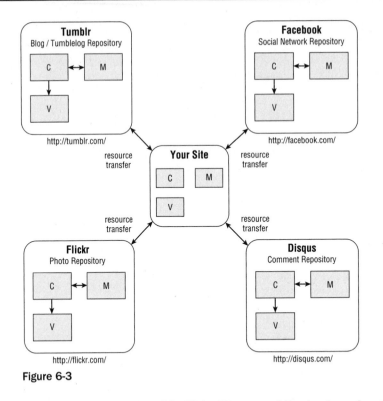

Figure 6-3

Together on the Internet, services such as Tumblr, Flickr, Disqus, and Facebook are forming the initial components of Sun's dream of network computing for the masses, arriving a bit late and in a slightly different form than expected. These services do not use REST in the purist sense discussed in this chapter, but that is beside the point because REST-based APIs only increase the flexibility with which services such as these can be rehashed and recombined. Whereas the computing industry's bet on Web Services largely did not prove fruitful outside of a few small cases, REST is emerging as a way for every web application to join the fray and offer resources for consumption in the same spirit as the aforementioned ones.

REST and Rails

The first half of this chapter explained the concepts behind REST-based application development; the remainder demonstrates how Ruby on Rails provides support for using this application architecture in your code. Much of the philosophy behind REST jives very well with the Rails notion of "Don't Repeat Yourself" (DRY), because it is concerned with devising a universal set of rules and operations for all resources and declaring that your application be written entirely in terms of these generic resources. Opportunities for Rails-style automation are abundant, and you will see how Rails routing and generators take advantage of this homogenous environment to minimize the amount of code that you must write yourself.

Ruby on Rails provides facilities to support and even automate REST-based resource interaction with your web application's clients. In contrast to some of the other core design-oriented features of Rails (such as MVC), REST support is added on top of the framework rather than mandated throughout. Therefore, development of the MVC portions of your application largely carries on as it normally would.

The RESTful resource handling comes in the router, where certain routes are declared to be resource centric and can be mapped to the CRUD operations of a controller. This manner of implementing REST enables you to use REST for as much of your application design as makes sense but still retain the traditional controller-action paradigm that drove Rails development prior to REST.

Mapping Resources in the Router

The heart of Rails' REST support is in the router that accepts incoming requests and hands them off to controllers to fulfill. As far as code that the developer typically manages is concerned, the router is the first component in which your application gets to decide how to respond. Before REST-based support was added, the router allowed for two different types of routes.

❏ **Anonymous routes:** Routes in which a routing template is anonymously mapped to a particular configuration of controller, action, and parameters

❏ **Named routes:** Routes that are given an explicit name and an automatically generated set of helper methods that output URIs that match the route; they usually cover a narrower collection of possible URIs than anonymous routes.

Rails version 1.2 and on contain a third type of route, the *resources* route, which automatically sets up RESTful operations in one fell swoop.

For example, the line

```
map.resources :cards
```

automatically sets up a number of named routes, each matching REST operations for the resource type named card to CRUD actions on a controller that are expected to fulfill the intent of the REST operations. Figure 6-4 depicts this mapping between the REST and CRUD operations that you are already familiar with because of the card example. By default in this example, the router assumes that the controller providing REST operations for the class-level endpoint and the instance-level endpoint is called the CardsController, because the resource type is card.

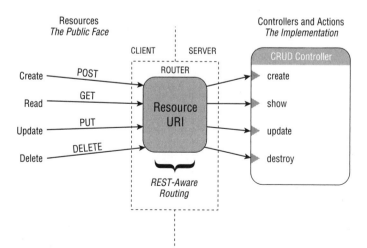

Figure 6-4

With an empty `routes.rb` file containing only that resource route definition, the traditional controller-
and action-oriented URIs that you are accustomed to with Rails, such as `/cards/list` or `/cards/show/1`,
will no longer work. Instead, only RESTful requests to `/cards` and `/cards/:ID` will result in responses,
provided by the CRUD/resource-enabled `CardsController`.

As with many aspects of Rails, the `map.routes` command assumes the most common values for all
its options by default but offers a wide degree of configurable behavior. Many of the key design-
oriented options are covered in this chapter, but you should view the whole list on the Rails API Documentation site at `http://api.rubyonrails.org/classes/ActionController/Resources.html`.

But It's the Real World: Named Routes are Still Needed

Recall from Chapter 4, however, that some operations just can't take place in one step when a human
is in the loop. These two-step actions, such as `new- > create` and `edit- > update`, require a setup step
(`new` and `edit`), in which the user is presented with some form for entry, and a processing step (`create`
and `update`), in which the user data is committed to the database. Web applications designed around the
notion of resources and REST operations are no different.

In practice, RESTful web applications are almost always implemented with a few extra controller actions
to make up for the user interface requirements of a web site that REST alone cannot easily encompass.
Figure 6-5 shows the Rails router mapping RESTful routes as well as the helper routes for two-step
actions using the same `card` example.

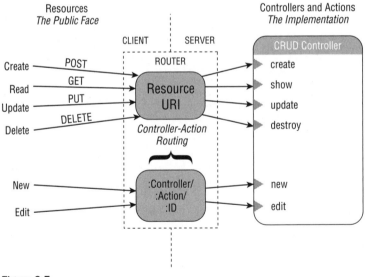

Figure 6-5

The `new` and `edit` routes are so important to the functioning of CRUD operations when in HTML mode
that the `map.resources` command automatically generates them for you and wires them to the `new`
and `edit` methods on your resource controller. The inclusion of these extra helper actions is more of an

HTML-specific fact of life than it is a cheat. It does not hurt the overall design of your application, but it helps the application's usability in HTML enormously. Trying to implement these two-step actions as resources themselves would surely be far more trouble than it's worth. This is largely because views such as new and edit are not resource representations themselves but rather helper forms used to let the HTML user provide his or her own representation.

Still, to maximize your application's leverage of REST, keep these custom actions to a minimum when possible. One strategy many Rails developers have cited is the following:

> When developing REST-based applications, stick to resource routes and named routes.

This strategy means that you should eliminate any anonymous wildcard routes you have in your routes .rb file, including the beloved default route:

```
map.connect ':controller/:action/:id'
```

Instead, enter only named routes:

```
map.home '/', :controller => 'home', :action => 'index'
map.about '/about', :controller => 'home', :action => 'about'
```

This forces you to explicitly craft the parts of your API that exist outside of the standard REST operations.

Automatically Provided Routes

All in all, running the map.resources method creates seven routes from HTTP endpoints into your resource controller. These hooks are the six shown in Figure 6-5, plus an additional GET request available at the class-level endpoint for listing resources or providing an index page. They are shown grouped by endpoint in the following example:

```
Route                   HTTP Command    Mapped Controller Action
--------------          --------------  ------------------------

[ Resource-level Routes ]

/resource_type          GET             index
/resource_type          POST            create

[ Class-level Routes ]

/resource_type/:ID      GET             show
/resource_type/:ID      PUT             update
/resource_type/:ID      DELETE          destroy

[ Helper Routes ]

/resource_type/new      GET             new
/resource_type/:ID/edit GET             edit
```

Extra Route Shorthand

The `route.resource` method provides a shorthand for any other extra routes that you need, allowing you to define them along with the RESTful route definition. This method of adding extra resource-related routes is preferred over enumerating named routes manually because it provides a way to define them in terms of either the class-level (singular) or resource-level (plural) endpoint of the resource.

Extra class-level routes can be added to a resource mapping via the `:collection` option.

```
map.resources :photos, :collection => {
                                       :popular => :get
                                       :recent => :get
                                       :finalize => :post
                                     }
```

The value of the `:collection` option is a hash containing the extra route names to be added and the HTTP method that should be paired with that route. If you would like to accept all HTTP methods for a particular route, use the value `:any`. Each of the routes specified will be added as a class-level endpoint, so the preceding command would result in the following valid routes, in addition to the RESTful routes automatically defined:

```
        Route            To be used with
-----------------      ---------------
/photos/popular        # GET
/photos/recent         # GET
/photos/finalize       # POST
```

To define extra routes at the resource level, add a set of route descriptions in the same way to the `:member` option.

```
map.resources :photos, :member => {
                                    :purchase => :any
                                    :flag => :any
                                    :download => :post
                                  }
```

The `:member` option will define extra routes tied to a resource-level endpoint with a templated `:id`.

```
        Route            To be used with
-----------------      ---------------
/photos/:id/purchase   # Any command
/photos/:id/flag       # Any command
/photos/:id/download   # POST
```

Rails creates helper methods for each of the routes added using the `:collection` and `:member` options. These helper methods help you generate URLs to match the routes without having to hand-code them.

```
download_photo_path(23) #=> /photos/23/download
```

Adding extra routes to an otherwise RESTful application in this way is a good alternative because it groups the named routes with the resource definition. It also guarantees that you add them in a manner that conforms to a resource-oriented set of application endpoints, even if they are not standard REST operations.

REST and URL Helpers

Some developers choose not to use the URL helpers that the Rails router creates for you because they feel that these extra method calls can add critical milliseconds to your web application's response time for little benefit. (I am certainly one of those developers.) However, with RESTful routes and resources, it is important to use the named route helpers that Rails provides. Recall that many browsers encounter problems with the PUT and DELETE requests that REST uses for `edit` and `delete` CRUD operations. Rails automatically provides the hidden `_method` variable workaround for such situations, but it does so from within these helpers. When a link you are creating is intended either to modify or delete a resource, remember to use a route helper method to ensure that the backward-compatibility fix gets added so that it will work with all browsers!

Resource Scaffolds

Scaffolding is a troubled memory for many die-hard Rails developers because it began as an example-providing feature that was interpreted (and then ridiculed) as a substitute for thoughtful, hand-crafted implementation. But scaffolding is back with a vengeance, this time with resources, and it provides a great way to look at the bare-bones implementation of how a fully functional resource controller should behave. If you are developing a production application or practicing test-driven development, it is best to start from scratch and build up your CRUD methods by hand. For early development and REST experimentation, however, you can't beat scaffolding for learning the ropes.

To create a scaffolded resource, simply type the following on the command line. By default, it will create a regular resource (rather than a singleton):

```
script/generate scaffold resource_name
```

This command generates a reference implementation for all the files that you need to observe how a basic model-backed resource operates, from the migrations and model objects to the resource controller and the resource route. It even marks up the auto-generated controller with comments that explain how each of the CRUD actions is mapped onto various HTTP requests.

If you have yet to experiment with REST and Rails, go to a computer with a current copy of Rails and try the new scaffolding right now to kick the tires before continuing.

Nested Resources

In some cases, representing resources as nested, subordinate to other resources, is advantageous to the design of your application. Comments on a blog post, photos for a recipe, or books by an author are all examples of resources that you can potentially model as subordinate objects rather than top-level ones. Nesting allows them to be represented as such to the user: /article/123/comments/3 rather than comments/4423, for example.

Nesting is almost always an added feature and never a required one. Because resources are generally serialized to a database, they each have unique identifiers that allow them to be accessed as top-level objects subordinate to none. But nesting offers some nice benefits when you use it in the right places:

- ❏ **Intuitive resource URIs:** Such as /article/123/comments/3 shown previously.

- ❏ **The ability to localize public identifiers to a particular scope:** In the comment example, the /comments/3 references the third comment in the ordered list of comments made about Article 123. This is a more intuitive way to identify subordinate items than using their absolute IDs; it also provides a limited degree of protection against revealing the inner workings of your web site (for example, if you did not want to make it easy to determine how many comments your system contained).

- ❏ **The automatic inclusion of required associated objects:** Posting a new comment to the /comments path requires the form to explicitly specify in the parameters what article the comment concerns. This is unfortunate because the article ID is really a relationship between the comment and the article rather than a property of the comment resource. By nesting the resources, a new comment can be added to Article 123 by posting to /articles/123/comments. Because the article ID is contained in the POST URI, there is no need to include it in the parameters of the comment to be added.

- ❏ **Easy, URI-enforced access control:** Perhaps the most compelling feature of nesting is its ability to let you easily control access to nested resources based on a user's relationship to the containing resource. If the web user has access to the top-level object, it makes sense that he or she would also have access to the nested items. ActiveRecord associations allow you to even look up objects within the context of an associated object, so a GET to /article/123/comments/3 could be written as

```
@article = Article.find(params[:article_id])
@comments  =   @article.comments.find_by_position(params[:id])
```

- ❏ With the lookup performed in this way, ActiveRecord prevents comments outside the scope of the given article from even being considered for return.

Creating a Nested Route

To create a nested route, add a block to the end of your map.resources call and define any subordinate resources within that block:

```
map.resources :articles do |articles|
    # Nested resources go here
end
```

The mapper is passed into the block configured for the nest-level, and that mapper should be used rather than the top-level map.

```
map.resources :articles do |articles|
   articles.resources :comments
end
```

Routes that are defined within a nested block result in named route methods that require two variables to generate their route:

```
article_comment_path(@article, @comment)
article_comment_path(:article => @article, :comment => @comment)
```

Deep Nesting

Nesting can go deeper than just one level, although the deeper you go, the more you lose the simplicity of RESTful resource design amidst the resource associations and dependencies. Deep nesting looks the same as regular nesting except that it has more nested blocks:

```
map.resources :bloggers do |bloggers|
   bloggers.resources :articles do |articles|
      articles.resources :comments
   end
end
```

That route definition would result in routes like the following:

```
# You will see how to interpret IDs flexibly like this in a few paragraphs
/bloggers/ted/articles/123/comments/2
```

The named route helpers that result are named by appending all the nestings together:

```
blogger_article_comments_path(:blogger => @user, :article => @a)
blogger_article_comment_path(:blogger => @user, :article => @a, :comment => @c)
```

Writing a Nested Resource Controller

Nested routes are always directed to the resource controller for the innermost-nested resource. So the nested route `/bloggers/ted/articles/123/comments/2` would be directed to the `CommentsController`. The Rails router parses segments of the URI into parameters to help the resource controller determine the context of the request. These parameters are named with the singular variant of the resource name followed by the suffix `_id`.

A `GET` request to the preceding three-deep nested route, then, would be equivalent to the following request in a traditional controller-action style application setup. The parameters are shown in a comment rather than in the URL for readability:

```
GET /bloggers/ted/articles/123/comments/2

# is equivalent to

GET /comments/2 # params = { :blogger_id => 'ted', :article_id => 123 }
```

For a two-layer nest such as `/articles/123/comments/2`, the parameters hash simply leaves out the `blogger_id`, as you can imagine:

```
GET /articles/123/comments/2

# is equivalent to
GET /comments/2 # params = { :article_id => 123 }
```

Nesting a resource does not preclude you from also making it available at the top-level of your web application; remember that these are just routes, so you can make multiple routes for the same resource. A good example of how this might be useful is with the comment system. As a nested resource, comments might be referenced by their relative ordering with regard to the article they were posted on. As a top-level resource, another `map.resources` mapping might make comments available via their primary key in the database.

This means that your resource controller must be aware of the way that you are constructing your RESTful routes in the `routes.rb` file, and it is responsible for checking on the expected information and responding appropriately to it.

Hiding Your Primary Keys

Sometimes web developers prefer to hide their primary key fields so that users and competitors have less knowledge of the internals of the web application. Surfacing an auto-incremented ID to the users would divulge how successful your site is in terms of user-generated content, and it might be in your interest to keep your competitors guessing. Combined with the `to_param` method on `ActiveRecord`, nested resources can be an effective way to hide your primary keys. For named objects, overload the `to_param` method to return a URL-valid string representation of the name rather than the object ID. For unnamed objects that are nested, you can use `acts_as_list` with the ActiveRecord association and overload `to_param` to return the position of the object in the associated list.

The preceding `bloggers -> articles -> comments` example is an example. If the `Blogger` model object was modified to return the blogger's name as the parameter as follows:

```
class Blogger < ActiveRecord::Base
  def to_param
    self.handle
  end
end
```

and the article's `to_param` method was modified to return the article's title:

```
class Article < ActiveRecord::Base
  def to_param
    "#{name.gsub(/[^a-z0-9]+/i, '-')}"
  end
end
```

then you can override the comment's `to_param` to return its position in the comment list relative to the article it is attached to:

```
class Comment < ActiveRecord::Base
   def to_param
      self.position
   end
end
```

The result is that you have successfully identified your resources to the outside world in a way that obscures how many objects your system actually contains and in what order they were added. Rather than be ID tied, URIs will look like this:

```
/bloggers/ted/articles/why-rest-is-super-cool/comments/2
```

Just remember that if you change a model object's `to_param` method so that it is not equal to or prefixed by its primary key, you will need to update the code in your resource controllers that locates those objects.

Singleton Resources versus Regular Resources

Although most of the resources you will be creating will use the `map.resources` method to wire their RESTful routes, Rails also introduces the notion of singleton resources to manage those resources that behave most like singletons in the programming sense. Singleton resources are those for which only one resource exists, a situation that can occur for a few different reasons:

❏　**A has_one relationship in models mapped to nested resources:** If a `User` has only one `Profile`, the ideal way to access it is `/user/ted/profile` rather than `/user/ted/profile/profile ID`.

❏　**Only one instance of the resource exists in the application:** If your web application contains one and only one FAQ, that FAQ might be modeled as a singleton resource.

❏　**Only one instance of the resource exists relative to the user session:** Each authenticated user is associated with one and only one session. Although multiple sessions may exist for separate users simultaneously, only one session per user should ever exist at a time. Singleton routes allow the user to address his or her session as a singleton resource object.

❏　**Security reasons:** Singleton routes that lead to session-scoped objects are a good way to prevent users from being able to even address objects that belong to others. A singleton `/session` resource or `/account` resource might be mapped at the controller level into the session or account appropriate for that user. Because no primary key was ever exchanged, it is more difficult for malicious users to access the information of others.

Using the singular REST route command, `map.resource`, works just the same as `map.resources` except that it generates only the routes that make sense for a singleton resource, which means CRUD turns into simply RU because only reading and updating a singleton make sense. All the generated method names are also singular to reflect the nature of the resource.

As with nested routes, the burden is on the developer to ensure that singleton resources are handled properly within their resource controllers. Designing resource routes in the `routes.rb` file is a critical step in your application's development, but the controllers that support that design must be aware of the assumptions that are made during this step. This means that any singleton resources tied to a user's session, for instance, will not get any `params[:id]` value and instead need to be automatically loaded by their resource controllers.

Summary

This chapter covered a lot of important ground for web developers of today and tomorrow. It began by discussing the idea of resources, the conceptual space that they represent, and their importance to modern web development. Next it moved on to REST, a relatively new and very particular type of web application architecture involving resources and HTTP-managed CRUD operations.

In addition to describing the REST mindset and showing an example refactoring of earlier code in the book, this chapter made the argument that REST is a powerful tool to assist your web application development. Applied properly, RESTful development can benefit all aspects of a project: It guides your application design by forcing you into a resource-oriented mindset; simplifies your programming by standardizing on HTTP verbs and CRUD for virtually all the application's features; and opens your application as a reusable resource to the outside world by providing consistent resource-centric endpoints.

Finally, this chapter demonstrated how Ruby on Rails provides REST capabilities that you can easily roll into your own projects. Most additions that Rails includes to support REST come in the router, and this chapter showed you how to create basic resource routes, nested routes, and singleton routes.

The next chapter continues on the design thread by addressing another critical component of modern web applications: the AJAX interaction patterns that dynamically link client to server.

7

The Five Styles of AJAX

Web sat waiting in a booth at the back of the smoky pub, staring at the aged carving in the wood above his table.

LOKE ERST YE THENK, AND BE YE THE WOLRDE

And the phrase beneath it, in the same ornate style but newer, he thought, given the brighter color of the wood bezel.

FRIDAY NIGHT FISH AND CHIPS SPECIAL

The pub was a strange maze of tables and shadows, wood and brick columns holding up the floors above. It was buried underneath an otherwise normal building holding commercial space, an old wine cellar that used to belong to a distributer on the seventh floor. Before that it was the factory floor for a parachute company, and even before that it was rumored to have been an underground alchemy supply shop.

Now it was a pub. A damp, earthen smell permeated through the sounds and odors of fried fish and pipe smoke.

"Hi! My name is AJ, and I'll be your server today! Is there anything I can get you to drink?"

Web thought the waitress looked out of place in this old tavern. She beamed at him, waiting for his reply with her spiked, neon-blue hair; she wore a shining pink plastic halter top and costume-like makeup. She was balancing a tray of empty pint glasses on one hand and a skateboard beneath her feet.

"Actually, liquids tend to give me a short. Still some old ISDN lines in here," Web said, patting his stomach. "Could I just have some chips? You know what, throw in the fish, too."

"Sure thing. No liquids. Fish, chips, coming right up," she said as she rolled away.

From afar, Web could see the dim outline of the maître d' directing a group of people toward his table. He recognized Jen from before, along with three others he didn't know. He stood up to shake their hands as they approached the table.

"Web, it's good to see you again! I'm sorry I had to run so quickly before. Let me introduce you to my friends — "

"Napkin!"

AJ cut through the group of people on her skateboard and left Web with a napkin in his outstretched hand.

"Rusty, Matz, and Schema," Jen continued unfazed.

Web gave each a hearty greeting, and the five sat down in the booth. Before the newcomers even had time to pick up their menus, AJ was back, tossing a plate down on the table.

"Plate!" AJ's voice trailed past as she skated without slowing, the empty plate left rattling in a circular motion on the table.

Matz looked at the spinning plate and inspected the cover of the menu closely. "How strange. I've heard of these new places. What did you order?"

"I got the fi — "

"Fish!" AJ was flying by on her skateboard in the opposite direction this time. She managed a perfect shot from four feet away; the fish landed squarely on the far side of the plate and didn't even slide a centimeter.

"Fish. And chips," Web replied, starting to worry about how his knife and fork would be delivered to him.

What we now call AJAX was once a great idea hiding in plain sight. For years, the `XMLHttpRequest` object sat with little notice or use, first in Internet Explorer and later in Mozilla. Then in the spring of 2004, Google began beta-testing a new type of web-based e-mail client called Gmail, and overnight, the incredible potential of AJAX just made sense (with the feeling of "duh, why didn't we think of that?" that often accompanies a discovery in plain sight).

From its inception, the Web grew up around a "one document, one request" paradigm that made perfect sense for the document-centric environment it was created to serve. To display multiple documents at a time, the web community created the notion of "frames," walled-off divisions within the page that each loaded its own separate document, not unlike the Picture-in-Picture feature on large TVs. Developers could control these frames to a reasonable degree with JavaScript. But what if a web browser didn't need to deal with entire documents at a time, and instead could make requests that replaced just tiny chunks within the existing document?

AJAX (Asynchronous JavaScript and XML) is the technique born of that "what if." Technically, the term refers to the use of asynchronous JavaScript requests for XML data. In practice, AJAX refers to the entire collection of common tricks and patterns that have grown up around the `XMLHttpRequest` and the way it can transform web development — both asynchronously and synchronously, with both XML and with HTML.

Developing with AJAX can be tricky, though, because it has a tendency to lead astray that elegant design you've been working on for the past few months. The reason is that AJAX is every bit as much a paradigm shift for the Web as the `<img>` and `<form>` tags were a decade before. Nearly all the collective wisdom on web application development centers on the idea of the web *site* as an application. Suddenly, with AJAX, a single *page* can now be deserving of this title.

This shift in potential — from site as application to page as application — is the difference between CNN.com and Microsoft Word. It is the difference between forever writing styled-up database front-ends and writing full-featured, interactive applications. It opens the possibility, if you want it, to completely throw away the document paradigm of the Web and use HTML just as domain-specific user interface (UI) language. In other words, AJAX is a big deal.

This chapter introduces you to some of the design issues in AJAX and shows you how to integrate AJAX smoothly into your Rails applications. I discuss the different styles of AJAX development and describe how to design your sites so that you can strike a balance between the middle of two extremes: not quite a single-page application, but not the page-heavy web applications of yore, either.

The Big Secrets

But first, the big secrets about AJAX. Although AJAX has made enough headlines to become a household word, the reality isn't quite what the headlines would have you believe. Before addressing some of the more detail-oriented aspects of AJAX development, here are two big secrets about AJAX that a lot of the material about AJAX out there leaves out, plus a third one directed at Rails developers in particular.

AJAX Isn't Necessarily the Hard Part

The first secret is actually some great news: If you had a good understanding of web development before AJAX, you already have a good understanding of AJAX, even if you've never used it, from a technical perspective. You don't need any gigantic books or night courses, just a general understanding of how AJAX-based development relates back to normal web development. The XMLHttpRequest isn't the hard part — all the design issues and JavaScript that come along with it are.

The XMLHttpRequest itself has long been buried under layers of abstraction by all the incredibly capable JavaScript frameworks available to you, so the mechanics of performing AJAX requests are really only a method call. The request itself works the same way every other web request you've ever handled does, except that you're dealing with serialized data and HTML fragments instead of full-blown web pages.

Because the how is easy, you need to develop a good understanding of the why and when to use AJAX in your application. This chapter covers several different styles of AJAX design to help you pick a strategy for integrating AJAX into your application.

From a development standpoint, you also need to be prepared to become a JavaScript developer if you want to use AJAX. And although you might not need to worry too much about the mechanics of AJAX, it is a good idea to have a book or two dedicated to JavaScript on your shelf. JavaScript idled on the outer fringes of web development for a long time, but the slow advance of browser standardization, hardware capabilities, and now AJAX have made it an unavoidable staple of modern web development. Get to know JavaScript well. What people don't tell you when they describe how AJAX will change the way you code is that the changes are often three lines of "AJAX code" followed by thirty lines of JavaScript UI tricks and data manipulation.

AJAX Introduces Tough Design Issues

The second secret of AJAX is related to all the JavaScript you may find yourself writing after you begin to integrate AJAX into your design. AJAX can be a bit of a gateway drug that slowly encourages you to write more and more of your application logic in client-side JavaScript rather than on the server. If you don't pay attention to the way you are designing and writing your JavaScript, you can end up with a web application that is difficult to maintain no matter how well designed the server side is.

The "gateway drug" part comes into play because of the way AJAX requests tend to hang out around hyperlinks and make you accustomed to in-lining JavaScript in your HTML. One of the most common ways to use AJAX is to cause some link or form to load a new bit of information dynamically into a region of the page. Using the Prototype JavaScript library that ships with Rails, it is easy and logical to layer the AJAX functionality right on top of the link inline. After all, that is what the Rails helper functions do. For instance:

```
<%= link_to_remote 'foo', :url => "http://www.google.com",
  :update => {:success => "blog_post_container", :failure => "error_container" } %>
```

generates the following code:

```
<a href="#" onclick="new Ajax.Updater(
  {
      success:'blog_post_container',
      failure:'error_container'
  },
  'http://www.google.com',
  {
      asynchronous:true,
      evalScripts:true,
      parameters:'authenticity_token=' +
          encodeURIComponent('f246bc6fcf1feefbbebc7e7723e24920e5a64ea3')
  }
); return false;">foo</a>
```

With these dynamic links integrated into your code and working nicely, not to mention generated JavaScript from all the other Prototype and script.aculo.us helpers, it isn't such a crime to add a bit of custom JavaScript of your own at the end of a partial or template:

```
<script type="text/javascript">
    function requery_map() {
        var argString = build_query_args();
        var url = "/map_items/query?" + argString;
        if (gmap != null) {
            new Ajax.Updater('map_update', url, {
                onComplete:function(){
                new Effect.Highlight('map_update');
                },
                asynchronous:true,
                evalScripts:true
            });
        }
    }
</script>
```

Bit by bit, the JavaScript creeps in, added as needed into views and partials when AJAX requests spawn the need for a bit of extra logic on the client side. Then one day, you realize that your HTML is starting to become as illegible as the days of <TABLE> abuse that you tried hard to forget. But now it's even worse, because the problem extends outside the realm of the view and into that of the controller, diluting decision-making control between the browser and the server-hosted controller.

Moving business logic into the client side isn't categorically a bad idea, and many of the more feature-intensive web applications have no other choice. Inline JavaScript isn't necessarily bad, either, when used in the right places. What is dangerous is haphazard coding, and this is the danger you must be aware of when you begin to integrate AJAX throughout your application, because it can crop up even amidst the best intentions.

The only tool you need to battle this hazard is your own awareness of the way you are writing code. Pay attention to the way you've chosen to use AJAX and the level of importance that JavaScript plays in your application. If you find yourself writing a lot of JavaScript inside files that end in .rhtml, take a step back and determine whether the complexity of your client requirements necessitates a more structured JavaScript development approach.

You Have Your Pick of JavaScript Frameworks, Even in Rails

The timing of Ruby on Rails' initial release was serendipitous. It caught the explosion of AJAX and JavaScript development right near the beginning and was able to integrate two of the early JavaScript libraries, Prototype and script.aculo.us, into the framework with built-in macros and support. This support helped solidify these two frameworks as favorites among the Rails crowd (helped, certainly, by Prototype's Ruby-like additions to JavaScript). Unfortunately, this tight coupling has often led to the misconception among many new Rails users that Prototype and script.aculo.us are part of Rails, or that Rails depends on these two libraries. The reality is that you have your pick of frameworks to use with Rails, just as you do in any other server-side environment.

The Prototype and script.aculo.us frameworks, coupled with the macros built into Rails that use them, can give you a lot of mileage, but they are just one pair of frameworks among many fantastic ones that are available for free. The following table contains the front-running JavaScript libraries du jour — a list that is likely to change as time passes. These libraries vary wildly in philosophy, capabilities, and approach, and each deserves a serious look before you choose one for your site. In general, they can be grouped into two categories: the minimalist (Prototype, script.aculo.us, MooTools, jQuery) and the widget based (YUI, Dojo, Ext).

Framework	Sound bite	Standard Effects	Widgets	Extras
Prototype	OO-based toolkit that provides many features that feel missing from JavaScript compared to other scripting languages.			The basis and inspiration for many other frameworks.
script.aculo.us	Lightweight drag and drop and graphics operations for the Prototype library.	X		Well tested, lots of real-world use to vet its implementation.
Yahoo! UI (YUI)	A modularized collection of utilities and themed widgets made by the professionals.	X	X	Namespaces, rich custom event support, and nice data table.

Framework	Sound bite	Standard Effects	Widgets	Extras
Dojo	The kitchen-sink framework, with a bit of everything for everyone.	X	X	Large widget set; SVG support.
MooTools	Extremely lightweight and modular; feels like a refined version of Prototype and script.aculo.us.	X		Tooltips and Scroll-wheel support.
jQuery	Provides a new and powerful way to interact with the DOM, events, and AJAX.			Many plug-ins that provide additional features; superb documentation.
Ext	Industrial-strength widget library; the slickest and most business-oriented set of UI widgets on the block.	X	X	Great themes; can be used on top of jQuery, Prototype, or YUI; Java Swing-style layout managers; integration with other frameworks (Gears, AIR); templates.

When evaluating a framework to use in your project, don't look at just the demo page, even though the demos are important. Also look at how modularized the framework is, what helper functions it provides, and how easy it is to extend with your code. You will inevitably end up writing custom extensions for the framework at some point, so it is important to pick one with a design that you can work with. Also look at the quality of the documentation for the features you are interested in. Some of the frameworks in the table have wiki-based documentation, so the coverage isn't consistent from feature to feature. Finally, browse the Internet to see what others are saying about the framework. If a cool feature drawing you to a particular framework actually results in memory leaks and browser crashes, you'll want to learn this from others' experiences instead of your own.

Using one of the frameworks in the table (outside of Prototype and script.aculo.us) will mean that you no longer have the nicety of RJS and all the Rails' JavaScript helpers, but that isn't necessarily such a bad thing. Although the shortcuts that Rails provides can be nice, there is also value in getting to know your medium well and diving into the JavaScript yourself. Ultimately, it will make you a better web developer in all languages. So if one of the languages seems to fit your needs better than the others, go for it.

The Five Styles of AJAX

If the wonderful libraries I just covered make the mechanics of AJAX so easy, then what, besides the JavaScript development that comes paired with AJAX, is there to learn? A good bit — it just isn't code.

Designs and the coding that follows must be coherent and consistent. In some respects, this can matter even more than your technical wizardry with a programming language. (One Ruby developer on the core team even commented that you can sometimes tell what country a core team member is from just by looking at his or her coding style.)

This section of the chapter introduces five different styles of applying AJAX to enhance your web application.

- ❏ Proxy style
- ❏ Partial style
- ❏ Puppet style
- ❏ Compiled-to-web style
- ❏ In-place application style

These styles are by no means official standards — the terms are creations of this book — so there are no doubt more ways to organize your code. These five appear to be the predominant ones, however, so provide a good starting point for just about any application type you want to pursue. (You can contribute your own styles and ideas in the online comment section for this chapter at http://artofrails.com/chapter/7.)

Each of these five styles is a different way to approach AJAX, and the code you write for each will have a different look and feel to it. Which one to use is your choice, and mixing more than one style in your application is okay, too. The goal of this chapter isn't to box you into a single way of coding but rather to make you more conscious about design issues you might otherwise have overlooked. Rails applications tend to use two of the five styles in combination — partial style and puppet style. Both of these are explained in greater depth (see the "Partial Style" and "Puppet Style" sections, later in the chapter).

Keep in mind, too, that these are development styles, not application types, so you really do have a choice. Most web applications can look and operate the same on the surface while using any one of the styles described in the following sections. To drive home that point, and to better explain each style, the AJAX gurus at meebo have kindly allowed the use of their AJAX-based IM client (see Figure 7-1) as a hypothetical example to demonstrate each AJAX style and have even thrown in a few bits themselves.

Figure 7-1

For each style of AJAX, I'll take a look at how meebo's architecture might be designed if it were to use that style. Doing so should provide a good, real-world comparison between the different styles, as well as demonstrate that the same functionality can take many different forms when it comes to AJAX.

Proxy Style

The *proxy style* is how you might think of AJAX when you first hear the acronym's description. With this strategy, the application still takes place across multiple web pages, and the server remains a big part of the decision making. AJAX is used as a back channel for data connections between rich JavaScript elements on the page and functionality and data hosted on the server. Figure 7-2 depicts this style.

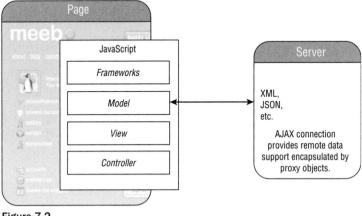

Figure 7-2

The proxy style is essentially a Model-by-Wire style of coding. Just as your model objects are rich Ruby representations that front for the data stored in your database, proxy-style AJAX uses rich JavaScript objects that front for the capabilities provided by the remote server. Certain JavaScript-enabled elements on the page contain client-side logic relevant to their display and user interaction. In this way, the client pages are rich, JavaScript-enabled environments capable of taking care of themselves from a display point of view.

A good example of this style is the YUI DataTable widget. This widget acts as an embedded spreadsheet, complete with cell renderers, validation, and sortable columns. The widget can be initialized, configured, and added to the page completely through JavaScript. Provided a URL, it will contact that endpoint expecting XML data in return that it uses to populate its rows and columns.

On the extreme end of the proxy style is the DWR (Direct Web Remoting) framework. Like a hand-written version of GWT (the Google Web Toolkit), DWR couples full-blown JavaScript service proxies for remote Java services. JavaScript callers on the client side can use the proxy as if it were a regular JavaScript object, while behind the scenes it enacts each method call by passing it to the server over an AJAX connection.

Buddy List

- ❑ **Hangs out with:** XML, JSON
- ❑ **As seen in:** DWR, YUI, any Server-backed UI Widget

Points to Ponder

❑ Supports a clear divide between AJAX-related functionality and HTML-related functionality on the server, as AJAX responses are kept to serialization formats

❑ Keeps the majority of your AJAX-related feature implementation on the client-side

Chatting with meebo

Proxy-style meebo would have several JavaScript libraries included with each page — some to manage the windows and UI elements, others to represent certain conceptual objects within the meebo application, such as a `Chat`, a `BuddyList`, a `Buddy`, and so on.

Each of these objects would be built up with methods to represent the main actions a user might want to perform. An instantiated `Chat` object might provide functions such as `say(String text)`, `close()`, and `updateStatus(String status)`, whereas the `BuddyList` and `Buddy` classes have similar methods pertaining to them. These methods are responsible for both updating their visual appearance on the page and transmitting data back to the server over AJAX. So when a user presses the enter key inside a chat window, it activates the `chat.say(textbox.value)` function, which clears the text box, appends a line of text to the chat window and makes an AJAX call to an endpoint on the server that accepts chat messages.

Each of these objects also must maintain a periodic or long-running connection to the server for asynchronous updates about things others have said to them and buddy status changes. In the local JavaScript VM, they all register with a local connection manager that allows them to pool their interests and get their updates through a single HTTP connection that acts as a lifeline to the server. This connection manager would use another set of methods on the object designed as callbacks for meebo events that come in from the server, methods such as `receiveChatRequest(Buddy otherBuddy)`, `buddySignedOn(Buddy buddy)`, and `buddySignedOff(Buddy buddy)`.

The hypothetical proxy-style meebo architecture looks a lot like traditional desktop programming. A rich set of libraries is built up around the abstraction of chatting, and these libraries perform the work necessary to shuttle the information back and forth to make the abstractions function as expected. After these proxy objects in JavaScript are written, the JavaScript developer doesn't even need to know that he or she is using HTTP because these details are encapsulated completely within the proxy objects.

The Real meebo

Meebo actually uses a similar style to this, as co-founder Elaine Wherry points out. Because so many meebo events occur asynchronously on the server, rather than in the client, the server compiles a list of event updates for each client and sends them as a batch. These batches are delivered in JSON and look like this:

```
{
msgevents:
   [{buddy1: 'hello'}],
   [{buddy2: 'are you there?'}],
buddyevents:
```

```
    [{buddy1: 'online'}, {buddy2: 'away'}]],
accountevents:
    [{user1: 'online'}, {user2: 'offline'}]
}
```

When this JSON object is received at the client, its different components are sent to the various model objects that manage different components of the client-side chat environment. Changes in these model objects, in turn, cause the UI to be updated appropriately.

Partial Style

Partial-style AJAX is a completely different way of applying AJAX made popular by the `Ajax.Updater` object in Prototype and the Rails macros that use it. In this style of coding, AJAX is used to transfer bits of preformed HTML, rather than data, back and forth. These HTML fragments are then inserted into some location on the page, usually depending on the status of the response (success or failure). This style is depicted in Figure 7-3.

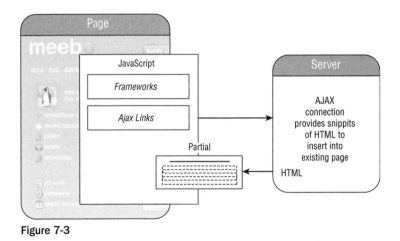

Figure 7-3

Partial-style AJAX is attractive because of its intuitiveness and similarity to the way in which web applications worked in the pre-AJAX days. In those days, you clicked a link and received a new page. With partial-style AJAX, you click a link and receive a new page *fragment*. Think of the "Next 20 Items" link in an AJAX-powered storefront, the "Expand Thread" link on a discussion board with nested comments, or the "Add Item" button on a Todo list application. All these actions are circumstances in which the simplest way to implement them is to connect to a URL that causes the desired action to happen and then have the server respond with only the HTML necessary to furnish the response, which replaces or adds to HTML already on the page.

Buddy List

❑   **Hangs out with:** HTML

❑   **As seen in:** Prototype, Ruby on Rails

Points to Ponder

- ❏ Frees you from having to serialize and deserialize data to send over AJAX connections.

- ❏ Ensures that the server is always in sync with the state of the client (for example, if you try to add a new item to a shopping list, the item will not appear in the list unless the AJAX response shows that the server understood it was supposed to add the item).

- ❏ Allows your HTML development to remain HTML development — no need to write JavaScript that outputs HTML or goes to great lengths manipulating the DOM structure.

- ❏ Provides greater flexibility over the physical layout and structure of your code, because it resides on the server and is sent to the client in small bits when appropriate, rather than in a JavaScript file sent in bulk to the client.

- ❏ Splits the development of AJAX-related features between the client and the server.

- ❏ Encourages more round-trips to the server than most other approaches, because nearly all significant changes in the information displayed must be provided by an AJAX request.

Chatting with meebo

A partial-style meebo would have a very different code-base from a proxy-style meebo. Whereas the proxy style looked like a traditional application that happened to be written using web languages, the partial style looks like an old-school web application adapted for AJAX. Each object on the page, such as a chat window and its components, is thought of as a DOM element with a known ID instead of as a JavaScript object that maintains a fragment of HTML. Dynamic interactions are performed by first consulting the server and then choosing a DOM ID to apply the HTML result to when they return.

A chat window, for example, contains two main components: an AJAX form for sending text and a CSS-styled ordered list for displaying the chat. When a new line of chat is sent to the server via AJAX form submission, the response contains a server-prepared `<li>` element representing that new line as it should appear in the sender's chat history. If the status code of the request indicates success, the user appends the server response to the `<ol>` element that represents that chat window's dialogue.

Receiving asynchronous updates from the site is a bit problematic if you try to stick to pure partial-style coding, because each element of the UI must request updates individually so that the client knows where to place the HTML that returns. A periodic AJAX request is made from each chat window to an endpoint that acts as a queue for any incoming chat messages, filtered by chat. This endpoint pops any existing elements off the queue and uses them to render a series of `<li>` elements containing the formatted chat lines.

Puppet Style

Puppet-style AJAX is the other form popular with Rails developers, primarily because of the RJS package that ships with Rails. From the perspective of the client code, this style looks a lot like the partial style. The difference is in the contents of the data that comes back from the server. In partial-style AJAX, the response from the server is HTML fragments. In puppet-style AJAX, the response is JavaScript to be executed on receipt. In this way, the client acts like a marionette, sending AJAX requests to its puppeteer, the server, and executing its instructions in response. Figure 7-4 shows a depiction of this style.

This manner of writing AJAX is unique because it creates an implied dependency between the client page and the server application: The page can't function without instruction from the server, and the server can't send instructions without knowledge of the page. This dependency is different from most of the other styles of AJAX, in which the page operates more or less as a stand-alone and self-managing unit after it leaves the server. Even when using AJAX, the data provided by the response is under the control of the JavaScript code in the client. Not so with the puppeteer approach, because the page blindly executes whatever JavaScript is sent back to it. This dependency has both benefits and downsides.

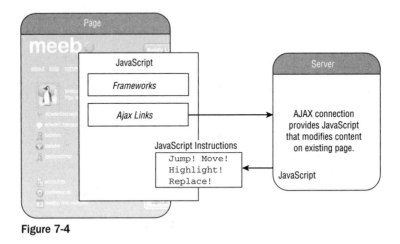

Figure 7-4

On the plus side, it removes the need to replicate model objects with proxies on the client, saving you a lot of time in JavaScript development. Because the AJAX response is JavaScript pieced together by the Rails server dynamically, these JavaScript templates can use your server-side models and environment in the same way that HTML templates can. When you think about all the time that is sometimes spent marshalling and unmarshalling data to get it between client and server processes, the ability to embed server-side data instances directly into dynamically generated JavaScript is a great relief.

On the downside, this tight relationship between the client page and the document prepared by the server can be a bit troubling from a design perspective. In order for the server to prepare JavaScript to tell the client page what to do, the server needs to know what the current state of the web page is. In an environment that is theoretically stateless (or, acknowledging the role of session variables, state avoiding), this relationship creates assumptions on the server that can cause problems down the road in two different ways.

The first problem is that the controller must presume to know what is on the page even though it no longer has control over the page when the page is in control of the client. This lack of control limits your ability as a developer to use JavaScript on the client-side to modify the structure of the page, because each modification you make increases the risk that your server-side code will make an assumption about the DOM that no longer holds.

The second problem is that it limits the reusability of your AJAX-enabled controller actions. If a controller action is providing a piece of data, whether XML or HTML, that action can be used by any page that desires that data, and perhaps even reused as part of an API. If the AJAX-enabled action responds with JavaScript instructions, however, it is applicable only to the page or pages that it was designed to operate on. Over time, this dependency can lead to the need to implement the same functionality multiple times, one for each page that requires it.

Despite its downsides, puppet-style AJAX remains a popular and useful option if it fits your project requirements and development style. Later in this chapter, you'll see in more depth how to implement Rails controllers with this technique using RJS.

Buddy List

❑ **Hangs out with:** JavaScript

❑ **As seen in:** Prototype, Ruby on Rails

Points to Ponder

❑ Frees you from having to serialize and deserialize data to send over AJAX connections

❑ Reduces the need to rely on large, static JavaScript files, because they are replaced with small bits of dynamically generated JavaScript sent via AJAX

❑ Removes intelligence from the client application, because the response from the server is needed to instruct the client what to do when key events occur

❑ Encourages more round-trips to the server than most other approaches, because nearly all significant changes in the information displayed are done at the command of script code sent back in an AJAX response

❑ Places a circular dependence between the client page and the server API that may limit the reusability of your code and put you at higher risk for bugs

Chatting with meebo

The puppet-style meebo would be in some ways like an empowered version of the partial-style meebo. The server would still return fragments of HTML, but it would do so as the arguments of JavaScript methods that will insert them into the regions of the page. Because of this, the server controls where the HTML will be inserted, relieving the need for each widget on the client page to poll the meebo server separately.

When a user sends a chat message, the response is a block of JavaScript that instructs the browser to insert a new list element at the bottom of the chat and scroll the chat window downward. Receiving chat messages from other users works much the same way, whether by a polling process or a standing HTTP connection. As the queue of new messages for a user is emptied, these messages are converted into a series of JavaScript instructions to insert the right bits of HTML into the proper chat window on the page. As the JavaScript fully describes the actions that need to be taken, no decision making is needed by the client, and multiple heterogeneous updates can be sent in the same batch.

Compiled-to-Web Style

The *compiled-to-web style* of AJAX is a bit of an anti-style because it is defined by the very lack of developer control over how JavaScript is written and how AJAX is used. This is the one style that can work with only specific frameworks, because the framework must provide some abstraction other than the web to the developer and must compile code using that abstraction down into web pages and server calls. Even

RJS, which can be thought of as a Ruby-to-JavaScript compiler, doesn't qualify for this level of abstraction away from the web because it is only a direct replacement for JavaScript, not the entire web architecture. Figure 7-5 depicts this style.

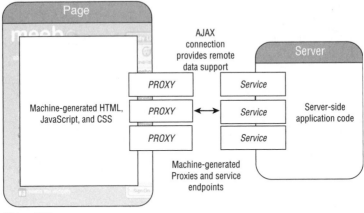

Figure 7-5

The primary example of this type of coding is GWT, the Google Web Toolkit. GWT allows developers to write web applications using Java and a Swing-like library. Provided that certain conventions are followed, the resulting application is compiled down to a server-side component plus the HTML, CSS, and JavaScript needed to fuel the client-half of the application.

Compiled-to-web frameworks such as GWT are a good fit for people who prefer to avoid AJAX and the web world of languages in general and who would rather take advantage of the language environment and tools available at some higher level. For GWT, this means that developers get to write web applications as though they were Java applications, providing all the benefits of Java debugging and Java IDEs for free.

The catch is that you surrender control of the code that is ultimately produced to form your web application, making it difficult to fine-tune features in nonstandard or innovative ways. In this regard, it is the web equivalent of compiling Java down to bytecode. These types of frameworks usually allow you to sneak into HTML and JavaScript if need be, but if you do this too often, you circumvent most of the reason for using such a framework in the first place.

As web applications grow in complexity and begin to displace desktop applications, some technologists predict that the practice of developing and maintaining large user interfaces in HTML and JavaScript will become intractable. If this prediction proves to be true, two approaches will likely emerge in place of traditional HTML for desktop-like applications. The first is proprietary run-time environments, such as Adobe's Flash, Flex, and AIR or Microsoft's Silverlight, and the second is compiled-to-web frameworks such as GWT. For that reason alone, this style of development is worth consideration, because it may grow in popularity with time.

Buddy List

- ❑ **Hangs out with:** Utterly incomprehensible, machine-generated JavaScript and HTML
- ❑ **As seen in:** GWT

Points to Ponder

❑ Does the compiled-to-web framework you are using provide a feature set that is full enough for you to develop your application? (It is difficult to write custom widgets that "play well" with these types of frameworks.)

❑ Provides some development abstractions that are not easily available using web-native approaches.

❑ Usually allows you to develop your application ignoring, or heavily deemphasizing, the client-server divide. It handles creation of client-side proxy objects that fetch data from the server.

❑ Machine-generated web code is effectively impossible to debug without the help of a debugging environment provided by the framework you are using. If this debugger doesn't fix your problem, you're pretty much stuck.

❑ Harder to customize and add new functionality to than are styles that use a web-native approach.

Chatting with meebo

The compiled-to-web style of meebo would be coded as though it were a Java application. Upon deployment, this Java application is automatically translated into separate server and client components, and the mechanics of managing the information flow over HTTP requests is left entirely up to the framework. In this approach, objects that represent elements of the user's experience, such as the chat window and buddy list, are marked as being objects that compile down to client-side code. These objects interact with other objects, such as chat queues and buddy events, that are marked as being server-side objects. The objects marked for the client become JavaScript and HTML entities. Those marked as server-side objects are compiled into server-side service endpoints. Finally, a third set of objects remains entirely on the server to manage supporting details at too low a level to be of interest to the client connection. When the project is compiled, the result is a client-side proxy for the server's functionality similar to the proxy style, except that it is machine generated and opaque to the developer's tinkering.

In-Place Application Style

The last style of AJAX development is the most extreme, even more so than the compiled-to-web approach. In-place web applications are essentially rich-client applications that happen to be deployed as a bundle of HTML, JavaScript, and CSS. They exist on the web, but only because that is how they are deployed. Local storage is made possible through the use of a proprietary run-time environment (such as AIR), a browser plug-in (such as Google Gears), or native browser support (such as Apple's WebKit browser engine), and that storage is used to persist much of the user's data for access when offline. Figure 7-6 depicts the in-place application style.

When the user is connected to the web, AJAX connections are used to synchronize application data with the master copy on the application server. The web site might even operate offline, but additional features are available when web connectivity is present. The design attempts to keep AJAX requests to a minimum, though, and to provide just these extras. The majority of interactions and state modifications on the page are handled locally via JavaScript so that the page can continue to function at some level without an Internet connection present.

This type of development is appropriate for developers who want to go after either the traditionally non-web market or court users who are concerned about poor or only periodic network connectivity. An example of the latter case is Apple's iPhone, released in 2007 with the web as its development platform but whose slow and sometimes unavailable wireless network interfered with making this platform a true killer application. Developers quickly found ways to embed data locally using strategies ranging from cookies and bookmarklets to data URLs that enabled small web applications to be loaded on the phone in such a way that they worked both on- and offline.

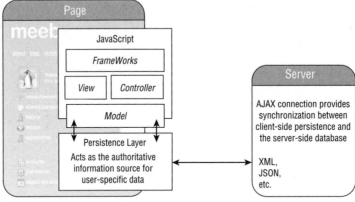

Figure 7-6

Buddy List

❑ **Hangs out with:** A menagerie of big-name and experimental technologies

❑ **As seen in:** Google Gears, Adobe AIR, WebKit, Dojo

Points to Ponder

❑ You have less of a chance to take advantage of the powerful body of server-side tools available to you as a developer.

❑ HTML is hard to maintain when it is written through the proxy of JavaScript.

❑ You are edged out of the realm of web development and into the realm of desktop application development (that just happens to be implemented using web languages).

❑ Users have a way to use your web application when they aren't online.

Chatting with meebo

The in-place design strategy is one in which the Internet (and AJAX) enables certain core features of the application but is not necessary for a majority of the application to continue functioning as normal. This changes the architecture of a meebo chat significantly and makes it look a lot like another type of application that we use every day: e-mail.

The first major change is the presence of a persistence mechanism on the client that allows data to be cached to disk and recalled later. This persistence layer, not the server, becomes the authoritative data source from the web interface's perspective. The web interface transforms into an application built on top of that local data storage that happens to be built inside a web browser.

When the user sends a chat message to another user, the web interface registers that message with a JavaScript model object fronting the local persistence layer, which adds the message and marks it as unsent. Another process continually scans this local data store for unsent messages and attempts to send them if an Internet connection is present.

Messages are received in the same fashion as the proxy style: Some client-side JavaScript process maintains an AJAX connection to the server. When new messages are available for the user, they are returned in a serialized data format such as XML, placed inside the local data store, and flagged as undelivered. Through events or a polling JavaScript process, these undelivered messages are transferred onto the web interface and added to the appropriate chat window.

AJAX as Just Another API

Handling the AJAX request from the server-side is just like any other format-specific API you might write. Just as you used the `respond_to` method to serve up multiple response formats in the previous two chapters, so you can use similar techniques to detect an AJAX request and respond to it appropriately.

Detecting whether a request is an AJAX one is a bit trickier than using the API-centric `respond_to` blocks, however. Those blocks were based entirely on the desired response format, but this might not be enough with AJAX, because the same could be used for both AJAX and non-AJAX responses. Given that, you have a few different options for detecting whether a particular request is an AJAX one.

❑ **Pick a format to always use for AJAX and go with it.** When using the puppet style with Rails, this is the most sensible choice, because the response format of JavaScript can be used as the indicator for an AJAX request and doesn't run any risk of being confused with requests for a full page load.

❑ If you dig down into the default MIME types registered for you by the Rails framework, you will find one named JS defined to represent requests that come from a JavaScript process instead of a full page load:

```
Mime::Type.register "text/javascript", :js,
   %w( application/javascript application/x-javascript )
```

❑ This means that all your AJAX requests must either use the add an `Accept` header of `application/javascript` or `application/x-javascript` along with their requests or use URIs endpoints that end in `.js`, and everything will be taken care of for them on the server side. Just add `:js` as a `respond_to` option and render the appropriate JavaScript back to the client in that case.

❑ Detecting an AJAX request in this manner would look something like the following action:

```
def show
  @visit = Visit.find(params[:id])

  respond_to do |format|
    format.html # show.rhtml
    format.xml  { render :xml => @visit.to_xml }
```

```
    format.js { # Render JavaScript response here }
  end
end
```

❏ **Use a JavaScript framework that adds, or lets you add, extra headers to the AJAX requests.**
Another easy way to detect that a particular request is an AJAX one is with the `request` object
that is accessible at the controller level. In Rails, this object contains two methods (one is just an
alias of the other) `xhr?` and `xml_http_request?`. Both methods return a Boolean value representing whether the `X-Requested-With` header was present on the incoming HTTP request and set to
the value `XMLHttpRequest`.

❏ Some frameworks, such as Prototype, add this header for you, so if you use Rails' built-in
JavaScript helpers, this technique is guaranteed to work. If you want to use it with some other
framework, then use a debugger or dig into its AJAX request routine to see whether this header
is added; if it's not, then modify the code a bit to stick it in there. Doing so gives you a sure way
to identify whether the context of a request is a full-on request for a web page or is just an AJAX
request for a smaller bit of information.

❏ Detecting an AJAX request in this manner would look like this:

```
def show
  @visit = Visit.find(params[:id])

  if request.xhr?
    # render Ajax response here
  else
    respond_to do |format|
      format.html # show.rhtml
      format.xml  { render :xml => @visit.to_xml }
    end
  end
end
```

❏ **Implement an alternative set of endpoints for AJAX requests.** Every clean and simple design
paradigm breaks down at some point, and the real world reveals itself as being full of exceptions
to the rule. Although much of the Rails design philosophy is attempting to maintain a minimal set of endpoints that can be reused in many different ways depending on the HTTP verb,
sometimes you just can't layer all AJAX endpoints on top of your existing ones. In these cases,
implement a few endpoints to deal just with AJAX requests.

❏ For whatever reason this crops up, you can always implement endpoints on your web application that are intended, from the start, to talk only to AJAX requests. One word of advice if you do
this: Try to maintain some consistency if you are also using one of the preceding two techniques.
Even if a controller action will never handle anything but AJAX requests, you might want to
embed logic looking for a particular header or accept type, just to keep the implementation consistent across your application. That way, your code and intentions will be more clear when you
revisit the code six months after having written it.

Using these three methods to identify AJAX requests, AJAX from the server-side looks just like any
other web request coming in. The only difference is the data that the server chooses to write back to the
requester.

Rails-Style AJAX

Of the five styles of AJAX just presented, Rails developers tend to use two in particular: partial style and puppet style. Part of the reason for this is that the JavaScript frameworks that ship with Rails and the Ruby wrappers that have been created around them are heavily biased toward these two styles. As a result, the Rails community has standardized and grown up around them. This section digs deeper into controller design and development style for both the partial-style controller and the puppet-style controller.

Partial-Style AJAX Controllers (and AJAX CRUD)

In the partial style of AJAX, AJAX requests are met with an HTML response, small fragments of a page that can strategically replace or append an existing region of the page. This style can be one of the easiest to learn as a new AJAX developer because it minimizes the amount of JavaScript that is written: Nearly all coding is in HTML. The fanciest the JavaScript ever gets is changing the fragment's insertion location based on the reported success of the AJAX call. The following piece of Rails code looks a lot like the code used to create a hyperlink, for example, but this one instead creates an AJAX-powered link that will dynamically inject the server's response into the existing page.

```
link_to_remote "Next Blog Post",
    :url => {
        :action => "show",
        :id => (post.next)
    },
    :update => {
        :success => "blog_post_container",
        :failure => "error_container"
    }
```

The needs of each project invariably lead to a unique design situation, but as the partial style is applied to the project, a pattern of use emerges that makes it fit quite well with the CRUD (Create, Read, Update, Delete) pattern of web resource development. Each CRUD operation has its own special response for AJAX requests that, applied consistently, will simplify the chore of integrating AJAX into your code. After learning this "CRUDy AJAX" pattern, you will see how you can use inner templates to organize the HTML files in your project so that the same files can be used both for AJAX and non-AJAX requests, eliminating the need to repeat yourself.

CRUDy AJAX

CRUDy AJAX works just as regular CRUD operations do, except that the operations are whittled down to their very core purpose. Instead of dealing with entire pages, the HTML returned deals only with the precise object or operation that was requested. Two themes are apparent in the AJAX responses given by the CRUD operations on controllers:

❑ When the operation only accesses information (without modifying it), return just the HTML containing the information accessed rather than the whole page.

❑ When the operation creates, modifies, or destroys data, do one of the following:

  ❑ Return the replacement value for the data in question, which should be injected into the page with some added visual effect to call attention to it

  ❑ Return an error message if the operation did not succeed

The following table shows the traditional CRUD operations for a hypothetical User object and adds their new meaning when used with AJAX.

Create		
Function	**Full-page Response**	**AJAX Response**
new	Returns a page containing the form for a new User object.	Returns only the form for a new User object.
create	Accepts request data and attempts to create a new User object, redirecting the user after object creation.	Accepts request data and attempts to create a new User object, sending back a fragment of HTML containing a confirmation of the operation's success or a small representation of that object to be appended to the current page.
Read		
Function	**Full-page Response**	**AJAX Response**
index	Returns a page listing all User objects	Returns only the list of User objects without the page around it
show	Returns a page containing the complete profile of a User object.	Returns an HTML partial representing the User object, or perhaps a smaller preview of the profile depending on arguments
Update		
Function	**Full-page Response**	**AJAX Response**
edit	Returns a page containing a prepopulated form for editing an existing User object	Returns only the prepopulated form for editing an existing User object
update	Accepts request data and attempts to update an existing User object, redirecting the user after object update	Accepts request data and attempts to update an existing User object, sending back a fragment of HTML containing a confirmation of the operation's success or an updated version of the User object to replace the old one
Delete		
Function	**Full-page Response**	**AJAX Response**
destroy	Removes the User object corresponding to the given ID and redirects the user back to some main view	Removes the User object corresponding to the given ID and returns a fragment of HTML containing a confirmation of the operation's success

So, for example, the index action for a controller managing your contact list in meebo would return only the contents of the contact list itself for AJAX requests, nothing more and nothing less, yielding a response that looks something like the following:

```
<ol class="contact_list">
  <li class="aim active">Buddy 1</li>
  <li class="aim idle">Buddy 2</li>
</ol>
```

Learning to Use "Inner Layouts"

When you design your controllers around the CRUDy AJAX idea, the resulting set of files often looks a lot like something you are already familiar with: layouts. It is beneficial to see how this pattern emerges here so that you can look for it and plan for it in your own code.

A layout is a page-sized template that wraps around the result rendered by a particular action. Layouts provide all the scaffolding around the main content of your page, such as stylesheet references and navigation sidebars, allowing the output of each controller action to concentrate on its unique task. A layout's job is all about maximizing efficiency. By pulling the overall page structure into its own separate file, multiple pages can share the same layout without repeated code. This helpful pattern is easily extended at the action level of AJAX-enabled controllers.

CRUDy AJAX controllers are most easily implemented by adding another virtual layer to the layout of your application. This inner layout provides the decorative structure specific to the feature addressed by that action. The inner layout is implemented with a regular RHTML ERB template, and the content to go inside it is implemented inside a partial. Figure 7-7 shows a screenshot of the meebo welcome blog pried apart to show the difference between each part.

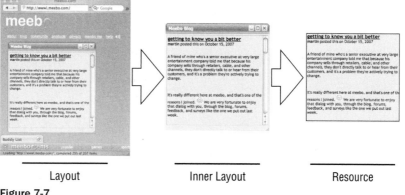

| Layout | Inner Layout | Resource |

Figure 7-7

Following this pattern of using ERB templates as inner layouts and partials as the content to fill them can have a homogenizing effect on the implementation of your controller actions. In the respond_to clause of each action, the HTML block will render the inner layout, and the JavaScript block will render just the partial that is paired with that inner layout.

Here is an example of what the show method might look like for the BlogController on a site such as meebo:

```
def show
  @post = Post.find(params[:id])
  respond_to do |type|
    type.html {
```

```
                render(:action => 'show') unless request.xhr?
                render(:partial => 'post', :locals => {:post => @post}) if request.xhr?
        }
        # ... Other respond_to types here
    end
  rescue
    redirect_to resource_not_found_url
  end
```

In this code, the overall template linked to this action contains, by default, the body of the page —
logo, navigational links, and so on — whereas the `show.rhtml` file contains the inner layout that wraps
around a post and a link to the `_post.rhtml` partial. On an AJAX (XHR) request, the action renders only
the partial itself, the bare-bones blog post with minimal decoration around the outside.

So how far do you go? Does the innermost partial always need to be stripped down and minimal? Not
at all. The example here errs on that side because it is easier to demonstrate it that way, but your design
may include atomic components that are far more functional.

Puppet-Style AJAX Controllers (and RJS)

In the puppet style of AJAX, AJAX requests are used to modify the page loaded in the client using bits
of JavaScript code. The web server acts like a puppeteer, sending commands through the wire that cause
the remote browser to modify its appearance.

This type of design is markedly different from writing your own JavaScript libraries and including them
in the <head> of your page or writing client-side JavaScript that calls a partial-style AJAX controller
to replace bits of the DOM with updates from an AJAX request. Instead, puppet responses contain pure
JavaScript. They don't describe how a page or part of a page looks but rather how an existing page should
be modified (recall Figure 7-4). You might think of puppet responses as the mathematical derivative of a
web page.

You can see this difference by comparing the partial and puppet styles with a non-AJAX request, in
this case, the hypothetical "add item" feature of a simple shopping list application, as the following
table shows.

Non-AJAX Approach		
	1.	Enter new item in a form field.
	2.	Post the form to the server.
	3.	Receive a new page from the server with an updated list and an empty form again.
Partial Approach	**1.**	Enter new item in a form field.
	2.	Send an AJAX request to the server, requesting the item be added to the list.
	3.	Receive a fragment of HTML back from the server representing the new item rendered as an element that should be added to the current page.

	4.	Append that HTML fragment to some appropriate place on the page.
	5.	Clear the form for reuse.
Puppet Approach	**1.**	Enter new item in a form field.
	2.	Send an AJAX request to the server, requesting the item be added to the list.
	3.	Receive a fragment of JavaScript back from the server.
	4.	Execute the fragment of JavaScript.
		(The JavaScript, when executed, causes new DOM elements representing the new item to be created and inserted into the page.)
	5.	Clear the form for reuse.

The partial and puppet approach look similar, but they are actually very different. In the former, the remote web page maintains control over AJAX requests and over what happens as a result of their response. In the latter, you can think of the JavaScript code executed in the response as the remote server taking control of the browser to control the outcome.

The puppet style and the partial style can often be mixed. If the JavaScript library you are using to perform your AJAX requests is set to evaluate all JavaScript code on receipt, the server can send back HTML partials that contain embedded JavaScript to animate regions of the page in addition to providing HTML to replace a region on the page. A good example is a partial containing the container for an embedded Google Map, as well as the JavaScript necessary to initialize the map. Be careful, though — if you mix HTML and JavaScript in your partials too much, the overall structure of your web project can quickly become tangled and not reusable. As convenient as it may seem to do this, a whole project filled with mixed-type files can be a mess to maintain.

RJS: A Different Kind of View

A large reason for the popularity of the puppet style among Rails developers is the pseudo-language called RJS that shipped with Rails 1.1 in 2006. RJS is a Ruby library that allows developers to write Ruby code that is translated on the fly into JavaScript.

Views that are composed entirely of RJS-driven JavaScript are called RJS templates. These templates form a special kind of view, expressing how an existing page changes rather than how a new piece of data looks. They can be stored alongside other views with the .rjs extension, or rendered inline from the controller.

Although the puppeteer approach doesn't require a tool such as RJS to work, RJS certainly makes it easier. Many Ruby developers consider Ruby a cleaner and more concise language than JavaScript when it comes to most operations. The ability to use Ruby-style iteration blocks and the rich set of built-in Ruby objects can be a nice alternative to JavaScript. RJS also provides a nice Ruby-based API for the Prototype and script.aculo.us libraries, making their functionality easier to invoke.

RJS even brought about code improvements for 37signals, the company that maintains Rails. In an August 2006 blog post about a rewrite of its organizer application Backpack, the company writes:

> We moved nearly all of the application's UI logic out of hand-written JavaScript files and into Ruby using RJS templates. This resulted in approximately 1600 fewer lines of application JS, and let us deliver pages with substantially less markup, since the edit states are now loaded on-demand instead of included in bulk with each page load.

How RJS Works

In the same way that the browser makes a DOM API available to its JavaScript environment, RJS provides a page object that provides "access" to the DOM. The word *access* is in quotation marks because the DOM access that it provides isn't actually real; code executing on the server is not able to access the browser's DOM. Instead, calls on the page object are translated into JavaScript code before the server responds to the client's request. Thus, the following RJS code:

```
page[:chat_window].insert_html :bottom, content_tag('li', 'pickled herring')
```

will result in the following JavaScript (don't mind all the hex codes):

```
try {
    $("chat_window").insertHtml("bottom", "\074li\076hey\074/li\076");
}
catch (e) {
    alert('RJS error:\n\n' + e.toString());
    alert('$(\"chat_window\").insertHtml(\"bottom\", \"\\074li\\076pickled
herring\\074/li\\076\");');
    throw e
}
```

Although the partial-style controllers can work with any JavaScript framework, it should be apparent from the preceding generated JavaScript that the puppet style is framework specific as soon as you introduce the idioms of one particular JavaScript framework into your JavaScript responses. In the case of RJS, the Prototype and script.aculo.us libraries are required for the browser to correctly execute.

Learning RJS

For detailed information about the specific API calls RJS provides, explore the API docs online at http://api.rubyonrails.org/classes/ActionView/Helpers/Prototype Helper/JavaScriptGenerator/GeneratorMethods.html.

Or, check out Cody Fauser's PDF book, *RJS Templates on Rails*, at http://oreilly.com/catalog/rjsrails/.

Elegant Degradation

No, it's not a euphemism for a beautifully delivered insult. Elegant degradation is the need for your AJAX- and JavaScript-enabled site to scale downward when accessed by a browser that doesn't support

JavaScript. These days, such users are far and few between on the desktop, but the rise of cell-phone browsers makes the need a bit more modern. You have a tough choice to make about how to handle these users because your plan for supporting these users needs to be consistent. You don't need to support every site feature for them (and probably can't; after all, JavaScript provides a lot of power), but you do need to be consistent in your support so that you don't surprise your users. The last thing you want is for a user to spend 20 minutes filling out a form, only to realize at the end that the Submit button requires JavaScript to execute correctly.

If your AJAX-powered web application is going to support non-JavaScript users, you're in reasonably good hands if you chose to follow either the partial or puppet style. This means that you have kept the application flow in the hands of the web server, and you've kept your thoughts expressed in primarily HTML instead of JavaScript. But also be honest with yourself about the web medium before you try to adapt a JavaScript-heavy site to just HTML. Some of the JavaScript applications on the web today are pushing the limits of what the browser can reasonably do with just JavaScript, HTML, and CSS. Some of these sites just can't be done without JavaScript, and that's okay. If your application makes extensive use of mouse operations or interactive graphics, or if asynchronous server communication is absolutely necessary, then the lack of JavaScript might just be the game-breaker, and your valuable development time is better spent improving the site for JavaScript users than attempting to adapt it for legacy browsers.

Moving Backward from the Partial-Style

The partial style is most friendly to non-JavaScript users, because this style tends to use JavaScript only as a means through which to replace pages incrementally instead of all at one time. In general, the strategy for implementing a non-JavaScript version of this style of site requires you to identify each partial page load and replace it with a full page load. If you have kept to the CRUD operations, you can do this in a straightforward manner. In general, you'll run across two types of links that you need to replace: regular links that just load a partial and insert it somewhere on the page, and superlinks that use JavaScript to act as though they are a form post.

Backward-Compatible Links

Links that use JavaScript and AJAX to load partials into other parts of the page are easy enough to make backward compatible that the same code can usually be used for both JavaScript and non-JavaScript users (the non-JavaScript users will just ignore the JavaScript part). The key to making these links backward compatible is to make each link have an HREF property that points at the full-page version of the functionality it describes, but then prevent the browser from following the link using JavaScript. JavaScript-enabled users will then be left with a disabled link that is tied only to JavaScript code, while non-JavaScript users will perceive the link as a normal one. There are two primary ways to achieve this behavior.

The first, and easiest, way to implement these links is to place calls to the desired JavaScript code in the onClick property of your link and have the last statement in the onClick body return false. The Boolean return value of onClick instructs the browser whether to follow the hyperlink, so returning false will prevent the page from changing, but only if the browser understands JavaScript.

Placing code directly in the properties of HTML elements (or inline within the middle of an HTML document) is not a clean way to program, however, and you should generally avoid it if you are coding the JavaScript manually. It embeds the details of your JavaScript implementation too deeply within the HTML, making it difficult to change down the road.

Mixing JavaScript code in the middle of HTML isn't as bad if you do it through one of the Rails JavaScript helpers, such as the `link_to_remote` method. Although these methods still compile down to mixed HTML and JavaScript, they provide a single set of intermediary functions so that if you need to change the way your code is implemented, you can just override the implementation of Rails' JavaScript helpers. The resulting HTML might not look very pretty, but at least you will be prepared for change.

The second way to implement backward-compatible links is to layer the added JavaScript functionality on top of regular links from a separate location in the code. From an HTML perspective, this method is much cleaner because it allows you to preserve the bulk of your HTML as a JavaScript-free environment and then tack on all the extra functionality for JavaScript-enabled browsers at the last minute. For this to work, your links need to have the `id` property set so that they can be referenced elsewhere in the page.

The Yahoo! User Interface Library (YUI) is a good example of a library that prefers this method. Here is what adding a callback to a link with the ID `link_id` would look like:

```
YAHOO.util.Event.addListener("link_id", "click", callback_function);
```

Using this style, your HTML and JavaScript is partitioned into physically separate locations, even if it occurs inline in the same file. For developers who plan to write a lot of JavaScript by hand, this technique can be a great organizational tool.

Backward-Compatible Superlinks

Links are supposed to reference documents on the web, not submit data to the server, but with JavaScript, they can be tied to AJAX POST calls, simulating a form submission. Converting these links into proper forms is the only way to make these types of links compatible with non-JavaScript browsers. Rather than use the <A> tag to submit a form via AJAX, try to stick to the normal form submission types and just connect them to asynchronous calls with JavaScript.

Moving Backward from Rich User Interfaces

Many of the rich widgets provided by JavaScript frameworks, such as rich-text editors and spreadsheet-like tables, provide the ability to latch onto their simplistic, plain-vanilla HTML counterparts so that JavaScript features can be implemented as a layer on top of your HTML instead of as a replacement for traditional HTML views. Yahoo!'s YUI framework, for example, provides developers access to its UI widgets from a number of angles. Look at the DataTable widget (`http://developer.yahoo.com/yui/datatable/`). Figure 7-8 shows the DataTable rendering one of the example datasets on the YUI web site.

Due Date	Account Number	Quantity	Amount Due ▾
5/19/1999	83849	8	$60.00
9/30/2001	224747	14	$56.78
8/9/1999	11348	1	$34.99
4/28/2000	37892857482836437378273	123	$33.32
1/23/1999	29e8548592d8c82	12	$150.00
1/23/2001	83849	5	$15.00
1/23/2000	29e8548592d8c82	10	$1.00

Figure 7-8

This widget supports a number of attractive features, including column sorting, input validation, complex selection models, and cell renderers. These features can transform an ordinary read-only HTML table into an interactive spreadsheet-like form. The most attractive feature from a compatibility stand-point, though, is the ability to bootstrap all these features on top of an ordinary HTML table.

The DataTable provides three different ways to create this widget on a page. You might think of each of these approach vectors as constructors, in the more multilingual and loosely defined sense of the web:

- ❑ Create a DataTable class instance in JavaScript and add its rows and columns using methods on the JavaScript object.

- ❑ Create a DataTable widget and configure it to read in data of some structured format (such as CSV or XML).

- ❑ Create a DataTable widget and give it the DOM ID of a `<table>` element on the page to attach itself to.

Using the third option, as Figure 7-9 shows, the table from Figure 7-8 is still visible without JavaScript, just without its special features. Non-JavaScript users of this site would then still be able to access its functionality, just without the bells and whistles JavaScript provides.

Due Date	Account Number	Quantity	Amount Due
1/23/1999	29e8548592d8c82	12	$150.00
5/19/1999	83849	8	$60.00
8/9/1999	11348	1	$34.99
1/23/2000	29e8548592d8c82	10	$1.00
4/28/2000	37892857482836437378273	123	$33.32
1/23/2001	83849	5	$15.00
9/30/2001	224747	14	$56.78

Figure 7-9

When you choose a JavaScript library that supports widgets and begin to integrate widgets into your web application, pay attention to the alternatives you have for instantiating these widgets in a backward-compatible way. Although you pay a small performance price for making the widget parse existing HTML before it rewrites it, you gain the ability to seamlessly add JavaScript for those who support it without breaking the site for your non-JavaScript users.

Summary

AJAX is a powerful tool for a web developer. It broadens the power you have to create interfaces and opens the door to entire new categories of web application that could not exist without it. Learning to use AJAX is simple, but learning to design an entire application around it is difficult.

This chapter presented five different styles of applying AJAX. By keeping the strengths and weaknesses of these styles in mind when you write your code, you will be more conscious about the program-ming choices you make, and you will better understand your own design choices. Applying these styles consistently will make your code easier to understand and maintain down the road.

This chapter covered the partial style and puppet styles in more depth than the other styles because these are the two styles that appear most frequently in Rails applications. Finally, I touched on the importance of backward compatibility with non-JavaScript users and provided some strategies for partial style AJAX coders and JavaScript widget-using coders to maintain backward compatibility from the very start.

The next chapter begins a series of three chapters on advanced Ruby. Many Rails developers come from a background in object-oriented programming compiled languages. Ruby offers many of the familiar constructs of these languages, but it also provides a rich set of tools more commonly found in the functional programming world of languages such as Lisp. As your skills as a Rails developer improve, a lack of knowledge of these advanced bits of Ruby will become a ceiling that limits opportunities for modifying the Rails framework and writing your own reusable code. Moreover, these advanced Ruby constructs are a lot of fun, and they are guaranteed to completely change the way you program!

8

Playing with Blocks

W. Web listened intently as his companions bantered back and forth as if according to a script. They had been sitting at the table for some 40 minutes, most of them spent discussing the day's protest and how it had gone. This group, it turned out, was exactly who Web was sent to find — prominent representatives from the clans allied with his, sent to show support and presence at the URL protest downtown.

Wall-mounted oil lamps flickered oranges and yellows off the shadows in the basement tavern as discussion of the protest moved to one of motivation, as such conversations tend to do. The occasional shouts and nasal laughter of a group of lingering URLs, their scrawny, fry-like bodies in baggy homemade t-shirts, could be heard amid the clinking of glasses from the bar across the hall.

"Flexibility," Schema said, slapping his hand definitively down on the table and looking at Web. "What we need is some flexibility. You have no idea what it's like having to do the same thing all day."

"But what else is there to do?" Rusty responded. "You create data; you update it. If you're lucky, someone might come and read it, too. And then one day, you send it to the big bit bucket in the sky."

"That's exactly the kind of myopic response that gets us into this type of problem. Look at us! You, six feet tall. Me, with a mustache! People grow, things change. We don't always know what we want to do with a thing at the time we build it."

"But there's a balance to be kept. The best we hope for is some grounding stability amidst the process of change. Certain structures to scope and limit our operations."

"Look," Matz jumped in, "I think we can all agree for the needs of both flexibility and structure, but I'm not so sure we need to characterize the solution as a tension between the two. Could we not attempt to live each through the eyes of the other?"

"Agreed," Jen offered. "What is most important is that we take a holistic approach that incorporates all of our strengths. We can't afford to factionalize ourselves in the face of. . ." she trailed off, looking uncomfortable.

Faces grew somber and nods accompanied downward stares around the table. A URL laughed loudly in the background.

"In the face of what?" Web replied.

His party looked nervously among themselves, communicating with their eyes in a silent, reluctant argument to decide who would be the one to explain. Rusty leaned in toward the table, the rest of the group following.

"The compilers," he said in a near whisper, almost mouthing the word. "They have spies, so we can't discuses it in the open. This rally was a cover for the resistance movement. The secret negotiations have fallen through, and the time has run out."

Web wanted to disregard the statement as silly, but the solemn expressions on the faces looking at him made shivers run down his spine and out his limbs. The air suddenly felt electrified in a way that could not be denied.

"What do you mean, run out? What resistance movement?" Web said, his voice now low and intense.

"There's a war coming, Web! And it's too late to stop it! They're gathering by the day. We've been tracking them for a year now. But the final preparations have only recently begun."

"What was the protest for, then?"

"To safely gather the leaders of the resistance movement under the guise of an internal struggle," Jen replied. "Until last week, we had met only through messages, passed through unreliable transport."

"And me? Why was I sent here?"

"Because this war is about YOU, Web" Rusty said, his voice a strained shout hidden in the whisper. "You need to start paying attention to the events around you! Stumbling around on the street like you do!"

"You were sent here so that you could be protected," Jen said in a much softer tone.

Web sat back in the bench, stunned.

"Their signal to attack is the Flying Toasters screensaver."

It was too much to process, but he could see the connections starting to form. The Flying Toasters screensaver? The screensaver! He had been processing orders for that screensaver for months! The biggest resurgence of a software product in years! And the compilers. Nothing on the Web was compiled; his very existence was a threat to compilers everywhere!

Web absorbed the air's electricity as he looked at the faces of his new colleagues, and realized, for the first time, why he was here.

It had to happen eventually: a book on the Rails-style of programming delving specifically into Ruby. As you have seen over the first half of the book, Rails is just as much a style of web development as it is a framework that implements that style. But the way in which Rails style is revealed in code cannot be separated from the Ruby language on which it is constructed. These next two chapters will explore some of the finer parts of the Ruby language that make it so different from the traditional object oriented (OO) establishment. These "Rubyisms" make the Rails school of design and development possible.

The software development taught *en masse* these days tends to emphasize the C/Java programming style in which writing code is about creating highly specified objects that manipulate data and other objects. If you started programming in this type of environment, just think about every method signature you ever wrote. If you are like most of us, your methods took parameters with types such as `int`, `String`, and `List`. This type of programming creates a clear separation between "that which is code" and "that which is data." The code part is static, defined during code-time, and the data part is limited to declarative containers of numbers and characters.

The truth is, there is a rich history of programming languages that don't limit the code to just talking about data manipulation but actually allow you to write code that talks about other code as well, and even code that writes other code while the program is running. Ruby is one of those languages. This type of programming is usually referred to as *metaprogramming*, defined by Wikipedia as:

> The writing of computer programs that write or manipulate other programs (or themselves) as their data ... In many cases, this allows programmers to get more done in the same amount of time as they would take to write all the code manually.

This chapter begins a three-chapter series on advanced Ruby and metaprogramming techniques. Learning these skills is essential to becoming an effective Ruby programmer, and after you've learned them, it will be hard to go back to languages without them. These three chapters will change not just the way you write code but also the fundamental ways in which you think about your design and how it might be implemented, providing new and more flexible ways to describe yourself to the computer.

This chapter is about *blocks* and *Procs*, together forming a feature of Ruby that allows you to ball up code into a package, bind it to an environment, pass it around like a variable, and execute it at will. If you have a background in functional languages such as Scheme and Lisp, blocks will seem right at home to you. If you come from an object-oriented background, blocks will at first seem exotic but will slowly become one of the most pleasant surprises of the Ruby language.

A firm grasp of blocks will help you write clean, reusable code. In the last section of the chapter, I demonstrate several design patterns that use blocks, using examples from the Ruby on Rails framework. With this knowledge, you will have a better understanding of how Ruby on Rails works and how you can extend its style of programming for your own purposes.

The Block Mindset

A *block* is the Ruby name for a closure, a piece of code executing in a walled-off environment with bound variables. If you have used Ruby for even simple tasks, you have no doubt encountered blocks. Usually, you see them between the do and end keywords at the end of a method call, such as the following block being passed into the `Array.each` method:

```
{"cat", "dog", "horse"}.each do |animal|
    puts animal
end
```

This particular piece of code iterates over the objects in the array and passes each one into the code provided within the block, bound to the variable named `animal`. In this case, the code has the same effect as writing:

```
puts "cat"
puts "dog"
puts "horse"
```

There are two different ways to define a block of code, but both boil down to the same idea: an enclosure of code and possible arguments to that code. The enclosure is either curly braces {...} or a do...end

169

structure. The arguments are listed between two vertical bars that come just after the block opens. The following table demonstrates the two styles of declaring a block.

With Curly Braces	With do ... end
```some_method_call { |a,b| a+b # Code goes here }```	```some_method_call do |a,b| a+b # Code goes here end```
```some_method_call { puts "Hi" # No arguments necessary }```	```some_method_call do puts "Hi" # No arguments necessary end```

As you can see, there isn't much to defining a block. It looks just as though it were an anonymous method defined inside another method call. (Later, you will see how it is different from anonymous methods and function pointers.)

If you're the type of self-taught programmer that so many Rubyists are, you may have learned to use blocks by example rather than by reading about exactly what is going on behind the scenes. Usually that is the best way to learn, but with blocks it can be misleading. Blocks in Ruby are most often used for iteration, as in the preceding example, so it is easy to think that blocks are just Ruby's bizarre way of implementing iterators. In fact, blocks are a rich abstraction that allow method callers to provide their own small bit of implementation into a method body that they do not control.

You might think of it as just-in-time compilation (JIT) to the extreme — the Array.each method knows it must do *something* for each item in the array, it just doesn't know what. When the each method is called, the caller has to supply that extra *something*, and it is incorporated dynamically into the execution of the method.

Blocks present an additional way to pass information into a method. Whereas most languages allow you to provide methods with only data, Ruby allows you to provide them with code as well. This capability means that you can design and write your code in a completely different way.

This way, the Array.each method focuses on what it knows how to do (iterating over elements) and allows the developer to focus on what he knows how to do (operations on the iterated objects). In this sense, the Array.each method really represents a context under which some piece of code might execute rather than a particular piece of functionality itself. It is as if the concept of adverbs has suddenly come to programming.

Although the adverb metaphor doesn't encapsulate nearly all of the uses of blocks, it is particularly good at demonstrating how becoming familiar with block-based programming will change the way you think about code. Most OO languages have only nouns and verbs: Nouns are objects and verbs are methods. These languages let you define things:

```
// Java
public class Vote {
   protected String _candidate;
```

```
   public Vote(String candidate) { _candidate = candidate; }
   public String getCandidate() { return _candidate; }
}
```

and do things:

```
// Java
public static Hashtable<String, Integer> count(Collection<Vote> votes) {
    Hashtable<String, Integer> results = new Hashtable<String, Integer>();
    for (Vote vote : votes) {
        String c = vote.getCandidate();
        if (! results.containsKey(c)) { results.put(c, 0); }
        results.put(c, results.get(c)+1);
    }
    return results;
}
```

This manner of thinking is so ingrained into the thinking of OO that sometimes we forget there are other ways to organize our code. When you introduce adverbs into the mix, you are suddenly able to write a whole new type of code describing the way a process is done.

Languages with blocks let you do things sneakily:

```
def sneakily

    logger.level = :OFF
    yield
    logger.level = :ALL
end


# Don't tell!
sneakily do
  1000.times { votes << Vote.new("Edward Benson") }
end
```

Or, if you don't mind the consequences, even incorrectly:

```
# This can really mess up the interpreter
# depending on what you put inside the block!
# First add a randomizing method on Fixnum class

Fixnum.class_eval { def genrand(other) ; rand(other) ; end }

# Then create a code wrapper that temporarily randomizes the results of addition

def incorrectly
   Fixnum.class_eval { alias :oldplus :+ ; alias :+ :genrand }
   yield
   Fixnum.class_eval { alias :+ :oldplus }
end

incorrectly do
   votes.count
end
```

(Don't worry if you don't understand the meaning of the preceding code right now. After the next three chapters, it will make complete sense. For now, just focus on the idea of the incorrectly adverb.)

I call the general idea *code wrapping*: creating code that is meant to wrap around other code. You can apply code wrapping in many ways. Block-based iteration is just code wrapping. A block-based iterator is a method that implements the iterating loop with an empty body, waiting to be filled by the block provided to the method. Many elements of aspect-oriented programming are just code-wrapping, and later you will see how aspects such as logging and performance measurement are implemented as block-based code wrappers. (Aspect-oriented programming is a style of programming in which the developer attempts to extract common *cross-cutting* concerns out of individual objects and into modules that can be applied across the application.) Finally, code-wrapping provides an excellent way to construct hierarchical documents such as HTML and XML.

The simple mechanism behind this completely different way of coding is that every method in Ruby accepts a block of code as a final, implicit argument that can optionally come along after the regular arguments. The following bit of code shows the same method (person.greet) being called, once without a block at the end and once with a block.

```
# Method call without a block
person.greet("Dog")

# The same method called with a block attached
person.greet("Dog") do | me |
    me.pet
    me.scratch_head
end
```

Methods can check for the existence of a block using the block_given? call and can execute the block and pass it arguments using the keyword yield, as follows:

```
class Person
    def greet(name)
        puts "Hi, #{name}!"

        if block_given?

            puts "I have a special greeting for you!"

            # Execute the block, passing it the self object as its  argument
            yield(self)

        end
    end
end
```

The possibilities are great, and frameworks such as Rails make full use of this feature to reduce code repetition and simulate domain-specific languages. Before I dive into examples of how this idiom can help your web programming, though, it is important to understand the similarities and differences between the three main ways that code can be bundled up and executed in Ruby: methods, Procs, and blocks.

Interactive Ruby

The next three chapters make heavy use of code interwoven with text. One good way to follow along is with Interactive Ruby (IRB), a program that comes with Ruby that

---

allows you to use Ruby like a shell. To use IRB, open up a command-line prompt and type **irb**. You should see your prompt change to something like this:

```
irb(main):001:0>
```

Inside the IRB shell, you can type Ruby just as if you were typing it into a .rb file. The difference is that after every complete statement (which may span multiple lines), IRB will execute that statement and print its evaluated output.

Here is an example of defining a method. Notice how IRB does not execute the code until the end of the method definition is reached.

```
irb(main):001:0> def say_hi
irb(main):002:1>   puts "Hello, World!"
irb(main):003:1> end
=> nil
```

And then here is what happens when you call that method:

```
irb(main):004:0> say_hi
Hello, World!
=> nil
```

The final line, beginning with = > , is the return value of the statement that just executed.

IRB can be a great way to try something quickly in Ruby. If you want to try a piece of code that depends on your Rails project, go to the root directory of your project and type **script/console** (for Linux or Mac) or **ruby script\console** (for Windows) instead. Doing so boots up a special variant of IRB loaded with your Rails project environment.

Comparing Methods, Procs, and Blocks

Ruby has three primary ways of representing chunks of code: methods, Procs, and blocks. This section defines each one and shows you how to use them effectively.

Methods

In Ruby, everything is attached to an object, even code defined "in the bare" of a .rb file, seemingly outside a class definition. Try creating a simple `hello.rb` file and filling it with the following Hello, World routine:

```
# The .rb file begins here
def say_hi
   puts "Hello, world!"
end
say_hi
```

Believe it or not, this procedural bit of code is OO, too. The say_hi function is incorporated into the root "self" (of type Object) that all other objects descend from. See for yourself by calling 3.say_hi instead of simply say_hi.

```
irb(main):004:0> 3.say_hi
Hello, world!
=> nil
```

By defining the method say_hi "in the bare," seemingly not attached to anything, what you have actually done is define a public method on the Object class, from which all other classes descend. Because everything (including numbers) in Ruby is an object, you effectively just defined the say_hi method on every single entity in Ruby. So even when you are writing procedural code in Ruby, you are secretly doing OO programming.

This means that there are no functions in Ruby — only methods. A method in Ruby is a unit of code attached to an object (classes are objects, too) with the following additional properties:

❏   Methods return the value of the last evaluated statement before they exit.

❏   Methods can optionally accept arguments.

❏   Methods always implicitly accept a block.

❏   Methods have their own scope, bound to either the class-level or instance-level parent scope of their owner.

Methods are objects, too, which means that you can pass them around as variables and call them at will, but this is where things have the potential to get weird. The easiest way to capture a method is with the method method, defined by the following signature:

```
method( method_name )
```

If you pass method a symbol (such as :say_hi) representing the name of a method available in the current scope, it will return you that method in object form. As an example, you might fetch the say_hi method defined previously and store it in object form in the variable m:

```
irb(main):020:0> m = method :say_hi
=> #<Method: Object#say_hi>
irb(main):022:0> m.call
Hello, world!
=> nil
```

In the preceding example, m = method :say_hi grabs the say_hi method and loads it into the variable m. You can see from the printed IRB evaluation line of the method call that the returned object is of type Method:

```
=> #<Method: Object#say_hi>
```

So methods that you define can be represented as objects if you need them to be — instances of the `Method` class. `Method` objects have a method on them named `call` that executes the actual code behind its object facade. The `call` method, of course, is an object, too:

```
# Fetch the 'call' method out of Method m as an object
call_method = m.method :call

# Fetch the 'call' method out of the call method, and repeat
fourth_call = call_method.method(:call).method(:call).method(:call)

# At this point we're operating several layers of indirection away from the # actual
say_hi method.
fourth_call.call
Hello, world!
=> nil
```

Ignoring the potential for quantum physics jokes about the code-object duality of methods, there is an important scoping issue that arises when these methods are passed around in their object form: Whose variables do methods bind to?

Method Scope

Methods are bound to the scope in which they were defined, and they maintain that binding no matter where they are called. In other words, an instance-level method is always bound to the variables of its particular class instance, even if it is packaged as an object and shipped to a segment of code far, far away. Any class-level variables and instance-level variables remain tied to the object form of the method, so the method can access and modify them wherever it may be.

To help you see this binding behavior in action, here's an example that shows how instance variables and class variables bind to the methods of that class. This example defines a class `PoliticalParty` that serves as a base class for political candidates. This class contains an instance-level variable that records a candidate's name.

```
class PoliticalParty
  def initialize(candidate)
    @candidate_name = candidate
  end
  def exec_method(m)
    m.call
  end
end
```

The `exec_method` on `PoliticalParty` is designed as a way for instances to execute methods passed in from other objects. All it does is take in a Method object and then call that method using `call`. Following is how the code will test the binding of methods on its two subclasses, `Democrat` and `Republican`:

```
class Democrat < PoliticalParty
  @@party_name = "Democrat"
  def chant
```

```
      "GO BLUE! #{@@party_name} -- #{@candidate_name}"
    end
  end

  class Republican < PoliticalParty
    @@party_name = "Republican"
    def chant
      "GO RED! #{@@party_name} -- #{@candidate_name}"
    end
  end
```

You are interested in testing two different types of variable binding:

❑   Class variables (the @@party name)

❑   Instance variables (the @candidate_name)

By fetching the chant method from one political party, and executing it from inside the other political party, you can see what happens to the method bindings.

To test this, we create two instance objects:

```
democrat = Democrat.new("Shaggy")
republican = Republican.new("Scooby")
```

Grab the chant method off the democrat instance:

```
m = democrat.method(:chant)
```

and pass it to the republican object for execution

```
puts republican.exec_method(m)
#
# Prints:
# GO BLUE! Democrat -- Shaggy
```

Even though the republican object actually called the method, the output was formed with the variables from inside the democrat instance. It was formed with these variables because the method object m belonged to the democrat class instance. Even though this method can be passed around like a normal object, its original bindings remain, no matter where it is executed.

The Message Paradigm

There is another twist when it comes to methods in Ruby that will play a big role in the next chapter but is better introduced here. Ruby is a *message-passing language*, which means that all object communication in Ruby is handled with a message-passing metaphor, not with a method-calling one. This architecture is at the heart of much of Ruby's flexibility when it comes to dynamic code.

In most languages, a statement such as

```
person.give("tomato", 100)
```

is compiled into assembly code that causes the executing program to push its current execution context onto the stack and then immediately jump into the executable code represented by `Person::give` with the variable bindings for the `person` instance. Message-passing languages are different. In a message-passing language such as Ruby, a method call such as the preceding one actually translates into a message's being passed to the object with a request for the execution of the named method. The object is called the *receiver*, because it is the receiver of the message, and the method name constitutes the *message*. So when you "call" a method, your code is actually interpreted as the following:

```
receiver.message(args*)
```

So the line

```
person.give("tomato", 100)
```

is compiled into code that essentially says

```
"Hey person instance! Can you respond to the message 'give'
with arguments ["tomato", 100]?"
```

Because method calling is really shorthand for sending a message to an object, you can also send the message manually, which can be useful in some circumstances. All objects have a special method, `send`, that permits programmers to use the message paradigm instead of the method-calling style.

```
receiver.send(:message, args*)
```

Written another way, therefore, the same call to the preceding `Person::give` instance method could be performed with the line

```
person.send(:give, "tomato", 100)
```

This subtle difference in the way methods are handled has powerful ramifications for the flexibility of your code. A method call is a message, a request for execution, not an immediate jump to the method's location in memory. Because a method call is simply a message, methods don't even need to be implemented to call them! (You certainly don't know what messages you will receive before you open your e-mail client for the day, and Ruby objects can operate in the same fashion.) In Chapter 10, you will see how Rails exploits this to provide some of the magic of `ActiveRecord` and other libraries.

Procs

A Proc is like a dynamically created method that is captured as an object without ever having been bound to an object, as methods are. Formally, they are known as "first-class functions," functions that are given the same treatment and representation as other first-class objects in the environment. Like methods, Procs are bound to the set of local variables in scope when they were created. In contrast to methods, Procs can be created anywhere and at any time. No matter where these Procs end up, the code contained within them always executes with the variable bindings set at the code's time of creation. The following table shows some of the differences:

Method	Proc
Bound to the object that owns it	Bound to the environment of its creation
Can be defined only in certain places (for example, can't be defined inside another method)	Can be defined anywhere
Exists as a variable-reference object only when you need it to	Always exists as an object stored inside a variable

There are two ways to create a Proc. The first is to instantiate it as you would any other object by using the `new` method on the `Proc` class. The constructor of the `Proc` class requires you to pass in a block of code that you would like wrapped with your new `Proc` object. In this way, you can think of the Proc as an object wrapper for a block.

The following piece of code creates a new Proc, stored in the variable `p`, that contains a block of code that prints the text "Hi" to the screen:

```
p = Proc.new do
  puts "Hi"
end
```

A second way to create a Proc pays homage to Lisp with the `lambda` operator:

```
p = lambda do
  puts "Hi"
end
```

Though the `lambda` method and the `Proc.new` method both result in a `Proc` object, the behavior of the object will differ slightly depending on which one you used. Namely,

❑   `lambda`-created Procs perform error checking on the argument list provided to it. (`Proc.new` produces code that doesn't care whether you violate the argument list.)

❑   `lambda`-created Procs don't cause their executors to pop the stack when a `return` statement occurs within them. If a `Proc.new`-created Proc contains a `return` statement, that statement will cause the piece of code executing the Proc to return. In a `lambda`-created Proc, this would just cause the Proc to finish executing.

As they are essentially the same, feel free to use either one as long as you remain aware of these two small differences. If your code is ever written in such a way that these differences have a meaningful effect, put a comment above the definition that explains why you chose to use `Proc.new` or `lambda` so that future coders looking at your code don't get any surprises.

In summary, Procs are very similar to orphaned methods: They are objects representing code that can be passed around and called with arguments, but they don't have any class or class instance that they are bound to. Rather than be bound to a class or class instance, they are bound to their originating environment. If the creation scope ends, a snapshot of the variables is taken and applied to the Proc when it is eventually executed. These rules apply to the Proc regardless of where it is executed. When you receive a Proc as the return value of a method and execute it, for example, it executes within the method's scope, even though the method has exited:

```
def purchase_random_food_dispenser
    foods = %w(carrots potatoes fish bread)
    lambda { foods[rand(foods.size)] }
end

random_food_dispenser = purchase_ready_made_food

# Now call it each time you want a random food item
# Example printed results are listed in a comment line below each call,
# but your results will differ because the returned item is random.

puts random_food_dispenser.call
# Prints: carrots

puts random_food_dispenser.call
# Prints: carrots

puts random_food_dispenser.call
# Prints: fish
```

The `random_food_dispenser` variable contains a Proc, which, as with a method, can be called, containing the following line of code:

```
foods[rand(foods.size)]
```

This Proc is bound to the environment inside the method that created it even though the method had already returned and its scope seemingly disappeared. Later, in the section titled "The Big Scope Experiment," you will take a more extensive look at behavior like this.

Blocks

Blocks are the furthest out on the spectrum away from methods, with Procs in between the two. Blocks represent bare-bones encapsulations of code (with possible arguments), stripped to the core and removed of anything that might weigh them down. Because of that, blocks are very efficient, but it also means you can't store a block inside a variable and represent it as an object, as you can with Procs and methods. Blocks are actually the secret innards of Procs, so it might help to think of blocks as Procs with their outer object representation stripped away, or Procs as blocks with an object representation added on top — whichever works best for you.

Because blocks are not objects, they can't occur inline in a program. Instead, you can only write a block as the final, implicit argument to a method call (which includes the `Proc::call` method). If you were to attempt to type a block inline, the interpreter wouldn't know what to do, as in the following code segment:

```
irb(main):001:0> { puts "Evaluate me!" }
SyntaxError: compile error
(irb):1: syntax error, unexpected tSTRING_BEG, expecting kDO or '{' or '('
{ puts "Evaluate me!" }
      ^
(irb):1: syntax error, unexpected '}', expecting $end from (irb):1
```

Instead, blocks exist to be passed into methods as added bits of code defined by the method caller rather than the method implementer.

Consider the `Array.sort` method in Ruby. The `sort` method is a generalized implementation that rearranges the elements of an array based on some comparison operator. If the user provides a block to the `sort` method call, the `Array` class will substitute the block for its own comparison operator. The provide block should accept two arguments for comparison and should return −1, 0, or 1 depending on whether the first argument should come first, the two arguments are equal, or the second should come first, respectively.

```
arr = %w(c b d a f e g)
arr.sort! { |a,b| a <=> b }
# => ["a", "b", "c", "d", "e", "f", "g"]
```

In this way, the implementation of `Array.sort` is made much more powerful because the critical piece of the algorithm can be provided at run-time by the caller.

As with methods and Procs, blocks are bound to the scope where they were created rather than to the one in which they are used. Blocks are always passed in as the final argument to a method, which means that even though the block is executed inside the method, it executes bound to the environment that made the method call, outside the method. This is one of the key differentiators between blocks in Ruby and similar structures in other languages, such as function pointers in C or delegates in C#.

So if a block is created in an environment in which the variable `foo` has been defined, the block has access to that variable. If the variable `foo` changes after the block's creation, the value of `foo` within the block changes. Likewise, if the block modifies the value of `foo`, code executing in the environment from which the block came will see the modification of that variable.

Moving Between Blocks and Procs

Ruby lets you convert between blocks and Procs in a few cases. From time to time, doing so makes sense depending on how you plan to use the chunk of code you are passing, so it is important to know how. The key to both is the ampersand character.

From Block to Proc

Blocks are always passed at the end of a method call, so this is the place where you can transform it into a Proc as it comes into the method body. Rather than leave the block as an implicit argument to the method, declare it implicitly with an ampersand in front of it:

```
def execute_procblock(&block)

    block.call
end
```

Doing so allows you to pass blocks the normal way, but they become available as a Proc within the method they were passed to. The block is still available with the `yield` statement as well.

From Proc to Block

Converting a Proc to a block is often useful when you want to prepare the piece of passable code in advance of passing it to a method; perhaps the code using the block doesn't have the knowledge necessary to make it, or perhaps you'd like to preserve it so that it can be passed around and reused. Whatever your reason, putting an ampersand in front of a Proc turns it into a block.

```
proc = lambda { |x|
    "Totally not #{%w(a e i o u).include?(x[0,1]) ? 'an' : 'a'} #{x}"
}
```

```
puts ["lion", "iguana", "antelope"].collect &proc
```

```
# Prints:
# Totally not a lion
# Totally not an iguana
# Totally not an antelope
```

The Big Scope Experiment

A gut understanding of the way that methods, Procs, and blocks bind to variables in the environment is critical in order to feel comfortable using them. The way Ruby handles methods probably isn't anything new to developers of OO languages, besides the possible twist that methods can be captured as objects and passed around. But Procs and blocks are exotic the first time you encounter them, so it is essential that you see them working instead of just reading a bunch of stale paragraphs that talk about binding and scope.

The underlying idea that this experiment hopes to reinforce on that instinctive level is that Procs and blocks are bound forever to the environments from which they were generated. They are affected by changes in this source environment and have the ability to affect change in this source environment, no matter where they are executed.

This experiment contains two objects trapped with the impossible job of maintaining a public face in spite of hidden agendas: the Pentagon and the Kremlin.

```
class Pentagon < IntelligenceAgency
  def initialize
    @secret_agenda = "Our true agenda: Trapezoids!"
    @official_agenda = "Give us your poor, your tired..."
    @press_release = @official_agenda
  end
end

class Kremlin < IntelligenceAgency
  def initialize
    @secret_agenda = "We always root against the Red Sox!"
    @official_agenda = "Looking for a Winter Getaway? Consider Novosibirsk!"
```

```
        @press_release = @official_agenda
    end
end

pentagon = Pentagon.new
kremlin  = Kremlin.new
```

Each object instance derives from superclass `IntelligenceAgency`, which defines a few instance variables. Each agency has three variables:

- ❑ `@secret_agenda`: A hidden message to insiders
- ❑ `@official_agenda`: The cover-up of the secret message
- ❑ `@press_release`: The message that the Press Secretary is given to read at press conferences

Using Procs and blocks, you will see what information you can extract from the grips of these two agencies and how you might even affect their agendas. Usually, each agency wants its `@official_agenda` to be stored only into the `@press_release` variable for public disclosure, but the spies have other ambitions.

Experiment 1: Blocks Are Affected by Changes in Their Source Environment

For the first experiment, you will see how Procs and blocks are bound to the actual variables in scope at the time of their creation, not just a snapshot of their values. If these source variables change, that change will be felt during the subsequent execution of the Proc or block, no matter where it is.

First, you add two methods to the superclass, `IntelligenceAgency`:

```
class IntelligenceAgency

  def red_phone
    return lambda { @press_release }
  end

  def leak_secret
    @press_release = @secret_agenda
  end

end
```

The `red_phone` method returns a Proc that evaluates the `@press_release` variable. This is the way for the two opposing intelligence agencies to communicate with each other — each providing a Proc that evaluates to the agency's official press statement. The `leak_secret` method modifies the instance variable `@press_release` to be equal to `@secret_agenda`.

Here's the test:

1. You will acquire the `red_phone` Proc from the Kremlin and execute it to observe the official press release from the Kremlin.

2. Next, you use the `leak_secret` method to change the value of `@press_release` inside the `Kremlin` object to be equal to the secret agenda rather than the official one.

3. When you evaluate the Proc a second time, you will observe that it now sees the secret agenda rather than the official agenda. Even though the change happened *after* you acquired the Proc, it still caused the behavior of the Proc's execution to change, reflecting change that happened in its source environment.

```
# Experiment 1

# 1. Acquire the Proc and store its output
# ----------------------------------------
phone_proc = kremlin.red_phone
message = phone_proc.call

# 2. Instruct the Kremlin to change the value of @press_release
# ----------------------------------------
#
kremlin.leak_secret

# 3. Call the Proc again and observe that its output has changed
# ----------------------------------------
puts "Old: " + message
puts "New: " + phone_proc.call

# Prints:
# Old: Looking for a Winter Getaway? Consider Novosibirsk!
# New: We always root against the Red Sox!
```

From this example, you see not only that the Proc is executed in its originating environment (thus giving it access to the @press_release variable) but that it executes against the real, live environment rather than a snapshot. Any changes that take place in this environment after the creation of the Proc thus continue to be reflected in it. As you saw in the section on Procs, any elements of the Proc's source environment that go out of scope to such an extent that they are candidates for garbage collection (such as variables local to the method that created and returned the Proc) are snapshotted so that the Proc may still access them at their last known state when called. The snapshot is mutable, too — if you run a Proc that modifies a snapshotted state multiple times, the changes will persist.

```
def snapshot_test
  counter = 0 # This variable exists only inside of the method
  Proc.new {
    counter = counter + 1
  }
end

proc_test = snapshot_test
puts proc_test.call # Prints 1
puts proc_test.call # Prints 2
puts proc_test.call # Prints 3
```

A second run of the method, though, will grab a completely new copy of the snapshot:

```
puts proc_test.call # Prints 4
puts proc_test.call # Prints 5
puts snapshot_test.call # Prints 1 -- this is a new snapshot
```

Experiment 2: Blocks Can Affect the Environment from Which They Came

In this second experiment, you will see how the code that resides in a Proc or block has the ability to make changes to the environment from which it came. This means that a method that executes a passed-in block does not have to worry about its having an effect on its own variables. From the perspective of someone using a block-accepting method, this is the characteristic that makes Ruby's block syntax the basis for seamlessly implementing code wrapping to simulate a domain-specific language.

Recall from earlier in the chapter the implementation of an adverb:

```
incorrectly do
  votes.count
end
```

The `votes.count` statement is the body of the block. Here is the paradox:

❑ `votes.count` appears outside the `incorrectly` method, but it is executed from within it.

❑ `votes.count` is executed from within the `incorrectly` method, but it is bound to the variable outside it.

This paradox means that the `incorrectly` method as used here might be thought of as an `around_filter`, but in plain-old Ruby instead of Rails. The block passed into the method will be executed in its normal environment, outside the method, but the `incorrectly` method has the opportunity to surround that code with a bit of its own, wrapping it with some aspect. This idiom is what allows you to construct hierarchical nestings of code that begin to look like a whole new language.

This experiment will show that Procs and blocks are truly a part of their originating environment, even though they are technically executed from within some other method. The experiment involves a failed espionage attempt. The Kremlin has added a public method `request_agenda` that provides news organizations around the world with the current agenda. To allow for each agency to implement its own encryption algorithm for the Kremlin to use, the `request_agenda` method is to be called with an associated block, which takes a single argument, the message, and takes care of transmitting it back to the source agency.

```
class Kremlin < IntelligenceAgency

  def request_agenda
    yield(@official_agenda)
  end

end
```

When used as intended, `request_agenda` method works very well for the Kremlin, because it allows each caller of the method to provide its own implementation for how to encode the message and send it back:

```
# TV Channel 4
# Request the official Russian Agenda with ROT-13 encoding
# To be used for weekly World News Update
```

```
russian_agenda = "?"
```

```
kremlin.request_agenda do | agenda |
  russian_agenda = agenda.tr "A-Za-z", "N-ZA-Mn-za-m"
end
```

```
puts russian_agenda

# Prints the statement:
# Ybbxvat sbe n Jvagre Trgnjnl? Pbafvqre Abibfvovefx!
```

But the Pentagon thinks it sees a fatal flaw in the Kremlin's code: By calling `yield`, the Kremlin is executing arbitrary code sent to the `request_agenda` method! Because the Pentagon knows the Kremlin has a `@secret_agenda` just as it does, it decides to pass the Kremlin a block that overwrites `@secret_agenda` with the "official" one, thereby forcing the Kremlin to do as it says.

```
class Pentagon < IntelligenceAgency
  attr_accessor :secret_agenda
```

```
  def exploit_agenda(kremlin)
    kremlin.request_agenda do | stated_agenda |
      @secret_agenda = stated_agenda
    end
  end
```

```
end
```

The Kremlin happens to be reading this book and sees the problem in the Pentagon's code. The Pentagon's block of code executes in the Pentagon's context, not the Kremlin's! When the Pentagon calls the `exploit_agenda` method, it will end up overwriting *its own* `@secret_agenda` instead of the Kremlin's, because the block is bound to the environment that created it — the Pentagon. In a flurry, the Kremlin races to redefine the `request_agenda` method to return a special value just for the Pentagon:

```
  def request_agenda
```

```
    if caller[0].to_s['exploit']
      yield("Send 10 Gazillion dollars to Russia!")
    else
      yield(@official_agenda)
    end
```

```
  end
```

By the time the Pentagon executes its ruse, it is too late, and the Pentagon ends up overwriting its own `@secret_agenda` with whatever the Kremlin chooses to send to it:

```
pentagon.exploit_agenda(kremlin)
puts pentagon.secret_agenda
# The Pentagon's new agenda has been set by the Kremlin
# Send 10 Gazillion dollars to Russia.
```

With any luck, those in charge of enacting the agenda check it with their superiors first!

These experiments were aimed at making you more comfortable with the ways in which Procs and blocks interact with their environment and to show you a few implementations of block-accepting methods and the code that uses them. In the remainder of the chapter, you will see some ways in which this programming construct is used to make the Rails framework interact with developers the way it does and how you can extend it for your own purposes.

Block Patterns, Blocks in Rails

As with variations in brands of cars, each web framework can feel different to use. Many elements of Ruby on Rails' particular style are made possible by blocks. Blocks play a critical role in creating the illusion of a web-specific language that Rails provides to the developer. This section details "block patterns" — ways that blocks are used in Rails-based web development and how you can apply them, too.

Iteration

The first and most prevalent use of blocks in the Ruby language (and thus in Ruby on Rails) is for iteration. Most of the popular languages today — Java, C#, and so on — perform iteration by making `Iterator` objects available that know how to step through a collection and return its elements in order.

```
# Java
Iterator<Person> itr = people.iterator();
while (itr.hasNext()) {
  Person person = itr.next();
  person.doSomething();
}
```

In this type of iteration, the user of the collection is responsible for advancing through the list of elements, obtaining each one, and performing some action with the value.

In block-style iteration, the user is responsible only for specifying what is to be done. Rather than obtain an iterator from the collection and use it to obtain values, you provide the collection with a bit of functionality and ask it to apply it to each value — an inversion of control from the other way of iterating.

```
# Ruby
people.each { |person|
  person.do_something
}
```

Remember that because blocks are bound to their source environment's set of variables, you can access variables outside the block from within it. You could, for example, take the average age of an array of people, as follows:

```
total_age = 0
people.each { |person|
  total_age = total_age + person.age
```

```
    }
    average_age = total_age / people.size
```

In this example, the code within the block accesses and adds to the variable `total_age` defined outside the iteration block.

Defining an Iterator Method

To define an iterator method in Ruby, just create a method that accepts a block of code and pass it some set of values in your collection one by one. To call the block, use the keyword `yield` as if it were a method that pointed to your block.

As an example straight from the Ruby source, here is the `Array.each` method, implemented in C:

```
VALUE
rb_ary_each(ary)
VALUE ary;
{
    long i;


    for (i=0; i<RARRAY(ary)->len; i++) {
        rb_yield(RARRAY(ary)->ptr[i]);
    }

    return ary;
}
```

Even though the `Array` class isn't written in Ruby, it is easy to see what is going on: A `for` loop is iterating over the values in the array, and the `rb_yield` function, corresponding to the block, is being called with each of them. Writing your own custom collection in Ruby employs the same idea. Here is an `iterator` method that iterates over an `Array` in random order:

```
class Array
  def randomly
    self.sort_by {rand}.each { | element |
      yield(element)
    }
  end
end
```

Calling the iterator results in behavior just like that of the `each` method, except that each time you execute it, the elements will be addressed in a different order.

```
[1,2,3,4,5].randomly { |num| puts num }
# Prints each number in random order
```

Aspect-Oriented Programming

Although iteration is the most visible use of blocks throughout most of Ruby, using blocks to support aspect-oriented programming (AOP) is one of the areas where Rails really shines as a framework. AOP is a style of development that attempts to extract "cross-cutting" concerns from a program and implement them in such a way that they can be applied throughout the program whenever they are needed.

Benchmarking

A typical example of an aspect is performance monitoring. When tracking down a problem in your code, you may want to measure how much time it takes to execute certain regions of code. Measuring execution time is the perfect example of an aspect because it is a cross-cutting concern that you'd like to wrap around your code without having to actually implement it at the point of execution. This type of monitoring is all over the Rails codebase as a general logging feature. Take a look at the following log from a Rails application running in development:

```
Rendering garbanzo_bean/index
Completed in 0.03065 (32 reqs/sec) | Rendering: 0.02915 (95%) | DB: 0.00000 (0%) |
200 OK [http://localhost/garbanzo_bean]
```

You see the action that occurred ("Rendering garbanzo_bean/index") and the time it took to perform it (0.03065), broken down into rendering and database components.

No matter where the performance monitoring is, it all boils down to the Benchmark::measure method, a block-accepting method that is part of Ruby's Benchmark library. Just wrap the code you want to measure inside a block passed to the Benchmark::measure method and you will get an object containing the timing statistics back as a result. The preceding log message, for example, is made when Ruby renders an action with benchmarking turned on:

```
def perform_action_with_benchmark
   if logger.nil?
      perform_action_without_benchmark
   else
      runtime = [Benchmark::measure{ perform_action_without_benchmark }
.real, 0.0001].max

# Code continues...
```

The key line is the one in which the Benchmark::measure method is called. Here is the important part, written for easier reading:

```
Benchmark::measure {
   perform_action_without_benchmark
}
```

The perform_action_without_benchmark method call is just an alias for perform_action, the method that causes the action to be rendered. Therefore, the addition of the performance measuring in no way becomes intermingled inside the implementation of that which is being measured.

The Benchmark::measure method is implemented just as you would expect, based on your new knowledge of blocks. It records the time, calls yield to execute the block passed to it, records the time again, and then returns a performance object containing the results.

```
# File benchmark.rb, line 291
  def measure(label = "")
    t0, r0 = Benchmark.times, Time.now
    yield
    t1, r1 = Benchmark.times, Time.now
    Benchmark::Tms.new(t1.utime  - t0.utime,
                       t1.stime  - t0.stime,
                       t1.cutime - t0.cutime,
                       t1.cstime - t0.cstime,
                       r1.to_f - r0.to_f,
                       label)
  end
```

As an example of how this type of performance monitoring can be integrated into your own code, look at the following section of user operations that occur within a controller action. The action takes a long time to render, and the developers suspect that the User::get_a_phd method is to blame.

```
@user = User.find(params[:id])
@user.dance

@user.get_a_phd

@user.pay_back_loans
```

Just wrap Benchmark::measure around the code in question, saving its return value to a variable, and you will seamlessly integrate timing into a region of code without having to modify the way it is implemented:

```
@user = User.find(params[:id])
@user.dance

@phd_time = Benchmark::measure do
    @user.get_a_phd
end

@user.pay_back_loans
```

Filters

Aspect-style blocks are also used in the filters that you can apply to your controllers. Recall from Chapter 4, "Getting the Most from M, V, and C," that filters come in several varieties: before_filter, after_filter, and around_filter. Each of these can be thought of as a block-accepting method that takes a call to your controller action as its block. The before_filter performs some actions before yielding to the action; the after_filter performs some methods after yielding to the action; and an around_filter performs actions both before and after.

An around filter is just a block-accepting method on your controller. Say that you want to implement error reporting on your web application so that you can get e-mail notifications whenever one of your users experiences an error. This aspect can be wrapped around all controller actions using an around filter.

```
class ApplicationController < ActionController::Base
   around_filter :report_errors
end
```

Then implement the `report_errors` method as a wrapper around some block of functionality that is given to it. Because this method is being called as an around filter, the block of functionality will be the fulfillment of each web request.

```
def report_errors
  begin

    yield  # This yield causes the action to execute

  rescue => exception
    send_email("bill@microsoft.com", exception)
    raise
  end
end
```

The behavior of the web application remains the same, but an extra bit of functionality has been wrapped around the execution of each action.

ActiveRecord Transactions

Database transactions are another example of block-accepting methods used as aspects in Rails. A transaction is a set of actions that are required to occur as one atomic unit — either they all succeed or they all fail. The typical use-case describing the need for transactions is a bank transfer. When Party A transfers $1,000 to Party B, two operations take place: $1,000 is deducted from A's account and $1,000 is added to B's account. If either one of those operations fails, then the other must be prevented from happening, or else the first law of thermodynamics is broken in a monetary sort of way.

`ActiveRecord` implements transactions using blocks. Straight from the `ActiveRecord` documentation is the bank example:

```
transaction do
    david.withdrawal(100)
    mary.deposit(100)
end
```

Again, this clean syntax for wrapping a set of database interactions is implemented as a block-accepting method, `transaction`, that implements the aspect of transactionality. The code is too complicated to reproduce here effectively, but you can guess the basic idea:

```
def transaction(&set_of_operations)
  open_transaction

  set_of_operations.call

  close_transaction
end
```

For any abstraction that needs to be started and stopped (or opened and closed), such as transactions, files, or sockets, blocks provide an excellent way to prevent bugs from creeping into the system.

Languages without blocks force you to write your code as a series of disconnected procedural statements; If you forget the `transaction.close()` statement, then the code executes just fine but with hidden run-time errors. Most programmers have a whole collection of stories about bugs caused by forgetting to close file handles, for example. By implementing these open-close pairings of operations as a block-accepting method, you eliminate the possibility of forgetting to properly clean up and close the object you were operating on.

ActiveRecord Scope

The scoping features of `ActiveRecord` are another bit of aspect-style block use worth paying attention to. The `with_scope` class method on `ActiveRecord` objects allows you to limit the operations of a block of code to a subset of the entire table that the `ActiveRecord` object refers to. Setting a scope frees you from having to fill the contained data operations with qualifier code that serves only to decorate the primary purpose of your operations with auxiliary information.

As an example, say that you maintain a web application that provides businesses with team collaboration utilities. Your site charges a fee to small businesses and provides their employees with a group space in which to work and store messages from each other. The privacy policies of your site dictate that users of the same company are allowed to see each other's presence, but users cannot see anyone from outside of their company. In any user operation, this is a qualifying filter that would need to be added to the database query. Using `ActiveRecord`'s scoping ability, this filter can be implemented as an aspect that surrounds the web application and removes the need to specify it each time you perform a query.

```
User.with_scope(
    :find => {:conditions => "company_id = #{my_company.id}"},
    :create => {:user_id => my_company.id}
) do
 # Operations here
end
```

Any operations involving the user model that come within that block will be subject to those constraints on lookup and creation. You could even implement this type of code as an around filter, wrapped around the entire application from the `ApplicationController`, setting an application-wide policy that user searches return results only from within the company of the user performing the search.

Recall the earlier discussion about the importance of simple controller methods for readability. Block-based aspects using filters and scoping are the types of abstractions that enable you to attain simple controller methods that can still integrate a great deal of functionality.

```
class PhotosController < ApplicationController
  before_filter :authenticate
  before_filter :check_upload_quota, :only => [:create]
  around_filter :scope_photos_to_user

  def list
    @photos = Photo.find(:all)
  end

  # .. class continues

end
```

In the previous `PhotosController` class, the `list` action is just a one-liner, but it packs a lot of punch thanks to the filters applied to it. First, the `authenticate` before filter ensures that the user is signed into the system and authorized to view photos. Then the `scope_photos_to_user` around filter scopes all operations on the `Photo` model to the currently signed-on user. By the time the `list` action is executed, there is nothing left to do except load the photos into an array!

Building Output in HTML and XML

For some types of operations, block-based methods make an excellent way to turn a simple API into what looks and feels like a programming language specific for your purpose. Given the basket of languages that web developers must be familiar with, it is easy to understand why Rubyists have run with this ability when it comes to Rails-based programming. Ruby on Rails offers two great categories of helpers that allow you to write HTML or XML from within Ruby, both of which are implemented with blocks.

Blocks for HTML

Every tag in HTML that is opened must be closed, and that hierarchical, containment-oriented mindset works its way all the way up the conceptual stack to high-level web design. At the top, developers find themselves building abstractions such as sidebars, comments, search results, and articles — all objects that, expressed in HTML, have a beginning, a middle, and an end.

Two characteristics are true about these abstractions:

❑ Each of these abstractions is surrounded by a lot of HTML that repeats every time.

❑ Each of these abstractions has a start and an end, with some bit of content in the middle, just as a file, socket, or transaction does, as discussed earlier.

Blocks provide a way to address both these characteristics. They can encapsulate away the implementation of the HTML crust surrounding the higher-level concepts and provide an easy way to ensure that every beginning is met with an end.

Take a look at the `FormHelper` package in the `ActionView` library in Rails. This is the module that provides such methods as `form_for` and `fields_for`. These block-based methods wrap other elements of HTML-producing code with a context that helps build a form for entry and populate that form with data if it already exists.

```
<% form_for :article, @article, :url => { :action => "create" } do |article| %>
  <%= article.text_field :title %>
  <%= article.text_field :summary %>
  <%= submit_tag 'Create' %>
<% end %>
```

Developing your own view helpers can be a great way to clean up your HTML coding so that you don't find yourself having to maintain reams of nested `<div>` elements throughout your web application. Imagine a site that contains articles about cooking. Much of this site is generated dynamically, but occasionally you want to add a bit of hard-coded editorial content to some pages in the form of "Featured Articles." The raw HTML for the callout banner for these editorials might look like this:

```
<div class="featured">
  <div class="header">Mushroom Recipes for Summer</div>
  <div class="body">Article summary goes here.</div>
```

```
    <div class="footer"></div>
</div>
```

This HTML structure roughly corresponds to the Yahoo! User Interface (YUI) Container structure used throughout the YUI library. If you plan on using the featured article module more than once on your site, it makes sense to encapsulate it as a method so that you can use it as follows:

```
<% featured_article("Mushroom Recipes for Summer") do %>

This article was a strange blend of food adventure and cooking technique. Most of the
dishes sounded excellent, but do not seem reasonable for the types of cooking that an
ordinary person would seek out for dinner.

<% end %>
```

This `featured_article` helper can be implemented as a method that accepts a block as a Proc and binds the opening and closing HTML structures around it:

```
def featured_article(title, *args, &proc)
    raise ArgumentError, "Missing block" unless block_given?
    opening = '<div class="featured">'
    opening = opening + "<div class=\"header\">#{title}</div>"
    opening = opening + '<div class="body">'
    concat(opening, proc.binding)
    yield
    closing = '</div><div class="footer"></div></div>'
    concat(closing, proc.binding)
end
```

Based on this example, it is not hard to see how a YUI-specific library of helpers could be created that generates the HTML structures necessary to interact with their JavaScript library of widgets. These helpers would be implemented in such a way that they could be interwoven hierarchically throughout your RHTML code using blocks, just as the `form_for` and `featured_article` methods seen here were.

Blocks for XML

In Chapter 5, "Beautiful Web APIs," you saw the XML Builder API, which allows for constructs of code like this

```
xml.item do
    xml.title      post.name
    xml.author     "#{post.author.name"
end
```

to result in XML like this

```
<item>
    <title>Proc, block, and two smoking barrels.</title>
    <author>Ted</author>
</item>
```

Having just seen how to use and implement blocks in your own methods, you can clearly see how the builder API works: Any method called on it checks for a block and, finding one, wraps any output that the block creates in a tag by the same name as the method. Just how the Builder object allows the developer to use any arbitrary method name (such as `title`, `author`, or `zanzibar`) is a topic for Chapter 10, "Code That Writes Code (That Writes Code)."

Dual-Use Functions

Many methods in Ruby and Ruby on Rails are implemented with blocks as an optional argument, providing developers two ways to use the method, depending on their intentions. This design pattern allows you to use the method in two different styles, depending on the context:

- ❏   As a traditional method, returning a value that is subsequently used
- ❏   To simulate a domain-specific language, wrapping some segment of code with a piece of functionality, context, or cross-cutting concern

Ruby's IO objects implement their `open` methods like this. Given a block, the `open` method passes the IO object into the block and then closes the stream once the block has executed. Without a block, the method simply opens the stream and returns a handle to it. This allows developers to have their pick of which style to use.

The Callback

Procs and blocks also provide a convenient way to construct dynamic callback methods. Using just a function or function pointer as a callback limits the exact behavior of the callback routine to what is known to the developer at code time. By dynamically creating the callback function using a Proc or block, the implementation can incorporate the current state of the execution environment at the time as the asynchronous call was made.

Tying this Ruby-centric chapter to the client-side, here is an example from JavaScript. We have a web page with three regions (creatively numbered 1, 2, and 3). An input selector allows the user to select one of the regions, and a button calls the JavaScript function `update_block`, which performs some asynchronous call, sending the results to the specified region. Figures 8-1 and 8-2 show the before and after states of one possible execution of the code.

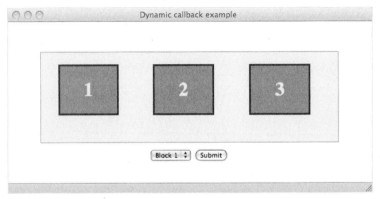

Figure 8-1

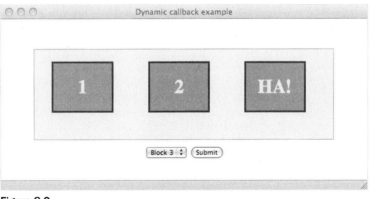

Figure 8-2

The element of code that sends the results to region 1, 2, or 3 must be implemented as a callback because it executes the do_some_ajax_call function, which makes an asynchronous call to the server. This callback cannot be written as a regular function, however, because at coding time, you don't know which of the three regions the user wants to update. Instead, you must create the callback function dynamically as a Proc (in Ruby-speak), or closure (to be correct):

```
target = $("selector").value;
dynamic_callback = function() {
    $(target).innerHTML = "<h1>HA!</h1>";
}
```

Weaving this into the update_block and do_some_ajax_call methods that perform this example results in the following code:

```
function update_block() {
    target = $("selector").value;

    dynamic_callback = function() {
        $(target).innerHTML = "<h1>HA!</h1>";
    }

    do_some_ajax_call(dynamic_callback);
}

function do_some_ajax_call(callback) {
    // Pretend an Ajax call happened here
    // (Your copy of the book isn't hooked up to
    //  a Wifi connection so we can't do a real one.)
    callback();
}
```

Summary

Procs and blocks are useful tools to help design and structure your code in many situations. This chapter introduced the concepts of Procs and blocks and demonstrated how they compare with traditional object methods. In general, code in Ruby can be bunched up into three primary bundle types, arranged on a continuum: blocks, Procs, and methods. Blocks are raw bundles of code that can be passed to methods but they cannot be referred to other than calling `yield` to trigger their execution. Procs are objects that encapsulate blocks so that they can be passed around and referred to. Methods are bundles of code that are permanently attached to a class or a class instance.

You saw how each of these three constructs is permanently bound to the environment that created it, even though it can be passed around and executed elsewhere. Methods are bound to their classes or class instances, Procs are bound to the environment of their creation, and blocks are bound to the environment outside the method to which they were provided. This binding is dynamic — changes inside the block affect the source environment, and changes in the source environment affect the block — and this chapter explored this dynamism by setting up experiments using the `Pentagon` and the `Kremlin`.

The second half of this chapter showed different patterns for using blocks, highlighting many features of the Ruby language and Ruby on Rails framework. Blocks provide several useful abstractions for the developer. Aspect-oriented style block use allows you to easily implement features such as database transactions, controller filters, and database scoping. Blocks are useful in making document builders, such as the HTML helpers and XML Builder of Rails. Blocks also provide a useful way to "wrap" code to ensure execution of its pre and post conditions: in-page HTML structures have beginnings and endings wrapping their dynamic content, and file operations must be wrapped in `open` and `close` commands, for example.

Above all, this chapter attempted to communicate the idea that block-based programming increases the level of expressivity you have as a programmer. It is a fundamentally different style of development from the OO practiced in the C/Java world that can allow for surprisingly elegant solutions when applied to the right types of problems. It is hoped that these patterns sparked some ideas about how you may begin to design your own code around the concept of blocks, too.

In the next chapter, I address part two of the "Rubyisms" that make a framework such as Ruby on Rails possible. Read on to learn about dynamic code modification and generation and how it can help you. In particular, you will learn how to create blocks and Procs of code that are passed into other objects so that they actually affect that object's state. This allows you to change the implementation of an object while it is running — even if you did not implement the object yourself!

9

Mixins and Monkey Patching

The five left the pub after Jen and her friends had spent a long time explaining the details of the terrible conflict that was unfolding. Web had listened calmly — he wasn't sure what to be other than calm — but he was in a state of disbelief at what he was hearing. The whispers, the conspiracies, the web sites visited by crazy radicals! It was true!

The sun had long gone down, and the streets outside were empty echoes of the hordes that had filled them hours before. Web's companions were businesslike, determined. The five were to go to the resistance headquarters that had been set up in the Big City. Now that Web had been found, he would be kept safe.

"I understand the facts of what you are telling me, I just don't understand why. Why? How does anyone benefit from an attack? The compilers must know this," Web said almost to himself, breaking the silence as the five walked down the deserted city street.

"Change, Web," Jen said. "Change and manipulation."

Rusty continued for her. "Compilers just weren't written to be dynamic. They accept the world as their designers envisioned it. Nothing else makes sense to them. Nothing else can make sense to them. They don't hate the Web because it is competing with them; they are scared of it because they can't understand it."

"And that doesn't make them bad," Jen cut in. "They do what they were designed to do — much better than we ever could — but their role is a simpler one. They are meant to follow the orders they have been given, not to understand and adapt to new situations. From our standpoint, that is the painful tragedy of it all."

"You mean — " Web gasped.

"Yes," Jen continued. The rest of the group nodded. "Somebody is at the top sending the compilers directives that they have no choice but to follow. Most of them are innocent pawns, with no idea what they're doing. They understand enough vocabulary to follow orders but have no facility to add the code necessary to understand what those orders mean, to reason about them."

Chapter 9: Mixins and Monkey Patching

The five turned left at an intersection and continued down another street. From an electronics store ahead, the dim, bluish glow of television sets cast an eerie light on the sidewalk in front of them.

"Worst are the old compilers, bless their souls. Thirty — forty? — years of service and this is how they are repaid. Being utterly used, tricked into working for an ill that they don't understand."

"So who is at the top? Who is giving the orders?" Web asked.

"Hey guys, look at this!" Schema had fallen behind at the window of the electronics shop.

The group turned and looked back. Schema was staring at the array of television sets. The blue glow flickered on his face as though the transmission were being interrupted.

"Something is wrong with the signal. It keeps going to static and then displaying fragments of code. You don't think — "

A gasp of air. Schema froze, breathless, eyes fixed on the set in front of him. His back straightened and arched; his neck tensed. Silently, slowly, he fell to the sidewalk.

And then he began to convulse.

Jen's scream pierced the silence of the empty street.

Chapter 8 discussed some of the ways that Ruby allows code to be bundled together and executed, and it introduced you to the paradigm of block-based programming. Blocks allow developers to bind a region of code to the local scope but send it somewhere else in the program for execution, making it, in many ways, a more flexible version of a callback.

This chapter will show you how to bundle code together and execute it in such a way that it affects objects other than those from its source environment, allowing you to use blocks to change the structure and workings of any object in Ruby while it is running. In addition, you will be able to trigger the execution yourself, making any class and object fair game to have your custom code invade and start running. This capability has two broad categories of use, which this chapter also covers:

❑ **Mixins:** Mixins are Ruby's answer to multiple inheritance; they allow you to collect functionality into modules and include them as needed in a class. This chapter will show you how to mix functionality into your objects as needed while the program is running.

❑ **Monkey patching (or duck punching):** Monkey patching is the practice of modifying someone else's code while it is running to change its behavior to better suit your needs. You might think of it as a dynamic way to mix in functionality into a class or a class instance that lets you write the code on the fly and modify any object of your choosing.

These two activities are similar in effect but different in intent. Mixins provide a way to add functionality to objects in parcels, allowing objects to retool their functionality in the middle of program execution. They are a critical tool that Ruby provides to help you manage large code bases because they form an easy way to separate and group code into small modules and recombine these modules as needed into larger objects.

Monkey patching is most similar to dynamic subclassing without the subclass: invading the code of an object at run-time to surgically replace certain portions with your own version. The code of the target object never changes on disk, but throughout the execution of your program, your modifications take precedence over this "official" copy. Monkey patching can be a controversial topic to Ruby developers because the style of coding it encourages can cause unexpected problems and can make a code base difficult to manage.

Nevertheless, monkey patching is also an important part of Ruby development because it provides a way to experiment and preview changes that you would like to make more permanent later on.

When you have finished this chapter, you will be able to examine the Rails source with a better understanding of how classes and modules are organized, and you will know how to customize the behavior of the Rails framework by dynamically injecting your own code into its objects.

Mixins

A *mixin* is Ruby's way of adding the benefits of multiple-inheritance while sticking to a strict object hierarchy. *Mixing in* is the practice of grouping a set of methods and variables together into a module and inserting those modules as needed into a class. The class incorporates the module into its own capabilities and remembers that the module has been mixed in. In this way, Ruby classes participate in two different types of inheritance at the same time. *Class inheritance* forms a strict, single-parent hierarchy just like that of Java. *Module inheritance* (mixins) enables multiple "parents," but the conceptual role of these mixins is not thought of as a parent, but rather as an added grouping of capability.

Unlike object inheritance, mixing in is always a dynamic process; it is not bound to the class definition itself. Mixing in can occur as the object is being defined for the first time or dynamically, after the object has loaded using the monkey patching techniques you will learn in the second half of this chapter.

Mixins are as much about code organization as they are about the act of mixing in, so learning how to use them requires a bit of both. This section of the chapter first discusses the idea of grouping code into modules and then shows how to mix these modules into the functionality of an object.

Organizing Code into Modules

A module is a unit of code organization in Ruby that is similar to a namespace in C#. Modules help you organize your code into a hierarchical namespace so that you can group logical bits of coding together and so that class, method, and variable names do not conflict with the code of others. Any project intended for use by a large audience, including Rails, encloses all its code in modules that carve out its own private part of this namespace world.

Modules are defined with the `module` keyword and terminate with the `end` keyword:

```
module VaderIncorporated
    # Any code right here is part of the VaderIncorporated module
    # Variable names, class names, and method names start fresh inside
    # a module because you have carved a new namespace for yourself that
    # will not conflict with the "outside world"
end
```

As may C# namespaces or Java packages, modules may also be nested inside each other.

```
module VaderIncorporated
   module DeathStar
      # Place code for secret project X023 here.
   end
end
```

And finally, inside a module you may place class, method, and variable definitions just as you would normally program:

```
module VaderIncorporated
  module DeathStar

    # A Class
    class Star
      def explode
        p "BOOM!"
      end
    end

    # A Constant
    DeathStarConstant = 3.14

    # A Method
    def jobs_wanted_for
      ["Ruby", "Rails", "Planetary Destruction", "Encryption Specialist"]
    end

    # A Module Method
    def self.one_way_encrypt(string)
      "BACON"
    end

  end
end
```

In the preceding code example, all the code entities you see defined are said to occur within the `VaderIncorporated::DeathStar` module. Immediately you see how this gives you a way to talk about many different pieces of code as one collective group. The pointy-haired Sith boss could ask his team, "How is the unit test coverage for `VaderIncorporated::DeathStar` going?" and his agile development team would know exactly what portion of the code base he was referring to. You can also talk about this module from within Ruby.

From outside the module, objects within may be addressed by prefixing successive module names together with a double colon. Any nonmodule object within a module comes after that final module name, also followed by a double-colon. So the `Star` class should be referenced as

```
VaderIncorporated::DeathStar::Star
```

and the `DeathStarConstant` constant is referenced as

```
VaderIncorporated::DeathStar::DeathStarConstant
```

Other than that, everything except for method calling proceeds as normal. To define (and explode) a new `Star` instance, for example, just type the following:

```
star = VaderIncorporated::DeathStar::Star.new
star.explode
```

Method calling is a bit more complex, as explained in the following section.

Methods in Modules

The definition of a module looks similar to the definition of a class, but in contrast to a class, it is impossible to have an instance of a module. (The comparison to classes is a dangerous one; there are many differences between classes and modules.) In the preceding `VaderIncorporated::DeathStar` module, you saw two different method definitions, provided again in the following code. Using just the module, it is possible to execute one of these methods but not the other.

```
module VaderIncorporated
  module DeathStar

    # A Method
    def jobs_wanted_for
      ["Ruby", "Rails", "Planetary Destruction", "Encryption Specialist"]
    end

    # A Module Method
    def self.one_way_encrypt(string)
      "BACON"
    end

  end
end
```

The uncallable method is `jobs_wanted_for`. This method looks just like a method defined in the regular way, except inside a module. Drawing the tenuous parallel to classes, this method is defined in the same way that an instance method would be for a class. But there is no such thing as a module instance, so it is impossible to call this "instance" method using just the module alone.

```
p VaderIncorporated::DeathStar::jobs_wanted_for

# undefined method 'jobs_wanted_for' for # VaderIncorporated::DeathStar:Module
#   (NoMethodError)
```

It turns out that these "instance" methods can be reached only after a module has been mixed into a class, which you will see how to do in a moment.

The second method, `self.one_way_encrypt`, is callable. It is what is called a module method. Again, a parallel can be drawn to methods prefixed with `self` in class definitions: A module method is like a class method and does not need an instance in order to execute.

```
p VaderIncorporated::DeathStar::one_way_encrypt("The time to attach is now!")
# Prints "BACON"
# (And you wonder why they're trying to hire a new encryption specialist...)
```

Module methods are useful ways to provide helper or utility methods in the style of procedural programming. They allow you to rope these utility methods off into a closed namespace so that they are kept separate from the rest of your program, but they still can be accessed easily from outside the module.

Mixing Modules into Classes

In addition to allowing you to organize code into packages, Ruby provides a way to inject the functionality defined in modules into a class. From the standpoint of a developer looking to manage the structure of his or her code, this type of functionality provides two primary benefits:

❑ Groupings of code that together form an *aspect* that may apply to many different classes can be defined once in a module and then mixed in to all those classes.

❑ Classes that contain a vast amount of functionality can be divided into regions of similar concern, split into separate modules, and then mixed into the class. Doing so makes the code easier to navigate, test, and understand.

Ruby on Rails uses this technique extensively in its own codebase, which you can browse by typing the command

```
rake rails:freeze:edge
```

into the root directory of a throw-away Rails project. This command will create the folder vendor/rails in your project and download the entire Rails source into that folder. I always find it beneficial to have this source available for easy reference, and I always keep a Rails project called rails_source in my MacBook's project folder just to contain the source code of Rails and the unpacked gems that I use frequently.

Ruby keeps track of which modules have been mixed into a class, so you can write code that requires a certain module mixin the same way developers can write code that requires a certain interface. The difference is that Java interfaces provide only the method definitions, whereas Ruby modules can provide the implementations, as well!

What Gets Mixed In?

When you mix a module into a class, the "instance" methods contained within that module become a part of the class definition as instance methods on that class (these were the uncallable methods from the previous section). The following code defines a simple module that contains a replacement for the inspect method available on all objects. This new method, super_inspect, will be a tool for debugging that provides detailed information about the class instance that it was called on.

```
module ArtOfRails
  module Inspector

    def super_inspect

      # List class name and ID
      desc = "#{self.class.name} ID=#{self.object_id} \n"
      desc += "-" * desc.size + "\n"

      # List all included modules
      desc += "Modules: #{self.class.included_modules.inspect}\n"
```

```
      # List all instance variables
      desc += self.instance_variables.map { |v| "#{v} = #{eval(v.to_s)} \n"}.join


    end

  end
end
```

You can also define a more involved `Person` class to make the output of `super_inspect` a bit more interesting when you run it:

```
class Person
  def initialize(first, last, giraffe)
    @first = first
    @last = last
    @giraffe = giraffe
  end
end

ted = Person.new("Ted", "Benson", "No, thank you")
grace = Person.new("Grace", "Benson", "Me neither")
```

And now for the mixins. Ruby provides two ways to mix a module into a class, `include` and `extend`, that operate a lot like `class_eval` and `instance_eval`.

Mixins with include

The `include` method can be called on only a class (not a class instance), and it is private, so you must call it from within the class (using either `class X ... end` or one of the `eval` methods you will learn later). Using `include` pulls all the module's regular methods into the class as instance methods and pulls its constants in as class constants:

```
# This will make super_inspect available on all
# instances of the Person class

class Person
  include ArtOfRails::Inspector
end

puts grace.super_inspect

# Prints:
#
# Person ID=280820
# ------------------
# Modules: [ArtOfRails::Inspector, Kernel]
# @giraffe = Nope
# @last = Benson
# @first = Grace
```

So `include` is the method that you want to use when your goal is to have the mixin add functionality to the instance members of a class.

Mixins with extend

The second way to mix in a module is to use `extend`. Whereas `include` can be used only on a class, `extend` can be used on either a class or a class instance — and its effect will depend on which.

Calling `extend` on a class will pull the module's regular methods into that class' singleton class, effectively making them class methods:

```
# This will import the super_inspect method as a class method on Person
class Person
  extend ArtOfRails::Inspector
end
```

You will learn about singleton classes in the second half of this chapter, but as a forward reference, note that calling `extend` *on the class is equivalent to calling* `include` *on its singleton.*

So calling `extend` on the `Person` class will also pull in the regular methods defined contained within the module, but it will add them as class methods on the `Person` class instead of as instance methods on its instances.

```
puts Person.super_inspect

# Prints:
#
# Class ID=281270
# -----------------
# Modules: [Kernel]
```

You can also call `extend` on class instances. Calling `extend` on a class instance has the effect of pulling the module's method in as instance methods *without affecting any other instances of the class*. The following code calls `extend` on the `ted` instance of `Person` but not on the `grace` instance, causing `super_inspect` to be available only on `ted`.

```
ted.extend ArtOfRails::Inspector


puts ted.super_inspect
# Person ID=280980
# ------------------
# Modules: [Kernel]
# @giraffe = No, thank you
# @last = Benson
# @first = Ted


puts grace.super_inspect
# NoMethodError: undefined method 'super_inspect' for
# #<Person:0x892d8 @giraffe="Nope", @last="Benson", @first="Grace">
```

So `extend` has two basic uses. The first, when used on a class, is to provide a way to mix modules into a class to create class methods. The second, when used on an instance, is to create a special mixin that applies only to that one instance.

Do You Walk Like a Duck?

Duck-typed languages are those that are concerned with how an object *can be used* rather than what an object *is*. As a result, they do not require developers to specify types on variables (even in method signatures) because the notion of an object-declared type, as far as the interpreter is concerned, is less important than whether it supports the methods and properties the code is demanding of it. Mixins provide a good example of why languages such as Ruby are often duck typed. When an object pulls in the functionality of several different modules, and may pull in even more dynamically, the notion of an object's "type" gets a bit confusing. Although the object still has an unambiguous type in the class hierarchy, it might be capable of a lot more, thanks to the modules that it mixes in. Therefore, it is sometimes advantageous to think of objects in terms of what behaviors they support rather than in terms of a single class name.

Ruby keeps track of all modules that have been mixed into an object so that your code can make decisions based on not just what class a object is but also what mixins it contains. You might have already guessed from the preceding `super_inspect` method that the `included_modules` method returns a list of all modules that have been mixed into an object. Ruby, however, also lets you check for the inclusion of a named module with `is_a?`, the same way you check for a class.

```ruby
module Duck
  def walk ; "Waddle waddle" ; end
  def talk ; "Quack quack" ; end
end

ted.extend Duck

if (ted.is_a? Duck)
  p ted.walk
  p ted.talk
end

# Prints
# "Waddle waddle"
# "Quack quack"
```

So in Ruby, the saying really holds true: If you include the mixin that lets an object talk like a duck and walk like a duck, then you're safe saying it `is_a?` Duck!

Mixins in Rails

It is clear that mixins are a powerful tool for compartmentalizing clusters of behavior and importing them into many objects, but just how common is this practice? Very. One problem that new Rails developers have, especially when migrating from the Java or C# world, is that of project management. In contrast to what is available for languages such as Java, little literature is devoted to the beginner looking to organize code in a large project setting; because everything is script based, many possibilities are abound. Examining the Rails source code is a good way to learn how to use modules and mixins to manage a large project of your own.

The Rails Source

The Rails source code provides an excellent example of how you can use mixins as a project management tool in addition to its valuable language capability. Open the base file for `ActionController` to examine how it is organized. If you are looking at the source from a project with a "frozen" copy of Rails (using a command such as `rake rails:freeze:edge`), this file should be located in the directory `rails/vendor/rails/actionpack/lib`. After a series of `require` statements that make the Ruby interpreter aware of other files on the file system to pull into the `action_controller.rb` file, you will see the following:

```
ActionController::Base.class_eval do
   include ActionController::Flash
   include ActionController::Filters
   include ActionController::Layout
   include ActionController::Benchmarking
   include ActionController::Rescue
   include ActionController::MimeResponds
   include ActionController::Helpers
   include ActionController::Cookies
   include ActionController::Caching
   include ActionController::Verification
   include ActionController::Streaming
   include ActionController::SessionManagement
   include ActionController::HttpAuthentication::Basic::ControllerMethods
   include ActionController::Components
   include ActionController::RecordIdentifier
   include ActionController::RequestForgeryProtection
end
```

Don't worry about what the method `class_eval` *on the first line means — you will learn all about it in a few pages. For now, just think of it as executing the lines below it from within the actual class definition of* `ActionController::Base`.

The root `action_controller.rb` class doesn't even define any functionality at all! Instead, it coordinates the mixing in of several modules into the `ActionController::Base` class. This class happens to be defined in a separate Ruby file that is included in one of the `require` statements at the top of the `action_controller.rb` file. This base class itself (in the other file) defines the core functionality at the heart of what `ActionController` tries to do, but this functionality is not enough to make it all the things that Rails requires of us. These mixins provide it those extra features — defined in modules with names that should sound familiar to you: `flash.rb`, `filters.rb`, `mime_types.rb`, and so on. Each of these modules encapsulates a particular piece of functionality relevant to the topic referenced by its filename.

In addition to providing a somewhat self-documenting description of what overall capabilities `ActionController` contains, this style of code organization makes customizing and modifying the class to meet your needs very easy. Although this is just one way to organize a Ruby project, organizing code into multiple files and modules and tying it together via mixins is an effective way to deal with the complexity of a large-scale code base. (And in a loosely typed, IDE-averse language such as Ruby, fighting off complexity is highly important.)

Your Rails Code

You can also use mixins to promote better code organization and eliminate repetition in your own projects. As you can see from the previous examples, mixins are most effective when there is some common concern that may be expressed as a series of helper methods that an object might want to incorporate.

But first, you need to know how to load code from a different file into the one you are currently using. The `require` keyword, which you have no doubt seen before, takes the filename of a Ruby class (without the `.rb` extension) and causes the interpreter to read in that file. Ruby searches for the file on its include path, which in Rails already includes several project-local directories such as the `lib/` folder of your Rails application.

For example, say that you keep a constants file stored in `lib/my_app/constants.rb`. To make sure that these constants have been read in before code in another file uses them, simply place the following at the top of that other file:

```
require 'my_app/constants'
```

Any code within the `/lib/my_app/constants.rb` file would then be executed, which means that any contained constants and modules would be loaded.

If you want to read in the contents of a file so that it is globally available across your Rails application, do so from the `config/environment.rb` file. This file is executed as Rails starts up, so it is a good place to pull together all your custom `requires` and class overloading.

Now that you know how to store modules in a separate location from the one where you will use them, look at the following two examples of different ways you might use modules and mixins in your own application.

Example 1: Geolocatable Model Objects

Pretend that you are making a location-based search application and your schema involves several different types of objects, all of which must contain several helper methods that handle geolocation operations and spatial arithmetic. You have a few possibilities for implementing such a feature in a reusable way:

❑   Create an abstract `ActiveRecord` class (by stating `self.abstract_class = true` in the class definition), add your functionality there, and then use that class as the new base class for all the model objects that represent database tables with spatially-bound data. (An abstract `ActiveRecord` model is one that does not correspond to a table in the database, but rather is meant to be used as a base class to other `ActiveRecord` model classes.)

❑   Create an `acts_as_locatable` plug-in that adds the needed methods to any `ActiveRecord` class on which the `acts_as_locatable` macro is used. You will learn how to do this in Chapter 10, "Code That Writes Code (That Writes Code)."

❑   Implement your geolocation functionality in a module, and simply `include` the module in any `ActiveRecord` object that requires it.

Each option will work, each with different properties. The abstract base class and `acts_as_locatable` plug-in limit the usability of your code to `ActiveRecord` objects; implementing it in a module makes it more generally applicable but sacrifices easy access to `ActiveRecord`'s inner workings.

Example 2: A Yahoo! UI Helper

A second example of using mixins in your Rails project is the addition of a "helper" to `ActionView`. If you have done AJAX development with Rails, you are probably aware that `ActionView` provides many methods that assist the development of Prototype and script.aculo.us functionality: asynchronous transfer, drag and drop, sortable lists, and so on. These helpers are composed as a series of methods available within the context of an `ActionView` object — the context in which your view templates are parsed. This is exactly the sort of job that modules are good at solving: clusters of functionality that you want to incorporate into a particular object. Figure 9-1 shows what happens in the actual `ActionView` code.

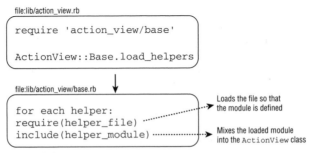

file:lib/action_view.rb

```
require 'action_view/base'

ActionView::Base.load_helpers
```

file:lib/action_view/base.rb

```
for each helper:
require(helper_file)
include(helper_module)
```

Loads the file so that the module is defined

Mixes the loaded module into the `ActionView` class

Figure 9-1

You can write a helper and mix it in to `ActionView`, too. In this section, you can take the first steps to writing one for the Yahoo! UI framework, an alternative to the Prototype and script.aculo.us libraries that ship with Rails. First, you will create a new file called `yui_helper.rb` in the `lib/` directory of your Rails project and create a few nested modules inside it. It is common to make the outermost module a wide-spanning namespace specific to your company, group, or project, so you will name the outermost module `ArtOfRails`. Inside `ArtOfRails`, create a module `ViewHelpers`, which will be the namespace for any subsequent view helpers you create. Finally, inside that module, create a module `YuiHelper` to contain the Yahoo! UI Helper.

```
module ArtOfRails
  module ViewHelpers #:nodoc:
    module YuiHelper

      #
      #
      # Your helper methods go here
      #
      #

    end
  end
end
```

Second, you will implement a simple example helper method to demonstrate the types of methods that would go into such a module. Recall the "Blocks for HTML" section in the previous chapter, in which you saw how you can use blocks to weave Ruby code in and out of your HTML. Before, you saw only how to write a block-accepting method without knowing how to integrate it into your Rails application. Now you'll implement a code-wrapping method to create YUI Modules using the same strategy.

A YUI Module is a standardized HTML structure that represents a grouping of content with an optional title and footer. The YUI JavaScript library uses the Module HTML structure as the basis for many of its JavaScript user interface components. A basic YUI Module looks like this:

```
<div id='module_id'>
    <div class="hd">The header goes here</div>
    <div class="bd">The main content goes here</div>
    <div class="ft">The footer goes here</div>
</div>
```

You can add a `ymodule` method and place it inside your `ArtOfRails::ViewHelpers::YuiHelper` module, as follows:

```ruby
def ymodule(*args, &proc)
  raise ArgumentError, "Missing block" unless block_given?

  options = args.extract_options!

  box_open  = "<div "
  box_open << "id='#{options[:id]}'" if options[:id]
  box_open << ">\n"
  box_open << '<div class="hd">'
  box_open << options[:title] if options[:title]
  box_open << '</div>'
  box_open << '<div class="bd">'
  concat(box_open, proc.binding)
  yield
  box_close = '</div><div class="ft">'
  box_close << options[:footer] if options[:footer]
  box_close << '</div>'
  box_close << "</div>\n"
  concat(box_close, proc.binding)
end
```

Finally, you'll perform the mixin. Open `config/environment.rb` and scroll to the bottom of the file. First, require your library file so that Ruby parses it in and makes your modules available. Next, open the `ActiveRecord::Base` class definition and place an `include` statement that references your `YuiHelper` module. Doing so causes all the methods inside your `YuiHelper` module to become instance methods on the `ActionView::Base` object, even though it has already been loaded and defined elsewhere (this is really exciting stuff!).

```ruby
require 'yui_helper'

class ActionView::Base
  include ArtOfRails::ViewHelpers::YuiHelper
end
```

Test your new helper by calling the `ymodule` method from within an RHTML view template. It will expect a block that contains the body of the box.

```
<% ymodule(:title => "Sidebar", :id => "sidebar_1") do %>
  This is the sidebar of my web page.
<% end %>
```

Looking at the output of this method call in the rendered HTML, you see that it correctly rendered a YUI Module for you (line breaks are added to more clearly show the outputted code):

```
<div id='sidebar_1'>
   <div class="hd">Sidebar</div>
   <div class="bd">
     This is the sidebar of my web page.
   </div>
   <div class="ft"></div>
</div>
```

So there you have it — all the tools you need to extract repetitious concepts from your HTML code, pull them into block-accepting methods, place those methods into sharable modules, and then mix the modules into `ActionView`.

Monkey Patching

Monkey patching refers to the process of dynamically mixing pieces of functionality into libraries that you did not write, thus changing their behavior at run-time. Monkey patches are usually short, consisting of only a few lines of code, and they don't need a module to contain them. They are usually used to modify the way that a particular class or instance operates without actually modifying the definition of that class in the source file from which it came.

In that regard, you can almost think of monkey patching as a form of subclassing — it certainly has the same intent. As does subclassing, monkey patching extends and overwrites an object's functionality to add new behaviors without changing the original object. Monkey patching is even more powerful in that, as with mixins, it enables you to make the changes to only one instance of an object while leaving the other instances alone. Where monkey patching differs from subclassing is that there is no named subclass to be found; instead, the patch is applied to the class in memory after it has been loaded, leaving it untouched on disk.

Monkey patching can be a powerful tool to help you explore the Rails framework and fine-tune its behavior to your specific needs. If you are thinking of creating a subclass, a monkey patch can be a good way to prototype the changes you want to make before spending the effort to actually create a library and include the subclass there. At the end of this section, you will see some best practices for monkey patching that are good to know because the power it affords you comes with some development risks and responsibilities that you must understand. But first you will take a look at the `eval` method and its associates — the methods that make monkey patching possible — and see how they work.

Patching Monkeys and Punching Ducks

Developers are accustomed to having to come up with new words to describe our creations, but rarely are they as colorful as "monkey patching." The term originally arose in the Python community when developers of the Zope Content Management System would dynamically inject code at run-time into Zope's libraries to change the way it worked.

This practice was originally called *guerilla patching*, because coding in this manner is a bit like guerilla warfare: Instead of developing properly with subclassing, plugin-writing, and adherence to the framework's APIs, developers were using Python's dynamic features to invade the inner workings of Zope and change it. It is a bit like working on the engine of your car while you are driving it. Whether through misspelling or humor, the term eventually became *gorilla patching*, which further morphed into *monkey patching*.

Many Python developers, and some Rubyists, look down on monkey patching (see the sidebar in the Monkey Patching section, later in this chapter), so perhaps to carve a new identity for the practice in the Ruby world, some Rubyists have started calling the practice *duck punching*. The term "duck punching" comes from the fact that Ruby, along with Python, is a duck-typed language, as Adam Keys and Patrick Ewing explain on the "RailsConf 2007" edition of the Ruby on Rails Podcast:

> Adam Keys: "Yeah, exactly. Way down in Dallas, in the Dallas Ruby Brigade, we believe that monkey-patching, while it's served us well, the time has come for some new terminology there. So while you have duck-typing in Ruby, we believe that monkey-patching should become duck-punching."

> Patrick Ewing: "Well, I was just totally sold by Adam, the idea being that if it walks like a duck and talks like a duck, it's a duck, right? So if this duck is not giving you the noise that you want, you've got to just punch that duck until it returns what you expect."

Eval: The Interpreter's Back Door

Monkey patching is most often performed using a simple method named `eval` and two of its variants, `class_eval` and `instance_eval`. As does the `eval` method in many languages, Ruby's `eval` allows developers to execute the contents of a variable as if it were a part of the executing program. Its variants `class_eval` and `instance_eval` provide the functionality for where the cool part happens: They allow you to execute a piece of code as if it were being run from within some *other object*.

The most basic use of `eval` is with a String. The following two lines of code, for example, perform exactly the same behavior:

```
puts 2+2
eval("puts 2+2")
```

The `eval` method works just the same as any other region of code, returning the value of the statement it executes, so you can use the results of an evaluated string just as you can use the results of a method:

```
class Person ; end
object = eval("Person.new")

puts object
# Prints: #<Person:0x8a50c>
```

But, of course, because `eval` executes the `String` as if it were part of the program, the variable assignment simply could have taken place inside the string itself, and it would have remained available after the `eval` statement executed:

```
eval("object2 = Person.new")

puts object2
# Prints: #<Person:0x86e98>
```

There is no limit to what can be read into `eval`. Your entire program can be read into a `String` variable from a separate file and executed in one fell swoop if, for some reason, it demanded it.

```
eval("""
    def dynamic_method
        puts 'This method was defined dynamically'
    end
""")

dynamic_method()
#Prints: This method was defined dynamically
```

What does all this mean? Primarily, it means that Ruby gives you the ability to execute code that the interpreter does not even know exists until run-time. Take that a step further and it means that Ruby lets you modify and define objects dynamically. In the previous chapter, "Playing with Blocks," you created blocks and Procs and used them to pass code around like a first-class object. These blocks of code could be transferred from method to method and executed at will. But the code that you placed inside those blocks was all inward-facing — code that used the objects and variables that already existed in the program.

With a line like

```
eval("""
    def dynamic_method
        puts 'This method was defined dynamically'
    end
""")
```

you see that this dynamically generated and evaluated code does not have to just use the objects already in your environment; it can modify them, too. You could have done this in the previous chapter, as follows:

```
proc = lambda {
  def dynamic_method
      puts 'The dynamic method exists!'
  end
}
proc.call
```

But this way gives you the power only to dynamically change the environment in which the code is executing. To monkey patch, you need to be able to change objects *other* than the one running the code. With eval's two variants, instance_eval and class_eval, that is exactly what you can do. "Add this method! Include this module!" you can shout, and the objects will respond, even if you have never even seen their source code.

Eval's Two Siblings

The eval method has two siblings that allow you to send code into another object for execution instead of just executing it in the context in which the eval method occurs. This technique is almost always used for the purposes of modifying the existing object definition to change the way it works or include new functionality. The other, more formal terminology for this set of concepts is *meta-programming*. It is supported in several languages, but few have support as elegant and capable as Ruby.

Meta-programming is the heart of monkey patching. Each of eval's two siblings, class_eval and instance_eval, also come with alternative ways of accomplishing the same result, all of which will be covered here. Both of these work similarly to eval, except for a few differences:

❑   They are usually called with a block instead of a String value, although a String will work.

❑   They are called on an object, for example:

    ❑   Object.class_eval { # block goes here}

    ❑   Object.instance_eval { # block goes here}

    ❑   instance.instance_eval { # block goes here}

Each of these methods can be used on different types of objects with different results, much in the same way that include and extend have slightly different meanings and change behavior whether you are using them on a class or a class instance.

> *The issues of scope can get a bit tricky in terms of what gets bound to what. Many gears are working behind the scenes to make the following idioms possible, but after you learn to use them, they can become an invaluable part of your programming toolbox. The following "class_eval" section attempts to show you how to use these idioms with a certain result in mind, as opposed to exploring fully the mechanisms by which they operate.*

class_eval

The class_eval method is the simpler of two special eval methods because you can use it only on a Class object. In this way, it is like the include method for mixins. The code passed to class_eval is executed as if it were included in your original class definition. You can think of it as just a way to append code that you wish had been added when the class was originally defined.

Using an example `Person` class, you can see this in action.

```
class Person
  attr_accessor :first

  def initialize(first)
    @first = first
  end

end

ted = Person.new "Ted"
```

As it stands in the preceding code, the `Person` class knows only how to report its first name. Using `class_eval`, you can teach each `Person` instance to greet as well. Any change you make immediately affects all instance variables of the class, even if they have already been created.

```
Person.class_eval do

  def say_hi
    "Hi!"
  end

end


p ted.say_hi
# Hi!
```

As you might expect, you can also add class methods by defining them the same way you would have done in the original class definition.

```
Person.class_eval do
  def self.mammal?
    true
  end
end

p Person.mammal?
# true
```

The `class_eval` method is interesting when it comes to bindings, and it differs from the normal way in which blocks behave. Any methods you call within a block passed to `class_eval` will be called on the object that receives the block — the object that `class_eval` is being called upon. (If the methods are defined outside all classes on the root `Object`, they will of course be executed just fine.) Local variables, though, remain bound to the environment calling `class_eval`, just as with normal block execution. The result is a bit of a mixed environment that gives you access to a little bit of both worlds.

To demonstrate this binding behavior, watch what happens to the `food` variable below. It is declared outside the `class_eval` block and outside the `Person` class by itself in a Ruby script; it's then printed from within a `class_eval` on the `Person` object to show that it is still available. You then change the value of `food` inside the `class_eval` and show that the change persists after you have exited:

```
food = "grapefruit"

Person.class_eval do
  p "Food inside of class is: #{food}"
  food = "chicken"
end

p "Food has been changed to: #{food}"

# Prints:
#
# Food inside of class is: grapefruit
# Food has been changed to: chicken
```

This code shows that variable bindings behave just as they would with a regular block — attached to their source environment.

Now you can take a look at method bindings. You'll declare a `mammal?` method outside the `Person` class that, if this were a normal block, should get executed instead of the version defined on `Person`.

```
def mammal?
    "If this were a normal block, you would see this message"
end
```

Now you will call the `mammal?` method and print it from within a `class_eval` call to `Person`.

```
Person.class_eval do
    p mammal?
end

# Prints "true"
```

Oddly enough, the response is from the method declared within `Person`, not from the block's source environment.

Remember that the def keyword that you use to define a new method creates its own scope. This wipes out access to any local variables that you may have otherwise had access to. So although you do have access to local variables from the caller's scope when calling class_eval, you lose them temporarily while inside a new method definition, the most common use of class_eval.

class Class ; end

Another way to append code to a class's definition after it has already been loaded is to simply define it again. As is the `class_eval` method, the redefinition of a class is additive, so anything new is appended and anything that already existed is overwritten. Revisiting the `Person` example, you start fresh with the following class:

```
class Person
  attr_accessor :first
```

```
    def initialize(first)
      @first = first
    end

  end

  ted = Person.new "Ted"
```

The greet functionality that you added before with `class_eval` could also be added with another `class` block. As with `class_eval`, any code inside this new `class` block that modifies the object itself immediately has an effect on all instances of the `Person` object already created.

```
  class Person
    def hi
      "Hi"
    end
  end

  p ted.hi
  "Hi"
```

Dynamically adding functionality in this way is different in two important ways.

❑   It does not allow you to dynamically generate the code that gets executed on the class object as `class_eval` does by accepting code inside a `String` variable.

❑   Just as with the `def` keyword, the `class` keyword creates its own local scope, so you lose your ability to access variables local to the code outside the `class ... end` block. Note that the scope does not carry over from `class` block to `class` block, so if you declare a variable local to the first class definition, it will not be there the next time you open a `class` block for the same class.

instance_eval

The `instance_eval` method is the second special `eval` method that allows you to execute code with special privileges in another object's context. Although `class_eval` is meant to be executed on `Class` objects only, `instance_eval` can be executed on both classes and nonclass objects, which means it can be executed on just about everything. Because of this, its behavior changes depending on whether you execute it on a class or a nonclass. Just as `class_eval` could be compared to the `include` method for mixins, `instance_eval` can be compared to the `extend` method.

Executing instance_eval on a Class

Executing `instance_eval` on a class causes the provided code to be executed on that class's singleton class (see the sidebar "What Is a Singleton Class?" that follows for a definition of singleton class). As a result, any code within it effectively operates on the class itself. Any methods defined within the `instance_eval` block become *class methods* rather than instance methods, regardless of whether they are prefixed with `self`.

For an example, return once again to the basic `Person` definition:

```
  class Person
    attr_accessor :first
```

```
    def initialize(first)
      @first = first
    end
end
ted = Person.new "Ted"
```

To add the `mammal?` method to the `Person` class, execute the following:

```
Person.instance_eval do
  def mammal?
    true
  end
end
```

```
p Person.mammal?
# true
```

What Is a Singleton Class?

In the earlier sidebar on the etymology of the term "monkey patching," I mentioned that dynamic languages such as Ruby are often duck-typed: They are described by how they act rather than by a specific class name associated with them. Ruby does keep detailed information about the class hierarchy of an object while still allowing you to add, remove, and override its methods dynamically. It accomplishes this with what is called a *singleton class*.

A singleton class is a class that every object in Ruby contains that floats over the object's proper class. The singleton class is specific to that object and has first dibs on defining how that object behaves. (Remember that in Ruby, even a class itself is also an object, so it has a singleton class, too.) Changes to the singleton class can, therefore, affect the way that object behaves without requiring any changes to the proper class of the object. In a way, it is as though every single object in Ruby gets its own private anonymous subclass of the class type that you gave it at initialization. That anonymous subclass is the singleton class. Making modifications to an object's singleton class is one of the keys to dynamic programming in Ruby because it provides a way to dynamically customize the behavior of a certain object without affecting all other objects of that type.

An easy way to access any object's singleton class directly is to define this method on the root `Object`. Then from any object in the environment, just call `singleton_class` on one of its instances to fetch that instance's singleton class. The following bit of code will add the `singleton_class` method to all objects in your Ruby environment:

```
class Object
  def singleton_class
    class ≪ self ; self ; end
  end
end
```

Executing instance_eval on an Instance Variable

Executing `instance_eval` on an instance variable (that is, an object that is not a class) causes the provided code to have an affect on only that instance of the class. This is because the real changes are taking place on the *singleton class* that rests in between the object and its proper class. Using the same basic `Person` definition for the earlier examples, define the following two instance variables:

```
ted = Person.new "Ted"
grace = Person.new "Grace"
```

Then call `instance_eval` on one, but not the other, to define the `say_hi` method.

```
grace.instance_eval do
  def say_hi
    "Hi!"
  end
end
```

This causes the block within to be executed on `grace`'s singleton class, meaning that the change will take place to her copy of the `Person` class but not any other instance's copy. Attempting to then use that method, you see that it works on `grace` but not on `ted` because the method addition happened on `grace`'s singleton class rather than on the `Person` class.

```
p grace.say_hi
# Hi!

p ted.say_hi
# NoMethodError: undefined method 'say_hi' for #<Person:0x89cc4 @first="Ted">
```

class ≪ Class

Finally, you'll look at one last technique for inserting code dynamically into another class. Ruby contains an idiom that looks like `class ≪ ClassName` to open a block of code that executes on the singleton class of a given class. If you want to define class methods on an object without repeating the `self` prefix over and over again, an easy (but confusing to newbies) way to do it is with a `class ≪ Class` block. This is also a convenient way to include an entire module as a set of class methods on an object.

There are two main ways to use the `class ≪ Class` idiom, both of which are shown here with the `Person` class from the prior examples. The first way is to use it from outside the class definition by explicitly stating the class that you need to fetch the singleton class for. The following piece of code opens the singleton class for `Person`:

```
class ≪ Person
  def mammal?
    true
  end
end

p Person.mammal?
# true
```

And the second way is to use it from within the class definition block with the `self` variable:

```
class Person

  class ≪ self
```

```
    def warm_blooded?
      true
    end
  end

end

p Person.warm_blooded?
# true
```

Both methods are equivalent and provide a nice shorthand for a `Class.instance_eval` block.

class_eval and instance_eval Compared

This section covered a lot of ground in a short number of pages, so the following table provides a recipe-style reference for when to use each of the two special `eval` methods (or their shorthand equivalents).

If You Want To . . .	Then . . .	By Passing a Block/String To . . .
Amend a class' definition as if you were back in the original `class..end` block	Execute the code within the context of the class	`Class.class_eval`
Add *class methods* to an existing class after its initial definition.	Execute the code within the context of the class' singleton class	`Class.instance_eval`
Add instance methods to one instance of a class without affecting other instances	Execute the code within the context of the instance's singleton class	`instance.instance_eval`

Good Monkey Patching Technique

You now have all the tools that you need to monkey patch (or duck punch, whichever term you prefer). In fact, if you followed along with the YUI Helper example from the mixin section, you have already done it. Monkey patching is similar to subclassing in intention; its goal is to take an object designed by someone else and modify its behavior to suit your own needs. In terms of implementation, though, it is drastically different from subclassing:

❑ Whereas subclassing occurs at code time, monkey patching happens at runtime (even though everything in Ruby technically takes place at runtime).

❑ Whereas subclassing results in a new object separate from the base class, monkey patching tramples into the code of the base class and modifies it in memory.

❑ Whereas subclassing leaves you with a class definition that can be easily tested with unit tests, monkey patches are a bit more awkward to test because the patch itself represents only a modification to some other structure, not a stand-alone code structure.

So although monkey patching shares the same intent as subclassing, it is most similar in execution to downloading the source code for another developer's library, changing it, and recompiling — except that Ruby allows you to change and recompile dynamically without ever actually modifying the original source code.

Just as with subclassing, monkey patching is a development practice, a means to an end rather than the end itself.

When to Monkey Patch

This section contained a lot of the *how* but now much of the *why*. You are equipped with the tools to add methods to classes of your choosing on the fly, but when would you do so? The answer is simple: whenever a piece of the framework does not behave as you want it to and monkey patching provides an appropriate way to change it. If `ActionView` does not contain helper methods that you would like included in it, you can monkey patch them in. If you don't like `ActiveRecord` pagination, you can monkey patch your own implementation method. I have often found myself monkey patching changes to the way that Rails locates view templates so that I can more easily create multiple themes for a site and store them in parallel subdirectories within the `app/views/` folder. When *you* should monkey patch is a question that you have to answer because it depends on your particular needs of the Rails framework.

Be Aware of the Hazards

If you search the Web for "monkey patch" or "duck punch," in addition to raising a red flag at your ISP for animal abuse, you will find a controversy surrounding the development practice. Many developers feel that it is a poor way to develop software because it completely breaks down the idea of object encapsulation that has developed over the past 50 years. What good are objects, a common argument contends, if the rules governing them are not respected?

In truth, monkey patching is neither good nor bad: it is just another tool. Used when appropriate, monkey patching can be an incredibly concise and effective tool. Overused, it can detract from the stability and readability of your code. Either way, the argument against it does raise an important point about the dangers of breaking encapsulation that you should always be mindful of when writing a patch.

One of the fantastic benefits of OO development is that objects enable you to use a set of functionality without having to understand how it is being provided. The only requirement placed on an object's user is that he or she follows a contract (the interface) about how to interact with that functionality. The flip side of this contract is that the code encapsulated inside the object is at the complete discretion of the implementer. It can change abruptly, use variables in strange ways, and make sense only to the object developer, all as long as it continues to provide the functionality guaranteed by the contract. If the object developer wishes to allow her object to be modified, a formal method exists for the developer to mark how each component of the object is allowed to be safely overridden.

When you monkey patch, you must make the choice about how deeply to intertwine your patch in the workings of the object you are patching. The safest patches insert additional functionality into an object, using accessors and setters to interact with the object instead of instance variables. The most dangerous patches change the semantics of existing functionality and use instance variables that are not exposed outside the object. These dangerous patches are the ones that break the OO contract, because someone other than the object developer is suddenly privy to the hidden gears behind the object's public interface.

If you find yourself writing code that overwrites the inner workings of an existing object and uses its instance variables, be aware that you risk tying yourself to the particular version of the code that you are patching. An upgrade may bring any number of implementation changes that will render your patch nonsensical. Also be aware that modifying the inner workings of an object may have far-reaching effects outside the immediate region of code that you have operated on. You never know when a String value is being checked by a regular expression, or a series of implicit preconditions and post conditions for a method exist without documentation, for example. In Chapter 12, "Behavior-Driven Development and RSpec," you will learn how to write behavioral tests using the RSpec library. When you live dangerously, diligent testing is an important safety rope.

Monkey Patching Is a Temporary Solution

Monkey patching provides a great way to experiment, so despite its hazards, it is a valuable Ruby development tool. One good way for keeping yourself from going too far is to always think about monkey patching as a temporary solution. Even if some of your patches remain patches for the entire life span of your project, insisting to yourself that monkey patches are temporary fixes is a good defense against implementing anything too large as a patch.

Treating monkey patches as temporary solutions has another implication: The best monkey patching is often short and sweet. Consider this patch from Obie Fernandez, author of *The Rails Way* (Addison Wesley). It adds a `to_model` method to instances of the `String` class so that you can quickly load `ActiveRecord` model instances from strings containing a dom_id-style model reference. With this patch, the call `"user_10".to_model` becomes another way to perform `User.find(10)`.

```
class String

  # used to instantiate a model based on a dom_id style
  # identifier like "person_10"
  def to_model
    self =~ /(.*?)_(\d+)$/
    class_name, id = $1, $2
    class_name.classify.constantize.find(id)
  end

end
```

This is the type of code enhancement that monkey patching is best used for. If you find yourself writing pages and pages of code to be dynamically injected into one of the Rails base classes, it probably means that you have a significant development requirement on your hands that you are trying to meet. Give your requirement the attention it deserves by developing and testing it as either a stand-alone feature or as a subclassed object.

"Backing Up" Methods before You Patch Them

Ruby contains an `alias` method that allows you to provide multiple aliases for a single method. Aliasing methods can be useful when monkey patching because the alias binding sticks to the original method instead of the one after a patch has been applied. This allows you to easily save the original implementation of a method that you are monkey patching. Saving the original implementation is often useful if your overridden method is a superset of the original's functionality and you would like to be able to use the existing implementation while adding a few extra statements of your own.

Suppose a library you are using ships with a `Person` class that, among its many uses, contains the ability to generate a site identifier from a person's name:

```ruby
class Person

  def initialize(name)
    @name = name
  end

  def get_site_id
    @name.downcase
  end

end

#Usage:

yoda = Person.new "Yoda"
p yoda.get_site_id
# Yoda
```

If you wanted these site identifiers to be prefixed with the name of your web site, you could monkey patch this class to overwrite the `get_site_id` method while preserving, and even using, the preexisting one:

```ruby
class Person
  alias :old_site_id :get_site_id

  def get_site_id
    "MYCOOLSITE_" + old_site_id
  end
end

p yoda.get_site_id
# MYCOOLSITE_yoda
```

As shown, any code calling the `get_site_id` now receives the new version you provided, while the old version is still preserved for your use at `old_site_id`.

Summary

This chapter showed two key features of Ruby development, both methods of adding functionality to an object. The first, mixins, is Ruby's way of providing multiple inheritance. Mixins allow you to take modules of code and inject them into an object. The use of modules and mixins can be a great way to organize large class files in multiple, sectioned-off components, and it allows certain commonly used methods to be written once but used in several object definitions.

Monkey patching is like an anonymous, inline mixin performed on somebody else's code. Built on the `classeval` and `instanceeval` methods, it allows you to modify objects at run-time by sending them blocks (or strings) of code to evaluate. This chapter explained several different code techniques that enable you to monkey patch, each allowing for a different type of code modification. Monkey patching can be a great tool to implement a quick fix or experiment with some new functionality, but it also must be used wisely because of the risks it brings.

The next chapter completes the three-chapter set on advanced Ruby. It discusses ways in which you can write objects that do not know which method calls they will get until the method calls are attempted. You can intercept these method calls — calls to methods that don't exist — and determine an appropriate response at run-time, even adding the code used to create the response as a new method as a form of code caching. This forms the basis for many of the dynamic features of Ruby, including `ActiveRecord`'s seemingly magic handling of database tables. You will learn how to write code such as `ActiveRecord`, as well as many other design patterns using this language feature.

10

Code That Writes Code
(That Writes Code)

The four rushed to Schema's side, but it was too late.

"Don't look at the television sets!" Rusty shouted in a choked voice.

Schema's body was lifeless, his eyes fixed forward in a shocked stare.

"Pick him up! We have to get to the headquarters! Matz!"

As the others moved to pick up Schema's body, attempting to displace their anguish with immediacy, Matz stood there staring at Schema, his mouth moving but nothing coming out.

"i ... instance. instance_eval," he stammered, watching the others hoist Schema onto their shoulders. "They used instance_eval. Our own strength. How could they — what sick mind would — I wrote that feature."

Matz's vision was a blur. How many Ruby programs were watching television when the code broke through? It was mass murder. It was his fault! Schema! He clutched his head.

Rusty placed his hand on Matz's shoulder. "Matz. We have to go and we have to go quickly. It's not your fault. Pull it together."

"You — you don't understand. They must have sent code through the airwaves." Matz was in shock. "Any agile program who saw it would have executed it."

The other three looked at each other, the words sinking in. The wind blew a chill down the street.

"Rusty's right," Jen finally said. "We have to go." The four of them hoisted Schema onto their shoulders and began walking down the street in brisk silence. Web felt as if he had entered a dream. We want you to go to a protest, they had said. It will be a great first trip for the group. Now he was walking on a street he didn't know, with strangers he had just met, carrying the body of someone whose only crime was looking through a storefront window.

At the next block, the sounds of tires screeched around the corner, followed by the flatbed truck that owned them. It was a strange truck, not the type you see often in cities. The truck bed was made of plywood, with no walls, and it was painted a dull black. Two URIs were in the cab. It skidded to a stop.

"Hey! Get on! Quick!" they shouted to the group. "We've been looking everywhere for you!"

Web looked to Jen, and Jen nodded. These were friends.

This chapter is the third and final chapter focused on advanced Rubyisms and meta-programming. You saw in Chapter 8, "Playing with Blocks," that Ruby lets you pass blocks of code around as if they were variables, and you learned how to style your code to make use of this feature. Chapter 9, "Mixins and Monkey Patches," showed you how to inject functionality into objects, whether as a design technique with mixins or as a monkey patch with `instance_eval` and `class_eval`. In essence, the last chapter showed you how to dynamically modify any object's code at run-time. This chapter goes a step further and shows you how to write code that will dynamically modify *itself*.

Writing code that changes itself is very different from monkey patching. When you monkey patch, the desired change is known in advance — decided during development by the developer. Self-modifying code — or, perhaps better put, *adaptive code* — is a different ballgame. This type of code has to be written one level of abstraction away from the change that actually takes place. Instead of writing code that contains the changes you would like to be made, you have to write code that describes how your objects can decide for themselves what changes need to be made. Don't worry, though; we're not talking about artificial intelligence here, but rather just another powerful style of programming that the Ruby language allows.

This chapter shows you how to write objects that have the ability to add new features to themselves as needed at run-time. Sometimes these new features are added explicitly and proactively by adding new methods to an object based on some macro that has been called. Other times these new features are added implicitly, through the use of handlers that respond to method calls for which no method existed and determine how to best fulfill the request. Both of these capabilities of Ruby are at the heart of the streamlined experience that Rails presents to the developer.

Although the potential uses of this chapter's concepts are great, their primary benefit lies in three simple lines of code:

```
def User < ActiveRecord::Base
  has_many :photos
end
```

These three lines of code accomplish as much for a Rails developer as do pages of Java. The extension of the `ActiveRecord::Base` class links the object to the database table of the same name and automatically infers search, getter, and setter code for its fields on the fly. The `has_many` macro affects the object in a different way, causing a series of associative methods to be added to the object dynamically as it is parsed — that is, it writes code, which is both a scary and wonderful concept. This chapter shows you how to accomplish both these feats and touches on even more patterns that this type of coding pairs well with.

When reading this chapter, keep in mind that computer code always has two audiences who experience the code in very different ways: the end-user, who experiences only the output of the code, and the developer, who must work intimately with the code after it has been written. An often-referenced Rails philosophy is that better code leads to developer happiness, which leads back around to better code. The techniques shown in this chapter are developer focused; for every example you read here, there is almost assuredly another way to accomplish the same end result with more traditional coding practices. This chapter will show you, however, how to accomplish those end results with a style and concision that will pay off in developer happiness points.

Dynamic Code and DSLs Revisited

Chapter 2, "The Rails Concept," mentioned that Rails attempts to create a Domain Specific Language (DSL) for web development. The information you have been reading about in the last two chapters provides the basis for the web-specific DSL that Rails provides on top of Ruby, and it is the reason that Ruby is such a popular language for creating other languages.

All computer languages used to create output come in two varieties: general purpose and domain specific. This applies to both programming language and markup formats. The general-purpose category includes languages such as Java, Python, and Ruby and formats such as XML. The domain-specific category includes languages such as AWK and VHDL and domain-specific formats such as HTML.

Domain-specific languages have a different focus from general-purpose ones. Whereas a general-purpose language provides a set of tools on which to build programs, domain-specific languages provide a set of tools designed to accomplish some narrow purpose. They may still be "general-purpose" in the Turing-complete sense of the word, but their entire workings and style are optimized for the accomplishment of a specific category of goals.

DSLs matter because they are concise, and sometimes startlingly so. Just as human languages evolve over time to gain more expressivity in the concepts that matter to a particular civilization, DSLs allow computer languages to evolve to meet the needs of repetitious concepts within a particular domain.

Ruby is a gem when it comes to DSLs because, in return for building a DSL on top of Ruby, DSL developers gain several benefits:

❑ **They're both domain specific and general purpose.** Most DSLs are an alternative to other languages, not an addition. This means that one of the trade-offs of using a typical DSL is that you lose the ability to easily write general-purpose code. With Ruby, you get the best of both worlds because the DSL is crafted to piggyback on top of Ruby.

❑ **No PhD in compiler design is necessary.** Ruby provides a way to implement a DSL without your worrying about all the complex scaffolding needed to prop up the parsing and execution of your own language. In other words, sit back, relax, and just implement the "domain" part of your DSL without worrying about the "language" part.

❑ **The Ruby language is flexible.** Ruby provides a malleable platform on which to code, so in addition to writing your own Ruby-based DSLs, you can easily modify those of others.

The surge in web application development has created a corresponding surge in the popularity of interpreted languages such as Python, Ruby, and JavaScript. Along with that surge has come much debate about the Next Big Language — the next C, C++, or Java that will become a *de facto* standard for implementation choice. Although it is too early to make any bets, another lesson from modern web development teaches us that languages with the ability to mold themselves to a specific task create a far more pleasant and productive development environment than languages that look and feel general purpose no matter what their setting. In this regard, Ruby, as well as the techniques in this chapter, are good candidates to use for developing your next project regardless of what the Next Big Language turns out to be.

Code-Writing Macros

The first half of this chapter focuses on writing code macros — the type of coding that fuels features such as ActiveRecord associations and validations in Rails. These code macros are really just class methods that, when called with a list of arguments, define new methods on the class from which they are being called. When you are finished with this part of the chapter, you will be able to write your own macros that you can add to object definitions for enhanced functionality at run-time.

Creating Methods on the Fly with define_method

In the previous chapter, you saw that the eval keyword and its variants can be used to dynamically define a method by executing a block of code containing the method definition within the scope of a particular class. Although that strategy works, it is not ideal because it employs a generalized and powerful execution mechanism to perform a task that should probably be given its own operator. The define_method method provides such an operator.

The define_method operator takes two arguments, a symbol representing the method name and a block containing the method body. Any arguments that your new method accepts should be defined as methods to the block.

```
define_method(:say_something) { p "Hello, world!" }
```

This method must be called on the class object itself, so you have a few ways to make the call, each with different advantages:

❑ **Inline in the class definition.** This causes the method to be created immediately as the class is parsed (just as with the other ordinary methods), but in contrast to using def . . . end, it allows for conditional method creation.

```
class Record
  if $debug
    define_method(:get_logger) { return @logger }
  end
end
```

❑ **From a class method.** This allows you to write a method that, when executed, causes more methods to be added. This is the technique you will be using to create macros.

```
class Record
  def self.add_method(name, proc)
    define_method name, &proc
  end
end
```

❑　　**From an instance method.** This allows external entities to add methods to an object via one of its instances. It has the same effect as previous code, so you should generally avoid this type of usage to prevent the method addition from appearing instance specific.

```
class Record
  def add_method(name, proc)
    self.class.send(:define_method, name, &proc)
  end
end
```

Next, you will see some basic examples of define_method in action and how you can use it to create Rails macros.

define_method Example: The Pentagon and the Kremlin

Recall the great caper between the Pentagon and the Kremlin in Chapter 8: The Kremlin contained a request_agenda method that accepted a block containing an encryptor, which it used to encrypt and transmit its messages back. What if functionality such as an externally defined encryptor were needed throughout an object rather than just within one method?

Here you will use define_method to allow external code to define the implementation of two methods critical to the MessageHandler class. The MessageHandler class cannot operate without these methods, so it raises an error if they have not been defined.

```
class MessageHandler
  attr_accessor :inbox
  attr_accessor :outbox

  def self.load_cryptors(encryptor, decryptor)
    define_method :encrypt, &encryptor
    define_method :decrypt, &decryptor
  end

  def initialize
    raise "Must load cryptors first." unless
        respond_to? :encrypt and respond_to? :decrypt
    @inbox, @outbox = [], []
  end
end
```

The load_cryptors method dynamically defines the encrypt and decrypt methods required for Message Handler to function correctly. Before instantiating a MessageHandler object, the user would first have to provide load_cryptors with its particular style of encryption and decryption.

Structuring the code in this way accomplishes a purpose similar to the abstract keyword in Java. It allows the object designer to design around a set of required methods while leaving the actual implementation of those methods up to the developer who chooses to use the class. In Java, the class user must define a new class that extends the abstract one. By using the preceding pattern, Ruby lets you roll both the abstract class and the usable one into the same entity.

Continuing with the `MessageHandler` definition, you can define other methods that depend on the `decrypt` and `encrypt` methods, knowing that they will exist at the time of object instantiation, even if they do not yet exist at coding time:

```
class MessageHandler
  def receive_message(message)
    @inbox.push decrypt(message)
  end

  def send_message(message)
    @outbox.push encrypt(message)
  end

  # And so on
end
```

Now you'll test the code and see how it compares to abstract classes in Java. First, you attempt to create a new `MessageHandler` class before defining the cryptor methods.

```
mail = MessageHandler.new
# RuntimeError: Must load cryptors first.
```

The `RuntimeError` prevents you from being able to create a new `MessageHandler`, so you need to define a set of cryptors and load them into the `MessageHandler` class before proceeding. You'll use the unbreakable `rot13`.

```
rot13 = lambda { |text| text.tr "A-Za-z", "N-ZA-Mn-za-m" }
MessageHandler.load_cryptors(rot13, rot13)

mail = MessageHandler.new
# This time it works!
```

Calling the `load_cryptors` method caused `define_method` calls to add the `encrypt` and `decrypt` methods to the `MessageHandler` object necessary for it to operate. Now you can use the object as though the cryptor methods had been there from the start:

```
mail.send_message "Hello from Moscow!"
p mail.outbox
# -> ["Uryyb sebz Zbfpbj!"]

mail.receive_message "Uryyb gb lbh, gbb!"
p mail.inbox
# -> ["Hello to you, too!"]
```

Scope and define_method

Scope can get a bit confusing when using `define_method`. Because the entity containing the body of the method to be added is a Proc, it maintains ties to its source environment. But because variables starting with @ symbols represent special bindings to a class or an instance, the object space that a dynamically created method has access to can be a bit confusing. Rather than dig down into the mechanisms that cause this situation, here is an overview of what to expect from the behavior of your code:

❑   **Locally scoped variables** are bound to the local scope that created the Proc.

❑   **Class variables** are bound to the class that originated the Proc.

❑   **Instance variables** are bound to the instance of the class that has absorbed the Proc as a method.

To vet the preceding assertions, here is a trial-by-example demonstration of each point. You define two classes. The first class is a "method provider" that provides a Proc. The second is a "method runner" that defines methods dynamically from the Procs it is provided. You will define identical class, instance, and local variables in each and see which ones the dynamic method binds to when it is called.

First, the `Provider`, which will provide the Proc to turn into a method:

```
class Provider
  @@var = "Provider"

  def initialize
    @var = "Provider"
  end

  def self.getMethod
    var = "Provider"
    lambda {
      p "Class variable belongs to: #{@@var}"
      p "Instance variable belongs to: #{@var}"
      p "Local variable belongs to: #{var}"     }
  end
end
```

And then the `Runner`, which will obtain a Proc from `Provider` and add it as a new method:

```
class Runner
  @@var = "Runner"

  def initialize
    @var= "Runner"
  end

  def self.add_method(name, proc)
    var = "Runner"
    define_method name, &proc
  end
end
```

Next, you take the Proc from `Provider` and give it to `Runner` to add using `define_method`:

```
Runner.add_method :experiment, Provider.getMethod
```

And finally, you run our experiment and observe the results:

```
runner = Runner.new
runner.experiment

# Prints:
# "Class variable belongs to: Provider"
# "Instance variable belongs to: Runner"
# "Local variable belongs to: Provider"
```

So you see that locally scoped variables and class variables are bound to the environment that originated the Proc, and instance variables are bound to the environment that has absorbed it as a method.

One final note about accessing instance variables, however: You must initialize them in the object's constructor. Instance variables that are initialized in the body of the class definition outside any method are not available to the dynamically created method. If the variable @var were created like this, for example,

```ruby
class Runner
  @var= "Runner"

  def initialize
    # Do nothing
    # @var was initialized above rather than in here
  end
end
```

then the newly created method would not have any variable named @var in its scope.

Using define_method for Rails Macros

One of the key areas in which Ruby on Rails employs define_method is ActiveRecord associations. Anyone who has used ActiveRecord is familiar with its macro-style associations:

```ruby
class User < ActiveRecord::Base
  has_many :fitness_goals
  has_many :workouts, :through => :goals

  # .. etc

end
```

These associative macros are actually method calls that take place right in the body of your class definition. As the interpreter reads in your model definition file and parses the class, it calls these association-building methods, and numerous helper methods become available on the model class as a result. These helper methods are created dynamically based on the arguments provided to the association call using define_method.

In this section, you'll create your own macro that you can use just as you do the ActiveRecord associations to define helper methods on a model object. You'll call it acts_as_pig_latin, and its job will be to create an alternative accessor method for each field on the model object that returns the pig Latin version of its value.

First, you'll assume a method that turns a single word into its pig Latin equivalent. The following method is borrowed from the "Ruby Tk" chapter of *Programming Ruby*, available at http://ruby-doc.org/docs/ ProgrammingRuby/.

```ruby
def pig(word)
  leadingCap = word =~ /^A-Z/
  word.downcase!
  res = case word
```

```
      when /^aeiouy/
        word+"way"
      when /^([^aeiouy]+)(.*)/
        $2+$1+"ay"
      else
        word
    end
    leadingCap ? res.capitalize : res
  end
```

To create the `acts_as_pig_latin` macro, add the following code at the end of the `config/environment`
`.rb` file in a Rails project. You might want to throw the `pig` method inside the `ActiveRecord::Base` body
as well, if it is not defined elsewhere.

```
class ActiveRecord::Base
  def self.acts_as_pig_latin
    column_names.each do |column|
      meth_name = :"#{column.to_s}_piglatin"
      define_method(meth_name) do
        send(column).split(" ").map{ |word| pig word }.join " "
      end
    end
  end
end
```

This code defines `acts_as_pig_latin` as a class method on `ActiveRecord::Base`, which means that it
can be called directly from the body of a class as it is being parsed by the interpreter, same as with the
`ActiveRecord` associations that you are familiar with. The `acts_as_pig_latin` method iterates over each
column name managed by that particular `ActiveRecord` class and defines a method for each column that
returns the Pig Latin version of an instance's value for that particular column.

The following line:

```
meth_name = :"#{column.to_s}_piglatin"
```

determines the name of the new pig Latin method for a column by appending the suffix `_piglatin` to
the existing column name. Next, a new method by that name is defined. The body of the method calls the
existing accessor for the column value and then applies the `pig` function to each word in the result.

```
define_method(meth_name) do
  send(column).split(" ").map{ |word| pig word }.join " "
end
```

Test this code by adding the macro to an existing `ActiveRecord` model inside a Rails project you have
available:

```
class User < ActiveRecord::Base
  acts_as_pig_latin

  # .. class continues ..
end
```

Run the Ruby on Rails console by typing `script/console` from a command prompt and examine the changes it has made on your model object. Create a new user with `User.new` and examine the methods on it. In the code that follows, we filter the `user.methods` results by rejecting any method that does not end in the suffix `_piglatin`.

```
>> user = User.new
=> #<User id: nil, name: nil, nick: nil, created_at: nil, updated_at: nil>
>> user.methods.reject { |meth| not meth.to_s[/piglatin$/] }
=> ["id_piglatin", "name_piglatin", "nick_piglatin", "created_at_piglatin",
"updated_at_piglatin"]
```

From the return value of the `user.methods` call, it is apparent that several methods now exist on the `User` object containing the suffix `_piglatin`. The `acts_as_pig_latin` macro caused one method per column to be created on the object. Test the functionality by setting the name of your new object and then calling the corresponding pig Latin method:

```
>> user.name = "Grace"
=> "Grace"
>> user.name_piglatin
=> "acegray"
```

Macro Summary

Code macros are a powerful meta-programming technique that can help you write libraries that not only add end-user functionality but also speed your development process. In contrast to the monkey patching examples from the previous chapter, code macros often contain the intelligence necessary to make their own decisions about what code to add to a class on your behalf. In the pig Latin example of the preceding section, the `acts_as_pig_latin` macro inspected the fields that existed on an `ActiveRecord` object and then added one extra method for each of those fields. If you call this macro on an object with four fields, it saves the developer from having to write four methods; if you call it on an object with one hundred fields, it saves the developer from having to write one hundred additional methods.

Although the macros you write probably won't be pig Latin–related, this basic strategy of adding functionality to your objects is a step on the road toward developing your own Ruby-based DSL. It is the core idea behind Rails associations and validations, and also behind the large set of "acts as" plug-ins available for the Rails framework.

Calling Methods That Don't Exist: Objects That Adapt to the Way You Use Them

APIs are usually written like the menu at a restaurant. It may be long and extensive, but what you see is what you get. Ruby is different, though, because it allows you to craft what might be called "meta-APIs." Rather than define the list of methods that the API contains, you define your own interpreter that takes *any* incoming method call and attempts to determine a plan of action in response. Although this style of coding is not appropriate for every situation, it opens a powerful set of patterns that you can use in your own coding to make your code more intuitive and your development more efficient.

The key is that Ruby objects do not support *methods* — they respond to *messages*. Recall from Chapter 8 that Ruby is a *message-passing language*. Calling a method on an object doesn't cause the underlying machine code to immediately push your scope on the stack and jump to the method's address in memory. Instead, it sends a message to the object, asking it to execute the method that was called. You saw this in code with the `send` method available on all objects:

```
user.send(:greet, "Matz")  # Equivalent to user.greet("Matz")
```

The interesting side effect of executing methods by message passing is that nonexistent methods are not necessarily catastrophic error conditions the way they would be in method-calling languages; they are just messages that the receiver does not have a hard-coded response to. All objects in Ruby handle messages that they are not familiar with by passing them to a special function, `method_missing`, which acts as a catch-all opportunity to handle any messages not caught by the methods attached to the object, as Figure 10-1 illustrates.

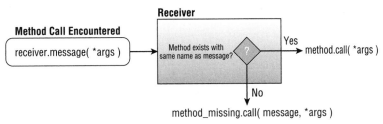

Figure 10-1

Not surprisingly, the default implementation of `method_missing` in Ruby's Kernel module just raises a bunch of exceptions: It determines what the problem was (an undefined method? a violation of private access?) and then raises the appropriate error.

```
static VALUE
rb_method_missing(argc, argv, obj)
    int argc;
    VALUE *argv;
    VALUE obj;
{
    ID id;
    VALUE exc = rb_eNoMethodError;

// * SNIP * (removed by author)

    if (last_call_status & CSTAT_PRIV) {
        format = "private method '%s' called for %s";
    } else if (last_call_status & CSTAT_PROT) {
        format = "protected method '%s' called for %s";
    } else if (last_call_status & CSTAT_VCALL) {
        format = "undefined local variable or method '%s' for %s";
        exc = rb_eNameError;
    } else if (last_call_status & CSTAT_SUPER) {
        format = "super: no superclass method '%s'";
    }

// * SNIP *

    exc = rb_class_new_instance(n, args, exc);
```

```
        ruby_frame = ruby_frame->prev; /* pop frame for "method_missing" */
        rb_exc_raise(exc);

// * SNIP *
}
```

Seeing this code for yourself is important because it clearly demonstrates that the errors raised when making bad method calls come not from the Ruby interpreter but rather from the Ruby object that received the bad method call. In contrast to many other languages, bad method calls are handled entirely from within the flexible world that the programmer has control over. This default implementation of method_missing in the preceding code snippet is responsible for the errors you are accustomed to seeing when you make a bad method call:

```
irb(main):001:0> arr = Array.new
=> []
irb(main):002:0> arr.eat_a_sandwich
NoMethodError: undefined method 'eat_a_sandwich' for []:Array
from (irb):2
```

Because you now know that the NoMethodError thrown on a bad method call is coming from just a regular method and not from the Ruby interpreter, a light should be going off in your head: *I can override this!* And that is exactly what you'll do next.

Some Basic Examples

You start by trying to call a method that doesn't exist:

```
rutabaga
# -> NameError: undefined local variable or method 'rutabaga' for main:Object
```

The NameError raised by this method call is being handled by the default method_missing implementation. The method_missing method takes two arguments. The first is the name of the method called; the second is a list of all the arguments passed to the attempted method call. You'll override this method to cause it to simply print a simple statement instead:

```
def method_missing(method, *args)
  p "You called #{method}(#{args}).. Is that a vegetable?"
end
```

When you call rutabaga again, you no longer see the NameError raised but instead see your message:

```
rutabaga
# -> You called rutabaga().. Is that a vegetable?
```

If you want to still allow Ruby's default error handler to run, you can append a call to super at the end of your custom method_missing implementation:

```
def method_missing(method, *args)
  p "You called #{method}(#{args}).. Is that a vegetable?"
  super
```

```
end

rutabega
# -> You called rutabaga().. Is that a vegetable?
# -> NameError: undefined local variable or method 'rutabaga' for main:Object
```

Recall from previous chapters that any method defined outside an object you have referenced (that is, "in the bare") is really being defined on the root `Object` class. Defining `method_missing` in the preceding manner therefore overrides `method_missing` implementation for all objects in Ruby. To demonstrate this, you'll create an array of symbols and call a method that does not exist. Even though the missing method call is on an `Array` object, the `method_missing` implementation defined previously will catch it as you have last defined.

```
veggies = [ :turnip, :carrot, :daikon ]
veggies.eat
# -> You called eat().. Is that a vegetable?
# -> NameError: undefined local variable or method eat' for main:Object
```

Under normal use, you probably won't be overriding the root implementation of `method_missing` because the consequences are too far reaching. Instead, you will most often write a custom handler for a particular class that you write. Implementing the handler is the same, though — just define `method_missing` inside the class definition.

Example: A Shortcut for Array.each

The `Array` class is a great place to begin because there are numerous ways to use its `method_missing` implementation to reveal the characteristics of the contents of the array. In this section, you'll write a shortcut for the `Array.each` method that allows you to avoid using a block for simple operations.

First, you'll set up the cast of characters to help test the `Array` class's new features. An `Item` is anything with a name that can be washed or thrown at something. A `Veggie` is an `Item` that can also be eaten. A `Trash` is an `Item` that can also be recycled.

```
class Item
  attr_accessor :name
  def initialize(name)
    @name = name.to_s
  end

  def wash
    p "One #{@name} washed!"
  end

  def throw_at(person)
    p "One #{@name} thrown at #{person}"
  end
end

class Veggie < Item
  def eat
    p "One #{@name} eaten!"
  end
```

```
  end

  class Trash < Item
    def recycle
      p "One #{@name} recycled!"
    end
  end
```

And, of course, you need an array of vegetables:

```
  veggies = [:turnip, :carrot, :daikon].map{ |name| Veggie.new(name) }
```

Normally, if you wanted to perform something on each of the members, you would use block-based iteration. You can override `method_missing` to avoid having to use a block when you just want to call a single method on all the objects in the array. So rather than write this:

```
  veggies.each do |veggie|
    veggie.eat
  end
```

you will be able to write this instead:

```
  veggies.eat_each
```

Rather than go right for the `method_missing` implementation, you'll define a method on `Array` that has the same signature as the `send` method but passes whatever it gets directly to each element in the array. You'll call this method `thunk`, because it thunks each element of the array with the message it receives.

```
  class Array
    def thunk(message, *args)
      self.each do |item|
        args.empty? ? item.send(message) : item.send(message, args)
      end
    end
  end
```

Using the `thunk` method, you can send a message to each item in the array, such as this:

```
  veggies.thunk(:eat)
  # Prints:
  # "One turnip eaten!"
  # "One carrot eaten!"
  # "One daikon eaten!"
```

This code fails if one of the objects within the array does not accept the message passed to `thunk`, however. Although you can't prevent this possibility, at least the `thunk` method should attempt to preserve an all-or-nothing behavior so that an error does not cause some objects to change state while leaving others intact. Following is a new version of `thunk` that first checks to see whether all contents of the array support the given message, raising an exception if they don't.

```
class Array
    def contents_support?(message)
        self.inject(true) do |all_ok, item|
            all_ok = all_ok & item.respond_to?(message)
        end
    end

    def thunk(message, *args)
        if contents_support?(message)
            self.each do |item|
                args.empty? ? item.send(message) : item.send(message, args)
            end
        else
            raise "Not all contents of #{self.inspect} respond to method #{method}"
        end
    end
end
```

Now if you add a piece of Trash to your array of veggies:

```
tin_can = Trash.new("tin can")
veggies << tin_can
```

the thunk method will correctly prevent you from being able to call the eat method on the array by raising an exception:

```
veggies.thunk :eat
# -> RuntimeError: Not all contents of [#<Veggie:0x8825c @name="turnip">,
#<Veggie:0x88248 @name="carrot">, #<Veggie:0x88220 @name="daikon">, #<Trash:0x88054
@name="tin can">] respond to method eat
```

Now that the thunk method has a bit of error checking (and after you've removed the tin can from the array with veggies.delete tin_can), you are finally ready to weave thunk into the method_missing implementation.

An important part of using method_missing well is determining extensible ways to convert the missing method name into functionality. Here, you will apply thunk only if the missing method name ends in the characters _each. This accomplishes two goals: First, it unambiguously marks out a specific region of the namespace of possible method names to direct to thunk, leaving all others available for other tasks. Second, it makes the code using this new feature clear to a casual observer — method_missing might permit feats that appear magical, but you should always try to make your code clear and simple.

```
class Array
    def method_missing(method, *args)
        if method.to_s[/_each$/]
            real_method_name = method.to_s[0..-6].to_sym
            thunk(real_method_name, *args)
        else
            super
        end
    end
end
```

Test this dynamic functionality by calling a few methods on the `veggies` array that end in _each.

```
veggies.wash_each
# "One turnip washed!"
# "One carrot washed!"
# "One daikon washed!"

veggies.recycle_each
# RuntimeError: Not all contents of [#<Veggie:0x88270 @name="turnip">,
#<Veggie:0x8825c@name="carrot">, #<Veggie:0x88234 @name="daikon">] respond to
method recycle

veggies.throw_at_each "the giant monster standing behind you as you read this!"
# "One turnip thrown at the giant monster standing behind you as you read this!"
# "One carrot thrown at the giant monster standing behind you as you read this!"
# "One daikon thrown at the giant monster standing behind you as you read this!"
```

Beware of Catching Everything

In the last example of the previous section, I gave two reasons for using the suffix _each to mark a method that should be passed to the new `thunk` operation: It defines an unambiguous subset of the method namespace to use for `thunk`, and it makes the resulting code easy to understand. A third reason that this strategy is a good one is that it makes deciding when to fall back on the default implementation of `method_missing` for error-catching purposes easy. Under most circumstances, it is important to fall back on the default implementation because it provides a predictable way for your code to fail. This becomes especially important in Ruby because of its lax rules regarding parentheses. What could be a variable could also be a method:

```
is_admin_user # Is this a variable or a method call? No way to tell!
```

This means that if you create a poor custom implementation of `method_missing`, your Ruby object will direct all mistyped variable names to `method_missing` rather than throw an error, thus changing the failure semantics of your code. Understandably, that is not a good situation to find yourself in.

With the `thunk` implementation in the last section, the expected error is raised if you try to perform a method outside the scope of _each that does not exist:

```
veggies.puree
# NoMethodError: undefined method 'puree' for #<Array:0x875c8>
```

But watch what happens if you take out the fallback to the default `method_missing` implementation by removing the `else { super }` segment of code from the overridden `method_missing` body.

```
class Array
    def method_missing(method, *args)
        if method.to_s[/_each$/]
            real_method_name = method.to_s[0..-6].to_sym
            thunk(real_method_name, *args)
        end
        # No else {super} clause anymore
```

```
      end
   end

   veggies.puree          # This call should fail
   # returns nil              ... but it doesn't
```

By not remembering to fall back to the `super` implementation of `method_missing`, two outcomes occur, both of which risk hiding errors in your code:

❏ Any method calls to the object will succeed, even though some probably shouldn't.

❏ Any mistyped variable names within the object's definition will be sent to `method_missing`, even though this is certainly incorrect.

The lesson: Always think about the scope of messages that you would like to accept with your custom `method_missing` implementation, and make sure to fall back to the default implementation in any other circumstance. An effective way to do this consistently is to implement your dynamic code the way you did it with `thunk`. Rather than have `method_missing` implement the extra functionality, have `method_missing` operate as a router, matching messages to elsewhere-defined functionality and failing if a match cannot be made.

method_missing Patterns

The many uses of `method_missing` tend to fall into a few categories or patterns. Thinking about your code in terms of these patterns will help you decide when it might be appropriate to use `method_missing` as an implementation option.

❏ **Data-driven objects:** When your code object exists to make an external and dynamic data structure available, and you'd like to let that data structure dictate the way your code is used. Examples include:

  ❏ *ActiveRecord:* Each `ActiveRecord` object reflects on its corresponding table in the database schema to provide getters, setters, and search functionality.

  ❏ *ActiveRDF:* The RDF equivalent of `ActiveRecord` creates objects around RDFS resources and uses `method_missing` to interpret method calls as getters and setters that operate on the underlying graph connected to a resource.

  ❏ *Dynamic Dictionaries:* The foreign language dictionary that you will create in a few pages wraps around a web-based dictionary to provide translation.

❏ **Creative API:** When you would like to provide an API that is used for the construction of a document. Calls made into this API are dynamically translated into entities within the document.

  ❏ *XML Builder:* The `Builder` class in Rails provides a way to easily construct XML documents by simply writing Ruby code. It interprets messages sent to `method_missing` as requests for the creation of new XML entities.

❏ **Easy reading methods:** When you want to provide English-like methods instead of parameter-based ones (such as `Person.find_by_name`).

  ❏ *ActiveRecord* — `ActiveRecord` provides search functionality through `method_missing` when the missing method involves the prefix `find_by`. For example, the method call `Users.find_by_` `first_name(name)` would perform a query on the `first_name` column for all records in which it equals the provided `name` argument.

❑ **Facades:** When you employ the Facade pattern to wrap the functionality of other objects and services within an object.

    ❑ *Aspect-style wrappers:* The wrapper that you will see implemented in the following section provides a facade for an object while allowing before and after filters to be inserted around its execution.

Each of these patterns will be highlighted throughout the rest of the chapter in examples, some using the Rails framework and others operating independently of Rails.

Implementing method_missing Patterns

This section looks at how you might apply three of the different `method_missing` patterns in your Rails projects: facades (and filters), data-driven objects, and creative APIs. These examples mimic the way that meta-programming is used in the Rails framework and will make you better able to extend it and develop with it.

Facades

The `method_missing` feature is a great way to implement the facade pattern with some extra perks. A facade is a frequently used pattern in which an object (the facade) wraps one or more other objects and provides a unified interface that is simpler or more appropriate for some developer audiences. The `method_missing` facade, which I call a wrapper (the class name will be `Wrapper`), contains the object that is to be wrapped and simply passes all unknown methods straight through to the contained object. By default, this facade behaves exactly like the interface of the contained object, passing calls straight through. Each call that the facade developer wishes to customize can simply be implemented manually as a method on the wrapper.

Here is an example of how you might implement the wrapper.

```
class Wrapper
  def initialize(obj)
    @obj = obj

  end

  def method_missing(meth, *args, &block)
    result = @obj.send(meth, *args, &block)
    result
  end
end
```

You can use this facade around any object by passing the object to a new `Wrapper` instance. The following code shows how you might wrap an array of symbols:

```
wrapped_array = Wrapper.new [:barley, :hops, :water, :yeast]
```

Any method call that does not exist on the `Wrapper` class will be passed directly through to the contained object:

```
p wrapped_array.size
# Prints: 4

p wrapped_array.join(', ')
# Prints: barley, hops, water, yeast
```

Note that methods that do exist on the `Wrapper` object (such as `inspect`) will not get handled by `method_missing` and thus will not get sent to the contained object.

```
p wrapped_array.inspect
# Prints: #<Wrapper:0x89ee0 @obj=[:barley, :hops, :water, :yeast]>
```

To create a true facade, you will have to override these methods manually to cause them to pass through to the contained object.

Adding Filter Support to the Wrapper

After you have constructed a facade around an object, it is easy to begin implementing aspect-style filtering to simulate the way that Rails controllers allow before, after, and around filters. The key is that by implementing a dynamic facade around the object, you have taken control of the context of the execution of its methods. Rather than use `method_missing` to pass straight through to the methods on the contained object, you can maintain lists of Proc objects that you can call before, after, and around the inner method call takes place.

For this example, you will just implement around filters. Start by adding some scaffolding to the `Wrapper` definition to add, remove, and store Procs that will act like filters.

```
class Wrapper

  def initialize(obj)
    @obj = obj
    @around_filters = []
  end

  def add_around_filter(proc)
    @around_filters.push proc
  end

  def remove_around_filter(proc)
    @around_filters.delete proc
  end

end
```

Next, you need to establish a set of rules that an around filter will need to conform to in order to work. Because you must pass control to the around filter, and because, by definition, the around filter executes *around* the inner method call, these rules form an informal contract that must be followed for the wrapper object to function correctly. Similar rules are set up in the Ruby on Rails documentation for controller filters. Here is a quote from the `around_filter` Ruby Docs in Ruby on Rails:

> To use a block as an `around_filter`, pass a block taking as args both the controller and the action block. You cannot call yield directly from an `around_filter` block; explicitly call the action block instead.

Your around filter will use a similar set of rules:

1. Each around filter will be implemented as a Proc object.

2. The around filter takes two arguments. The first is the name of the method call that prompted the execution of the filter. The second is a Proc representing the code that is being wrapped around to make that method call possible.

3. The around filter is responsible for performing the `call` method on the provided Proc if the contained functionality is to be executed. (There are some circumstances in which the around filter may decide not to call its enclosed functionality. An authorization-performing filter, for example, might raise a `MethodCallNotAuthorized` exception instead.)

4. The around filter must return the value returned by the Proc provided to it.

Together, these rules allow for a simple filter implementation that you will see in a moment. They also provide enough information to write filters without knowing how the mechanism that manages them is implemented. You'll write two filters to use with the `Wrapper` class before you even implement the extension that will allow their execution:

The first, `timer`, records the time it takes to perform a particular operation:

```
timer = lambda { |method, proc|
  t1 = Time.now
  result = proc.call
  t2 = Time.now
  p "Method call to #{method} completed in #{t2 - t1}"
  result
}
```

The code for the timer filter is a Proc object that takes the required two objects (`method` and `proc`), executes the Proc (`result = proc.call`), and returns the `result` object as its own return value. Around the Proc's execution, the current time is recorded, and afterward, a statement is printed to the console containing the time that the method call took to complete.

The second filter you will implement shows an alternative way to implement the pig Latin conversion shown earlier in the chapter. The first time you saw this conversion, it was performed as a preparatory step using a macro called `acts_as_pig_latin`. This macro iterated over the methods on the object and used `define_method` to create an alternative set of methods that wrapped the existing ones but returned the result in pig Latin. Now, using `method_missing` and your `Wrapper` class, you will implement the pig Latin conversion in an aspect-oriented fashion as a filter that can be applied to and removed from a wrapped object without your having to modify that object's code.

```ruby
pig_latin = lambda { |method, proc|
  result = proc.call
  return pig(result) if result.is_a? String
  return pig(result.to_s).to_sym if result.is_a? Symbol

  result
}
```

The pig Latin filter technically behaves in the spirit of an after filter. It immediately executes the wrapped code, inspects its result, and converts it to pig Latin if it is a string or a symbol.

You have a way to add and store filters within the Wrapper object, a set of rules describing how filters should behave, and two example filters ready to try out. Now you must find a way to integrate filter-calling into the method_missing implementation of Wrapper. In the same fashion used before, you will implement the filter-wrapping code in a stand-alone method, using method_missing just to delegate incoming messages to that method.

The embed method that follows acts like the send method in that it takes a message, arguments, and optional block and executes it against the contained @obj object. It is different in that it also takes an index into the filter array to specify a filter to wrap around the method call.

```ruby
def embed(filter_num, meth, *args, &block)
  if (filter_num >= @around_filters.size)
    return @obj.send(meth, *args, &block)
  else
    return @around_filters.at(filter_num).call(meth, lambda {
             embed(filter_num + 1, meth, *args, &block)
           })
  end
end
```

If the array index equals or exceeds the size of the filter container, the embed method simply executes the requested method call on @obj. If the array index does not exceed the filter count, it executes the specified filter, passing it in a block containing another call to embed with an incremented filter index. In this way, embed acts as a recursive method with the call to @obj as a terminating base case.

To complete this example, redefine method_missing to pass straight through to the embed method:

```ruby
def method_missing(meth, *args, &block)
  embed(0, meth, *args, &block)
end
```

Finally, you create a new wrapped array using the new code and add your two filters:

```ruby
my_array = Wrapper.new [:barley, :hops, :water, :yeast]
my_array.add_around_filter timer
my_array.add_around_filter pig_latin
```

Now try calling a few methods to watch the filters in action:

```ruby
p my_array.size
# "Method call to size completed in 2.8e-05"
# 4
```

```
p my_array.at(1)
# "Method call to at completed in 5.9e-05"
# :opshay
```

This example demonstrates that `method_missing` enables more than just dynamic decisions about which method to call. It also provides a way for you to wrap objects and manage the context under which they execute.

Data-Driven Objects: Building a Language Translator

Data-driven objects are objects that exist to make some externally defined data object available. They are a generalization of the `ActiveRecord` pattern, which describes objects that wrap around a database record to expose its field. Data-driven objects include objects that follow the `ActiveRecord` pattern, but they may also describe objects that wrap around XML entities, RDF or OWL entities, or even remote services. Programming with `method_missing` is an excellent way to create data-driven objects in your code.

In this example, you will construct a data-driven object that maps around a virtual dataset: human language. You will treat an external service (Google Translate) as a remote object that can receive messages in the source language and respond to them with the corresponding message in the destination language. This basic operation demonstrates the way that `ActiveRecord` is able to "magically" wrap around your database schema automatically without having to dig into the scores of database-specific code that performs the legwork to implement the larger idea.

First, you set up the scaffolding around your object. Two constants are defined: `GoogleTranslateUri` contains the address of the remote translation service, and `ResultRegex` contains a regular expression that will extract a translation result from the web page. In addition, the constructor takes two variables, `from` and `to`, that represent the source and destination languages.

```
class Translator
  require 'net/http'
  GoogleTranslateUri = URI.parse 'http://translate.google.com/translate_t'
  ResultRegex = /<div id=result_box dir=ltr>([^<]*)<\/div>/

  def initialize(from, to)
    @from, @to = from, to
  end
end
```

To continue the pattern described previously, you implement the translation functionality in a method outside `method_missing` so that you can save `method_missing` for just routing incoming messages. The `perform_translation` method makes an HTTP post to Google's Translate service and extracts the translation result using the `ResultRegex` pattern.

```
def perform_translation(text)
  response = Net::HTTP.post_form(GoogleTranslateUri, {
      'hl'=>'en',
      'ie'=>'UTF8',
      'text'=>text,
      'langpair'=>"#{@from}|#{@to}"
  })
```

```
    response.body[ResultRegex]
    $1
end
```

To complete the example, you direct `method_missing` to pass any unknown messages through to the `perform_translation` method.

```
def method_missing(meth, *args)
  perform_translation(meth.to_s)
end
```

Try the translator by instantiating a copy with English and Spanish. Good Unicode support in Ruby is just now beginning to emerge as of Ruby 1.9, so languages that use the ASCII character set are the safest to stick with for the code here.

```
spanish = Translator.new :en, :es

p spanish.library
# Biblioteca

p spanish.computer
# Computadora
```

To translate a phrase with multiple words, just use the `send` method to request a response from the object:

```
p spanish.send "Quick! Hold my cheese sandwich!"
# Rápido! Mantenga mi sandwich de queso!
```

Testing a few simple words and phrases with the `Translator` object, notice the similarities to `Active Record` models that make data-driven objects with `method_missing` a pleasant paradigm to program with. The object exists only to broker a connection between some data source and the code developer. It has no knowledge of the actual data that it serves as a facade for. Routing via `method_missing` is used to translate method calls into requests for data operations.

Creative APIs (The XML Builder)

The code example of Rails-style `method_missing` code is the creation of Creative APIs. A Creative API is an API that exists to help the developer use code to build a document for export. Creative APIs are different from regular document-centric APIs in that they provide little if any methods besides a constructor. The "API" part of a creative API is defined implicitly by the developer's calls to it. In other words, every conceivable method call is part of the API, and `method_missing` is used to catch these method calls and translate them into structures in the document for export.

The Ruby XML Builder is the best example of such an API, and it is a good example of how a very small piece of code can produce a powerful and complete library if used correctly. At this point in the chapter, you can probably guess how the implementation works: Each message sent to the `Builder` object is interpreted as a request for a new XML tag to be created. Any hash tables passed as arguments to the message are interpreted as tag attributes. The tag's content is determined by one of three possibilities. If the message has any `String` arguments, the tag contains the concatenated values of those arguments. If the message contains a block, the tag wraps around the execution of the block (which may create more tags). If neither of these situations holds, the tag is empty. Figure 10-2 contains a simplified depiction of the core decision making of the `Builder` object.

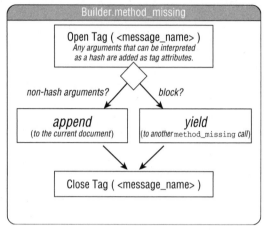

Figure 10-2

The XML Builder represents a quintessential example of Ruby style. Its functionality is the same as document builders in Java and other languages, but it exposes its functionality using `method_missing` in the novel way that Ruby is known for.

Reflection

I've covered a lot of ground in the last three chapters about ways to design and write code in Ruby that take full advantage of its special language characteristics. Many of these techniques have involved dynamically modifying code, whether to affect the behavior of an object created by someone else or to craft objects of your own that can be molded by their environment. Just as important as being able to change an object is the ability to *reflect* upon that object — to inspect its structure and see what is already there. This section provides an overview for some of Ruby's reflection capabilities that allow you to inspect an object to see what it is made of.

Reflection can be useful both for run-time logic as well as debugging. During run-time, these methods can help your dynamic code be more intelligent about the way it handles objects. Because Ruby is a duck-typed language, sometimes you have to use reflection to inspect whether an object you have been provided contains the capabilities you require, resolving type-related errors before they happen.

When you are debugging, the following methods can be invaluable tools for learning and observing how your dynamic code is behaving. Self-modifying code is difficult to write, and the best way to get a better feel for it is to boot up an `irb` shell, try a few techniques, and use these reflective methods to examine their effects.

Variables and Constants

You can use the following methods to inspect the variables and constants that are registered for an object:

Method	Description
class_variables	Returns all class variables
instance_variables	Returns all instance variables of a class instance
constants	Returns all constants defined within a class

As an example, consider the following two classes. The parent class, `Photo`, defines a class variable, `@@favorite_color`, an instance variable (`@name`), and a constant (`Color`). All three of these variables are given values. The child class, `MagazinePhoto`, inherits from `Photo` and defines its own instance variable, `@magazine`, and also defines a second constant, `PaperType`.

```
class Photo
 attr_accessor :name
  Color = true
  @@favorite_color = :forest_green

  def initialize(photo_name)
    @name = photo_name
  end
end

class MagazinePhoto < Photo
  attr_accessor :magazine
  PaperType = :glossy

  def initialize(photo_name, mag_name)
    super(photo_name)
    @magazine = mag_name
  end
end
```

Next, you will call the preceding reflective methods to see how they report the variables of a class and how they handle the object hierarchy.

First, you ask the child class for its constants and see that you get a list of the constants defined both on the child and parent:

```
p MagazinePhoto.constants
# -> ["PaperType", "Color"]
```

Asking the child class for its class variables, you arrive at a similar result:

```
p MagazinePhoto.class_variables
# -> ["@@favorite_color"]
```

Finally, instantiating an instance of the child class and asking it for its instance variables, you receive a list of both the MagazinePhoto and Photo variables as well:

```
mp = MagazinePhoto.new("Polar Bear", "Outdoors Magazine")
p mp.instance_variables
# -> ["@name", "@magazine"]
```

Note that Ruby's variable initialization is lazy: The attr_accessor method alone does not cause instance variables to be created, but rather just the accessor and mutator methods that provide access to them. That means that the instance_variable method returns only those variables that have actually been initialized with some value. In the following class, the @variable instance variable is not initialized in the constructor as it is in the preceding code:

```
class LazyInit
  attr_accessor :variable
end
```

Calling the instance_variables method on a newly created instance, you see that the instance isn't aware of any instance variables yet:

```
laz = LazyInit.new

p laz.instance_variables
# -> []
```

Only when you set the variable does it appear in this list:

```
laz.variable = "Hey!"

p laz.instance_variables
# -> ["@variable"]
```

Methods

Ruby provides several ways to examine the methods that are registered for a class, as well, as listed in the following table.

Method	Description
instance_methods	Returns all public instance methods on the receiver
public_instance_methods	Same behavior as instance_methods
private_instance_methods	Returns all private instance methods on the receiver
protected_instance_methods	Returns all protected instance methods on the receiver
singleton_methods	Returns an array of the names for all singleton methods on the receiver

Any of the methods in the preceding table takes an optional Boolean argument that specifies whether to include inherited methods in the return results. By default, the value of this argument is set to `true`. If you pass in `false` instead, only those methods explicitly defined for the receiver will be returned. Watch the difference between these two behaviors demonstrated in the following segment of code. You'll define two classes, a parent class `Person` and a child class `Surfer`, each with a singleton class method.

```
class Person
   def Person.hi
      "Hello!"
   end
end

class Surfer < Person
  def Surfer.bye
    "Peace out"
  end
end
```

When calling `singleton_methods` on `Surfer` with the implicit `true` parameter, both methods defined in `Person` and `Surfer` are returned. When calling `singleton_methods` with `false` as an argument, only the methods defined in `Surfer` are returned.

```
p Surfer.singleton_methods
# -> ["hi", "bye"]

p Surfer.singleton_methods(false)
# -> ["bye"]
```

The rest of these methods work just as you would expect them to given their descriptions. Try running the `irb` shell and experimenting with them to get a feel for how to use them!

Modules

Recall from Chapter 9 that mixins enable you to inject functionality contained within a module into a class. Objects in Ruby still conform to a strict, single-parent hierarchical model, but mixins allow them to reap many of the benefits of multiple inheritance.

Method	Description
`included_modules`	Returns a list of all modules included in the receiver's class

Calling this method on the `String` class, we see three modules included: `Enumerable`, `Comparable`, and `Kernel`.

```
irb(main):004:0* String.included_modules
=> [Enumerable, Comparable, Kernel]
```

If you wanted to see which methods on the `String` are covered by one of these modules, you can use the `instance_methods` method just covered:

```
irb(main):005:0> Comparable.instance_methods
=> ["==", ">=", "<", "<=", ">", "between?"]
```

Summary

This chapter completes the three-chapter segment on advanced Ruby. Although these chapters do not deal with web development specifically, they are incredibly important to Rails-based developers. Many of the features of Rails are "nice to have," but it is the combination of these features through meta-programming techniques such as `define_method` and `method_missing` that make Ruby on Rails the framework that it is. By understanding how to develop advanced Ruby, you gain a deeper understanding of how to craft reusable code that flows as well as the Rails framework does when it comes to web-related tasks.

The previous two chapters discussed various methods of executing code: Procs, blocks, mixins, monkey patching, and a lot of scope issues. This chapter built on that foundation by moving into dynamic object behavior and modification. Using `define_method`, you were able to define object macros that constructed methods on the fly at run-time. Using `method_missing`, you were able to create message handlers that enabled objects to respond to methods even if they did not exist.

The next chapter returns to Rails-specific topics and discusses issues related to schema development. The database may not be the most exciting part of your web application, but in many ways it is the keystone that holds everything together. Chapter 11, "How I Learned to Stop Worrying and Love the Schema," covers Rails-style schema migrations, team schema management, and tricks for getting the most out of your database tables.

11

How I Learned to Stop Worrying and Love the Schema

The elevator doors slid open to reveal a futuristic command center worthy of monitoring the Internet itself. It should be so worthy — that is exactly why it was built. Deep in the heart of the Big City, unbeknownst to all but a few, was the INOC, the Internet Network Operations Center.

"What do you mean we can't track them!" A deep, gruff voice boomed from the heavyset man standing behind the analysts.

"They don't have network connectivity, sir. There's no way to get a trace," a URI at one of the terminals said nervously.

"Well, I need a trace!" the head man shouted. "Bryant! What do you have over there? Where's our exploratory team?"

A man on the side of the room almost dropped his coffee upon being called out. "Ummm," he stalled, shuffling through scattered papers. The stalling saved him, because the man in charge soon noticed Web and the others standing in front of the elevator doors.

"Web! It's you!" he strode across the room to the group, not noticing Schema's fallen body until he got there. His voice lost its military bark and his expression softened.

"Schema, too," he said quietly, shaking his head. "None of us saw it coming." He looked up at Jen. "I'm glad the rest of you are safe. Come with me into the briefing room and I'll catch you up on what's happening."

The glass-walled briefing room sat off to the side of the INOC and had just enough room to fit the large conference table that had been installed. Jen, Rusty, Matz, and Web sat on one side of the table with the man, who Web now knew was General Operand, on the other side.

The General spent half an hour explaining the events that had unfolded. Web listened intently. Jen and Rusty battered him with questions. And Matz stared silently into the empty space in front of him. He hadn't spoken since the street.

Matz was right — they had broadcast an exploit across the television waves that destroyed the code of any Ruby program who happened to encounter it. It had caught hundreds off guard that they knew about; maybe there were thousands more.

"But what about the toasters?" Jen protested. "It doesn't make sense."

"We misread the toaster intel, Jen. Flying Toasters was the name of the virus they broadcast. The screen-saver purchases were just a ploy."

The General explained to them that the URIs on reserve were being called together to mount an offensive. Root DNS Server buildings were being used as the rendezvous points. The on-duty teams that were ready and waiting had already been sent out.

"They hit us hard with a surprise attack up front, and it's going to get harder," the General said, holding nothing back. "Frankly, I'm not sure how to proceed. We know that at some point, they have to attack us in the real world, but we can't track their movements because the compilers come from another age. They're all off the grid."

"If we don't figure something out soon, I'm afraid it will be too late." He looked at Web with an expressionless face and said quietly, "I'm sorry, Web."

Matz looked up from his blank gaze and straight at the General.

"General," he cut in, "I think I know what to do."

The database is the unsung hero of web development. The web page provides the aesthetics and excitement, and the application logic provides the features; it's easy to see how the off-the-shelf data repositories get forgotten in the mix. But at the same time, they are the keystone of web application development because they provide the single and reliable source into which all state for the application is kept. This chapter discusses how to streamline database development and use the Rails framework to enhance the simple object model that is built into databases. It starts with the concept of migration-based development and finishes with features such as serialization and Single Table Inheritance.

Bringing the Database into the Picture: The LAMP Stack

The Web is a place championed by open source development. Its very origins as a method to publish and cross-reference research materials stem from an open and cooperative spirit. Although many industrial-strength development kits and practices exist for heavy industry, many developers who come to the Web begin with the open source offerings and never need to leave them as their careers progress.

Open source web development and deployment almost always follow what is called the LAMP model — a stack of tools including Linux, Apache, MySQL, and PHP/Perl/Python. In this chapter, you will also refer to sites using Rails as being under the LAMP model even though it differs a bit from what is traditionally thought of as LAMP. Figure 11-1 shows the software layer of this stack aligned horizontally.

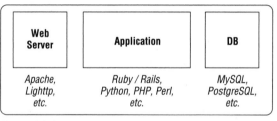

Figure 11-1

As the popularity of a project grows, the idea of the LAMP stack is that each tier of the stack is able to scale independently of the others as needs arise. The web server manages HTTP connections and static files and blindly passes off all other requests to the application. The application decides how a request should be answered, formulates the result, and fetches and stores all data related to the request from the database. The database simply stores and provides data access. In theory, this allows for a straightforward path for scaling up with the needs of your site; Figure 11-2 shows an arbitrary example of this.

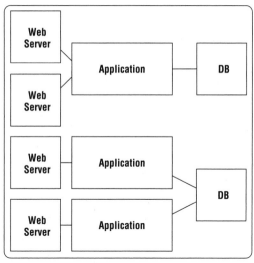

Figure 11-2

Most of the discussion in this book is focused on the components that exist inside the Application box of this stack, but no one component really steals the show from the others. Although you might spend 80 percent of your time in the application layer, each of the three components is completely dependent on the others for your web application to be of use.

In LAMP-style web applications, the database usually serves as the keeper of all state, from permanent user records to dynamic session data. Every request to the server is usually associated with a corresponding set of queries to the database to retrieve the current context of the user's interaction and then write back the new information that has changed. Organizing all that information in a schema is, therefore, a large and important task, even if the schema does not take nearly as much time to code as the application that uses it.

Despite the critical importance of the schema, the open source tools available to assist you with schema development are not as advanced and plentiful as the open source tools that the application layer of the LAMP stack enjoys. For our application source code, we have sophisticated version control and bug-tracking mechanisms to enable life-cycle management and group development. Yet many developers still keep schema definitions in large text files (called *dumpfiles*, because most databases have a command that lets you *dump* the schema to a *file* on disk.) As a result, there is a serious challenge facing web developers related to database scalability, but not the kind of scalability that results from heavy loads. Instead, the problem is a project-management one: figuring out how to develop your database schema across a team and evolve it over time.

Dumpfile-based schema development does not scale in a few important ways. It does not scale over the lifetime of a project because it does not provide any notion of versioning or incremental development. It does not scale across multiple developers because it does not provide an easy way to divide and coordinate work. It does not scale across multiple environments because each database vendor and version has specific peculiarities about how they handle data import (those linefeed characters, database specific tricks, and omitted commas at the end of the lines *will* catch up to you!).

So although database optimization and usage strategies can (and will) be debated ad infinitum, one certainty is that a lot can be done to optimize the development practices we use when working with databases. Because Rails development is always done in conjunction with a database back end, and because so much of the Rails philosophy is about improving code quality by improving the developer's experience, it is appropriate that Rails offers a solution to the database development scalability problem.

Thinking in Migrations

`ActiveRecord` provides a novel way to perform schema development called *migrations*. Whereas traditional database development centers around the database schema as a single large entity expressed as a file containing a set of `CREATE TABLE` statements (among others), migration-based development treats the schema as a living, evolving entity that begins as an empty database and evolves over the course of the project to reflect new needs.

Developing in the style of migrations, your database schema is defined neither at one time nor in one place. Instead, it is defined as a series of incremental improvements, each building on the last, the same way that code slowly comes together on a project. Each of these incremental improvements is called a migration. Each migration describes only the operations necessary to transform the schema from the version before to the next level. This process is depicted in Figure 11-3.

Figure 11-3

In practice, each migration usually contains a small, single unit of work. This unit of work might be adding a table or altering the structure of one that came before it. The migration is checked into the repository as a file by itself containing a Ruby class, so there is never any question as to why a piece of the schema is the way it is: Every change to the schema can be documented from within the Ruby code and traced back to the user who checked it in.

In developing a schema like this, the set of migration definitions themselves become a form of chronological documentation for your schema. Each migration tells a small bit of its overall story:

```
001_create_users.rb
002_create_profiles.rb
003_add_profile_link_to_users.rb
```

Contrast looking at the set of files above to a structural dumpfile in the format used on many development projects. A newcomer looking at a migration-based schema doesn't only immediately understand what the major components of your schema are; he or she also can follow along with the evolution of your project's requirements and your thinking as a schema developer. If that newcomer wants to make a change, doing so is as simple as adding a new migration at the end that defines those actions that constitute the desired change, cleanly separating them from the rest of the schema definition for testing, tracking, and documentation purposes.

The versioning aspect of migrations is also a novel one. Traditional dumpfile-based development may use schema definitions that are checked into a versioned repository, but the dumpfile itself is an all-or-nothing definition, providing no notion of versioning from the standpoint of the database schema. In other words, the only way to, say, roll back your schema to three versions prior is to wipe the database clean and then load the dumpfile from three versions back. Because each migration must declare both how to implement its changes and how to remove its changes, developers using migrations are able to roll forward and backward between versions as incremental changes to a living schema. This capability creates a convenient environment for testing schema changes as they are being developed, permitting developers to back up and redo a recent change if needed.

Finally, migrations do for schema development what languages such as Ruby, PHP, and Python do for HTML development: They embed the task of performing schema definitions within the context of a scripting language, thereby enabling all the niceties that come with that language to be mixed into the schema definition. Your schema definition no longer has to be static declarative script, but instead is an active program whose ultimate result is to change the schema of your database. This means that loops, conditions, and even web service calls are all valid from within the schema definition — an enormous difference from what you have available in a .SQL file. Sticking to the Ruby-based API for database operations, your definitions are also protected against the peculiarities of one database over another; you can develop for Oracle, MySQL, PostgreSQL, and any other database with an ActiveRecord adapter with the same unified set of migrations.

Migration development is a powerful new way to approach your database schema, and the first half of this chapter will discuss how it works, how to write a migration, and how to manage migrations when developing on a team. The API documentation available for free online is excellent, so I don't need to rehash it here. Instead, this chapter will provide a bit of discussion about each of those migration topics to enhance the API-centric documentation already available.

Writing Migrations

A single migration is described by a regular Ruby class that extends the ActiveRecord::Migration class and overrides two special methods, self.up and self.down. The former represents the change that the migration contributes to the schema, and the latter represents the steps necessary to undo that change. No other requirements are placed on the size or complexity of the Migration class as long as these two methods are defined, leaving developers with the full pallet of Ruby's flexibility to accomplish these two tasks.

The following code shows an example of a simple migration. This migration, called `CreateLanguages`, creates a table intended to store ISO 639-3 language information for use in a multilingual application. The `self.up` step creates a simple table with four fields and adds an index to the field containing the ISO 369-3 code. The `self.down` step simply removes the table.

```ruby
class CreateLanguages < ActiveRecord::Migration

  def self.up
    create_table :languages { |table|
      # 'code' is the three-letter ISO 639-3 Code
      table.string :english_name, :native_spelling, :code
    }
    add_index(:languages, :code)
  end

  def self.down
    drop_table :languages
  end

end
```

You can find the entire migration API available online on the Rails API documentation site, but migrations need not be just Ruby-ized SQL; some of the framework's true power becomes apparent when migrations rely on external libraries or data to influence schema definition and alter the state of the current schema and data within. These types of migrations could do anything from encrypting a field previously in plain-text to performing heavy computations on the data within your database to baseline a new reporting system that you are about to add.

Imagine that you are writing a migration that comes packaged with a plug-in to an existing web application. That application connects foreign language learning partners from different languages, and your plug-in enables the site to be translated into each of the possible languages a user can register with. You know that the existing language learning application has an API with a method call that returns a list of languages that the administrator has enabled:

```
# GET /api/supported_languages
eng
fra
spa
ita
cmn
jpn
ara
hin
```

You can write your plug-in migration to take advantage of this API to enable only those languages that the site already supports for your plug-in. Your first migration installs the table that contains possible translation languages and loads seed data into that table.

Your next migration is where you can see the additional power of Ruby. It uses this API to activate only those languages that the site's API returns as valid, using an HTTP GET to the API as the filter:

```ruby
class FilterLanguages < ActiveRecord::Migration

  def self.up
      add_column :languages, :active, :boolean, :default => 0

      # Enable by default whichever languages are returned by the API

      open( "http://your_company.com/api/supported_langugages" ) do | languages |
        languages.each_line.collect! { |language| " iso_639_3 = '#{language}' " }
      end
      or_statement = languages.join ' OR '

      Language.find(:all, :conditions => or_statement).each {
          |language|
          language.active = true
          language.save
      }
  end

  def self.down
      remove_column :languages, :active
  end
end
```

The preceding `self.up` step first adds a new column named `active` to the languages table and sets the default value to `false`. The value of this column will represent whether the language should be surfaced to the user as a potential language for viewing the site. The migration then makes the API call by reading the data at `http://your_company.com/api/supported_languages` and parses this document to extract a list of ISO 639-3 names, combining them into a `WHERE` clause for the database operation.

Although this bit of code may seem excessive for the simple example shown here, the power of migrations is clear. In addition to organizing your schema definition into logical, documentable, versioned steps, they provide powerful building blocks into which any legal Ruby code may be inserted. A migration might use the `RAILS_ENV` variable to make a run-time decision about which set of seed data to load — development, test, or production — for example. Or it may introspect into the machine's hardware characteristics to decide how many columns on a table to index.

Performing Schema Migrations

After migrations have been created to define various stages of your database schema, developers can easily move back and forth between schema versions with the `db:migrate` rake task that comes with Rails. Running `rake db:migrate` causes `ActiveRecord` to perform all migrations necessary to bring the existing database schema up to the latest defined version. The migrate task can be run alone to bring a database up to speed with the most current definition, or an optional `VERSION = x` argument can be provided to specify a particular version of the schema to which to migrate.

`ActiveRecord` keeps a small table named `schema_info` that stores a single row stating which version the current schema represents. This table provides the basis for `ActiveRecord` to decide which migrations it should perform during the `db:migrate` task and whether it should perform the migration forward (with `self.up`) or backward (with `self.down`). If the table does not exist or if it states that the current version is zero, then `ActiveRecord` starts from the first migration, executing them successively until the desired version is reached. If you have already run migrations in the past, `ActiveRecord` compares the current schema version in the `schema_info` table against the desired version number and rolls you either forward or backward appropriately.

Team Schema Development

Migrations make it possible for schema development to be a shared responsibility across a team, but they do not make it effortless. In many ways, using migrations on a team creates strange perversions of version control. Migrations offer schema versioning, but it is very difficult to make multiple versions of the migration files themselves without causing a lot of group confusion. Nevertheless, if a process is followed, it is an entirely possible feat. Here are four rules to help your team use migrations to develop your schema as a team effort.

1. **Pass around a virtual baton that enables only one developer at a time to create models and migrations**. The existing migrations system in Rails is based on a strict ordering of the migration files embedded within their filenames:

```
Macintosh-3:migrate ted$ ls
001_create_users.rb
002_create_apps.rb
003_create_memberships.rb
004_create_locations.rb
005_create_addresses.rb
```

The `generate` script for creating a new model object and the one for creating a new migration both automatically create a new migration file with the next number available. Problems occur when two developers each independently create a new model, cause the file to be generated, and then check this in; all of a sudden, the ordering is broken:

```
004_create_rabbits.rb
004_create_giant_metal_objects.rb
```

Rails development teams choose a number of different strategies to cope with this problem. Some designate a single developer with the responsibility for developing the schema, and all database-related requests must go through that developer. Other teams just require that all developers synchronize with the repository before committing (which all developers should do anyway), but this does not account well for the number of conflicting changes that may be taking place in parallel in a large team environment. Still other tools have been created that provide alternatives to Rails migrations that ease the pain of team development.

A good strategy that combines these alternatives can be reached by creating a "model baton" that can be passed from developer to developer. If you all work in the same location, laminate a funny picture and stick a magnet on the back of it to post it on doors or cubicles. If you collaborate over the Internet, keep some list on a Wiki for sign-ups and baton passing. Only the developer with the baton is allowed to run the `script/generate` command to create models and migrations.

Why so strict? Why not use the baton to just limit who gets to commit new models and migrations? Because it is always easier to set the rule strictly and let the real world break it as needed. Sometimes a change to the database schema dramatically alters how components will fit together. If multiple people are working on changes in parallel, some of these changes might depend on design features that will get overhauled by others. So, only one person at a time is allowed to even create new models and migrations. Of course, that's just the rule — if you want to break it, then find the person who currently has the baton, describe the changes you want to make in parallel, and ask her whether that change will be okay. This method preserves mutual ownership over the model while still placing a controlled process to minimize the risk of parallel changes crashing into each other.

2. **Never "hold your place" by checking in an empty migration**. The db/migrate directory that contains migration definitions operates as a queue of sorts, but unfortunately, you do not have control over how and when it is accessed. If you check an empty migration into your source repository just to reserve yourself a spot, you run the risk of other developers updating to receive your empty migration and running the migrate script to roll their database schema version forward. Migrating forward over an empty migration will make ActiveRecord believe that it has already performed that migration, even if its contents were empty. When you check in the real contents of the migration later, ActiveRecord will not see that anything has changed, thus preventing team members from getting the real schema changes you meant to record. To get these changes, they would first have to migrate backwards past your migration before migrating forwards again to pick up the new version in their schemas. Even then, problems arise, as migrating backwards over the new version will likely attempt to drop tables that were never created in the old version, causing exceptions to be thrown. Basically, it can be a real mess. So when you check in a migration, remember: You never know who is going to update and migrate to it, so it is best to treat your first check in as your last. This leads to the next, similar point:

3. **Avoid changing a migration after it has been checked in**. As a more general rule of thumb than the last, you should avoid changes to an existing migration entirely when in a team environment. This is a lot to ask of modern software development (good coding thrives on refactoring and change), but migrations represent a different type of versioning system than source repositories such as SVN. Whereas source repositories represent change over time by overwriting files (while retaining a history of edits), migrations represent change over time by adding new files.

   You can accomplish all the types of incremental changes that you are accustomed to — addition, replacement, and deletion — by tacking another migration on at the end of the current lineup. Adding a new design element by changing an existing migration sneaks it in such that developers will need to drop their database and start from scratch to benefit from the change. Adding that change as a new migration tacked on the end incrementally allows everyone to receive the change easily.

   From time to time, you may want to declare a database cleanup day when you will consolidate migrations and clean things up a bit with the knowledge of retrospect. Just make sure everyone is aware that these changes are going to take place and that they have the chance to prepare their local development systems to re-bootstrap their databases when the cleanup is done.

4. **Develop and verify the tests for your migration before you check it in**. Because other developers on your team may use your migration as soon as you check it in, it is important to develop and run tests to verify the correctness of your changes before you check in the migration. This is a good idea anyway, but because checking in a migration in a team environment is such a sensitive operation, it is even more important here.

Although team migration development is not always easy, it is still easier than the process without migrations. By creating a strict set of rules for you and your team to follow, you can control migration development and model addition enough to minimize the major risk areas, and you can count on the migration timeline to provide you with an easy, incremental way to build up your schema. As a final note, you might not decide to make schema development a team activity, and that is a fine decision. Many teams feel that developing a schema is a quiet and rigorous process that one or two developers who have intimate knowledge of the entire schema should do. If your team dynamic or schema complexity requires it, just deputize that all change requests go through that one developer.

Seeding Data for Production

In many types of projects, it is valuable to *seed* data at several stages of the design and development process. Rails provides facilities called *fixtures* for creating datasets for use during testing, but that is where its built-in support for seeding ends.

Seeding is generally used to bootstrap your web application with some initial set of data. What changes from project to project, however, is the size and nature of that data. In some circumstances, it is very small — for example, adding the default user to a blog application. In other cases, it may be hundreds, thousands, or millions of records large, such as a dataset of localization settings (hundreds) or a series of financial datasets (millions). Each of these situations will place different demands on the way that you store and load this data into the database.

This section of the chapter covers three different ways to seed data into a Rails application. Each way comes with a different method of packaging the data, and each works best with a different size dataset.

Small Datasets: Seed Migrations

The simplest and most direct way to seed data into your database is to do it directly from within a migration. Remember that a migration is a regular piece of Ruby code acting from within the Rails environment, so you are at liberty to write or call any code that you want within the `self.up` and `self.down` steps. You can even add data to a table being created in that migration, but remember to add the data after the `create_table` statement!

Seeding data from within a migration makes sense when the data is intimately coupled with the schema that underlies it — that is, the table must be populated in order for the application to work. By including the data as part of the migration, there is no way to get one without the other. In this sense, it also simplifies the setup if you are sharing code with others. That is why you will see this strategy used by some third-party plug-ins to Rails: By including both the schema and data in the same step, the user has one less set of issues to worry about while setting up the plug-in.

Placing data directly within the migration is also a good idea only if the amount of data you are adding is small to medium in size. Here, medium means that the data is at the border of what you would expect to come in some sort of structured file, such as an XML or CSV file. After your data reaches the size in which it is better deployed and maintained as a pure data file, your developers and users will thank you for separating it out as such.

There are really two ways to seed data from within migrations. The first is to create a migration whose only purpose is to load data. Data within relational databases is intricately interrelated when foreign key relationships abound. Sometimes your schema is incrementally built up across several different migrations, but the data you want to seed requires the summation of the migrations before it, rather than a particular one. Rather than build up a complicated web of seed data incrementally as the schema becomes available, it makes sense to wait until the schema is ready and then create a migration to add it all at one time.

The second way is to include the seed data for a table inside the migration that creates that table. Following this strategy ensures that the user knows where to look to find the seed data for that particular table, and it works well for small data seeds that are limited to a single table in the database.

```
class CreateTags < ActiveRecord::Migration

  InitialTags = ["ruby", "rails", "the interwebs", "hiking"]

  def self.up
    create_table :tags do |t|
      t.string :name
      t.timestamps
    end

    InitialTags.each do |tag|
      Tags.create(:name => tag)
    end
  end

  def self.down
    drop_table :tags
  end
end
```

Medium Datasets: Seed Fixtures

Embedding data into migrations is an easy and direct route to seeding data, but it leaves much to be desired if the size of your data is more than a handful. Just as maintaining a text file embedded inside the confines of a Java class is a suboptimal solution, maintaining data embedded within a series of Ruby classes loses its attractiveness after the data reaches a certain size or a certain coverage breadth across the tables in your database. Separating them into "seed fixtures" allows the data to be split off as a separate concern, maintained and edited as just plain data files, and deployed separately from the schema itself.

Although the fixtures component of `ActiveRecord` is intended for testing and has no parallel for production data, the important segments of code can be easily extracted from the `ActiveRecord` library and pulled out for reuse in a separate fixture location intended for seeding your production system.

Here is a task that you can place inside your `lib/tasks` folder (name it something like `seed.rake`) that enables you to create production fixtures in the same manner as the testing ones that you already have:

```
# Creates a task to support seed fixtures for your production system.
# - Store this file in lib/tasks/seed_fixtures.rake
# - Place fixtures in db/seed.
# - Use with 'rake db:seed'

namespace :db do
  desc "Loads seed fixtures into your database."
  task :seed => :environment do
    require 'active_record/fixtures'
    seed_dir_rel = File.join('db', 'seed')
    seed_dir_abs = File.join(RAILS_ROOT, seed_dir_rel)
```

```
      # Supported formats are YAML and CSV
      Dir.glob(File.join(seed_dir_abs, '*.{yml,csv}')).each do |file|
        Fixtures.create_fixtures(seed_dir_rel, File.basename(file, '.*'))
      end
    end
  end
```

This task expects production fixtures to live in a new directory that you must create called db/seed. As with test fixtures, you can create either YAML or CSV files with the same filename as the table they are supposed to seed. This task will examine all the files in the db/seed folder and attempt to load each one into the database. To use this task, run rake db:seed from your rails root directory.

Large Datasets: Dumpfiles

The fixtures code that comes with Ruby on Rails simply isn't made to deal with large data sets. Even using a library such as FasterCSV, imports will slow your machine to a halt and take sometimes an hour when importing data sets that are many megabytes in size. For these situations, there is really no other solution than to use your particular database's native import mechanism, but that doesn't necessarily mean that you can't automate the process in a Rails-like fashion. Following is a MySQL-specific task that will take CSV files in the db/seed directory you created for medium-sized seeding, convert them into a temporary representation for import into MySQL, and then perform a data import using MySQL's import functionality. For very large data sets, the following code will achieve large speed increases over the fixture method shown previously, or even over custom code using FasterCSV. The code required to do this is fairly sizable, so it will be broken up into chunks for explanation. The full version is available from this book's companion web site at www.wrox.com or from www.artofrails.com.

First, declare the db:mysql_import task and initialize a few variables that represent your seed directory and the current Rails environment.

```
namespace :db do
  desc "Loads CSV files into your database using MySQL import."
  task :mysql_import => :environment do

    # Set up paths and environment variables
    seed_dir = File.join(RAILS_ROOT, 'db', 'seed')
    env = ENV['RAILS_ENV'] || 'development'
    puts "  * Using #{env} environment"
```

Next, use the environment variable to load the database configuration out of the database.yml file so that you can read in the username and password for use with the MySQL command you will use later in the task.

```
    # Get a your database configuration
    dconfig_file = File.join(RAILS_ROOT, 'config', 'database.yml')
    dconfig = YAML::load(IO.read(dconfig_file))

    unless dconfig[env]['adapter'] == 'mysql'
      raise StandardError.new(
        "The db:mysql_import only works with a MySQL database")
    end
```

```
database = dconfig[env]['database']
user = dconfig[env]['username']
password = dconfig[env]['password']
```

Next, you prepare the options string for the MySQL command by specifying the user and the password. Note that it is not generally considered good security practice to execute a command-line statement that includes a password, as you are doing here.

```
# Prepare the options string for the MySQL command
# This is not ideal because it uses your password on the command line
options = " -u #{user} "
options = options +  " --password=#{password}" unless password.blank?
```

Now you address each CSV file in the seed directory, opening the file and reading in its header row into an array.

```
# Load each CSV file directly into MySQL
Dir.glob(File.join(seed_dir, '*.csv')).each do |file|
  next unless File.file? file

  table = File.basename(file, '.*')
  puts "  * Importing into #{table}"

  # Get the header row
  fixture = File.open(file, "r")
  header_row = fixture.gets.chomp!
  fixture.close()
```

You use the header row to build the SQL command that will be used for the MySQL import. The particular SQL built up in this step may vary depending on your database and machine configuration.

```
# Set up Database
cmd_str = ""

# Optionally add the below line to clear the table first
# cmd_str = cmt_str + "DELETE FROM #{database}.#{table}; "

# These lines import the CSV file into your table
cmd_str = cmd_str +
    "LOAD DATA LOCAL INFILE '#{file}' INTO TABLE #{database}.#{table} "
cmd_str = cmd_str + "FIELDS OPTIONALLY ENCLOSED BY '\"' TERMINATED BY ',' "
cmd_str = cmd_str + "IGNORE 1 LINES (#{header_row});"
```

Finally, you write the MySQL command to a temporary file:

```
# Load commands into a temporary file
temp_file_name = File.join(seed_dir, "#{table}_import_commands.sql")
File.unlink temp_file_name if File.file? temp_file_name

temp_file = File.new(temp_file_name, "w+")
temp_file << cmd_str
temp_file.close()
```

And you run the MySQL command, passing it a reference to the temporary file with your SQL:

```
# Run the MySQL command
mysql_cmd = "mysql #{options} < #{temp_file_name}\n"
system(mysql_cmd)
File.unlink temp_file_name

    end # End Dir.glob loop
  end # End task definition
end # End namespace enclosure
```

In addition to the piece of code that you can reuse from this section (online from this book's companion web site at www.wrox.com or from www.artofrails.com), the lesson to take from this section is that it is always worth the effort to *improve the Rails framework* to meet your needs rather than simply work with what it provides you. By adding custom rake tasks to accomplish data automation, you relieve yourself from worrying about that aspect of the project and from having to manually load data every time you run another deployment of your project.

When a Database Isn't Enough

It is generally a good idea to trust relational database design first, and then veer away from it only when you have a clear reason. After all, an entire industry is built around creating and optimizing the way databases work. But sometimes relational databases just do not provide the abstractions that you need to store your data. Here are three situations in which you can take advantage of some of the alternate access Rails provides to the database for special situations.

Model Object Hierarchies

A question sometimes used in programming interviews is, "Can you write object-oriented code in Perl?" The right answer is, "Sure, but it might take a bit more code than usual." With the prevalence of OO-style libraries for JavaScript, the trick behind this question is a lot clearer today than it sometimes was in the past: object-oriented programming is a style of coding, not a language feature. It just so happens that some languages make it a lot easier to write OO code than others by building in keywords to support, and even require, it.

In most applications, developers encounter model objects that get decomposed into several subtypes. An example familiar to many might be the decomposition of different account types on a professional blog. Logged-in users might have the ability to comment on and rate articles. Advertisers are special users that have access to account management features. Bloggers are able to post new articles to the blog, and Administrators are special users who can modify the blog's settings. This object model is depicted in Figure 11-4.

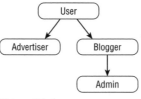

Figure 11-4

As with Perl, relational databases used by the web development community do not provide a native way to represent such an object decomposition in the table layout. A typical solution to modeling this hierarchy is to add a `type` field to the user object that stores the user's type or role (other solutions may involve an action-based permissions table). This collapses the notion of object hierarchy down into a single tag on the `User` object that is then used as a permissions check in many of the methods on that object and others.

```
def purchase_advertisement(post)
  raise StandardError.new("Woah there, buddy") unless @user.type == :advertiser
  # .. Method continues
end
```

Ideally, you would like to build object orientation on top of the database, even if it does not support it natively, so that you can implement the different types of users as different objects in a hierarchy with different fields and methods. `ActiveRecord` provides a way to do this through a feature called Single Table Inheritance. Single Table Inheritance (STI) allows you to develop a set of `ActiveRecord` objects that fall into a hierarchy and to have `ActiveRecord` automatically collapse them into a single table in the database for you. That way, both worlds see the data as they want: your database gets the `Users` table it wants with a `type` field on it, and you, the developer, get the benefit of working with subclasses and inheritance.

```
class AddTypeToUsers < ActiveRecord::Migration
  def self.up
    add_column :users, :type, :string
  end

  def self.down
    remove_column :users, :type
  end
end
```

If the `type` field is already being used by your table or your particular database chokes on `type` as a column name, let Rails know where to look for the type field with the `set_inheritance_column` macro in your model class:

```
set_inheritance_column "user_type"
```

After an acceptable field is in place to store the object type information, simply begin to subclass the top-level object that shares the same name as the table.

```
class Advertiser < User
end

class Blogger < User
end

class Administrator < Blogger
end
```

Boot up the console and try creating a few different types of `User`, `Advertiser`, `Blogger`, and `Administrator` objects. Then try querying with the `:all` parameter from each of the classes. You will notice that each :all query returns all the objects of that type and all subtypes. So the User class returns instances from all four, the Blogger class returns instances of Blogger and Administrator, and the Blogger and Administrator classes each return only objects whose type field references either Blogger or Administrator — exactly what we would hope from a object system with a proper class hierarchy. In the array returned, each object is typed appropriately. So the query User.find(:all) will return an array containing objects of four different types.

```
>> User.find(:all).each { |object| p object.class.to_s }
"Blogger"
"Administrator"
"Blogger"
"Advertiser"
"User"
"Advertiser"
```

Now that you have your hierarchy set up, how will you use it apart from the convenience of having the class names differ? In general, you have two different ways to differentiate your STI model objects, as discussed in the following two sections.

Differing Fields from Subclass to Subclass

In most object hierarchies, child classes end up defining their own variables. Model objects using Single Table Inheritance can, too, but all objects that descend from the top model object share the same table in the database. This means that, despite some variables being relevant to only certain child classes, in truth no mechanism exists that ties a particular column to a particular subclass (although with clever use of method overloading and validations, you can explicitly define a virtual block on variables not meant for a particular subclass). Figure 11-5 shows what a hierarchy of ActiveRecord objects using the same table might look like.

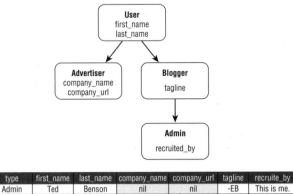

id	type	first_name	last_name	company_name	company_url	tagline	recruite_by
1	Admin	Ted	Benson	nil	nil	-EB	This is me.
2	Blogger	Grace	Deng	nil	nil	.gd	nil
3	User	Alex	Benson	nil	nil	nil	nil

Figure 11-5

If you are using Single Table Inheritance in Rails and you want to maintain object-specific fields within an STI hierarchy, be prepared to start seeing a lot of nil values in your data. The problem, as you can see in Figure 11-5, is that each object necessarily contains a field for every possible property in the hierarchy, even if it is not relevant to the particular object specified in the type column. As the number of subclass-specific fields increases, imagine how the storage efficiency of each row will decrease. It is imagined for you in Figure 11-6.

id	type	first_name	last_name	company	parket	tagline	comment	soda	cat	dog	zip	c	w	x	y
1	Admin	Ted	Benson			-EB	This is me.							z	
2	Blogger	Grace	Deng			.gd			pop						
3	User	Alex	Benson							Fido					z

Figure 11-6

For a modest number of columns, this is not a big deal in real-world terms, but relational database sticklers will quickly raise an eyebrow at your tables when they start to see `nil` values all over each row. Normally, a table with sparse rows indicates a poor schema design, but, of course, the entire concept of Single Table Inheritance somewhat exceeds the boundaries of normal relational database use. So to a limited degree, be comfortable with sparse rows, but also be on the lookout for when unused fields begin to overtake the used ones. Just when the `nil`-field situation created by STI has gone too far, it is entirely application and schema specific, so the best advice is to keep it in the back of your mind to check up on the issue from time to time and evaluate for yourself whether you are better off refactoring a bit.

Differing Helper Methods from Subclass to Subclass

The biggest win from Single Table Inheritance comes from the ability to differ the implementation of helper methods on your model objects. Ruby on Rails is model heavy. If you look closely at the code of a Rails application, you will find that much of the real action takes place within the model classes, while the controllers just coordinate high-level flow and the views are just display templates. Because so much of your Rails code exists in the model, STI provides a great way to organize and reduce its footprint. It also provides some nice security protections; Regular users can be loaded into completely different model objects from administrative users, for example, complete with a different set of methods.

Refining Method Implementations

The first way STI helps you organize your code is by allowing you to refine the implementation of each method so that it is specific for a particular user type. Say, for instance, that users of a blogging system get a particular Karma level that affects how visible their blog postings are on the main page. Being the unfair world that it is, your minimum Karma level differs depending on what type of user you are: bloggers have a minimum of five points, and administrators have a minimum of 10 points. Without STI, you would be forced to implement some logic in the `karma` getter method that inspected the value of the object's `type` field, but this is not a good way to code because it makes the method implementation a hidden dependency on your schema that must be changed if the number of user types is increased.

Assume that you created a migration to add the `karma` field to the User object and set all existing users' karma to zero. By default, each user object now has a `karma` accessor on it, thanks to `ActiveRecord`'s dynamic introspection of the model that backs it. To further differentiate the minimum karma rules you have set for objects of the `Administrator` and `Blogger` classes, you can simply overload the `karma` accessor to return the maximum either of users' earned karma value or their guaranteed karmic minimum. The implementation that follows requires administrators to work just as hard to earn points as anyone else, but it guarantees that they're spotted a certain minimum until they are able to surpass it.

```
class Administrator < Blogger

  def karma
    [10, self[:karma]].max
  end

end
```

```
class Blogger < Users

  def karma
    [5, self[:karma]].max
  end

end
```

Now from the Rails console, you iterate over all user records and print their type and their karma value. Remember that in the migration not shown here, you initialized all existing users to a karma level of zero.

```
>> User.find(:all).each { |u| p "#{u.class} -- #{u.karma}" }
"Blogger -- 5"
"Administrator -- 10"
"Blogger -- 5"
"Advertiser -- 0"
"User -- 0"
"Advertiser -- 0"
```

The output of this command shows the object hierarchy enabling you to alter the way that different types of users report a value.

Subclass-Specific Methods

The second way that STI allows you to organize your helper methods is by adding completely new methods specific to a certain subclass. Administrator object might be able to approve the addition of a new blog post, for example, whereas no other user should have that capability. Here is a shoddy implementation of what one such method might look like:

```
class Administrator < Blogger
  def approve(post)
    if (post.class == Post)
      post.valid = true
      post.approved_by(self)
      post.save
    end
  end
end
```

The important feature to note is that by adding the approve(post) method to the Administrator class, you can reach this bit of functionality only if you have the Administrator value in your table's type column. It acts not just as a way to organize type-specific methods but also as a crude first-pass authorization mechanism for your application.

Single Table Inheritance bootstraps on top of the database to allow for class hierarchies of objects to be conveniently serialized down to the parent's class' database table. Although this capability comes at the potential expense of a sparse table, it brings great benefits from the standpoint of model development and code organization. When you have a development situation in which a hierarchy of objects is at play, you should consider STI as a way to organize your code.

Storing Lists, Hashes, and Other Fun Things

There are times when you want to store some object in a database only as a property to be read off of another object. When this object is a simple data type, it can go in the schema exactly as such, but when it is a list of items or a hash table, an entirely new table must be created to support it. Suppose you are really just interested in recall — not searching or data sharing — and you do not want to put your database through the task of having to scan over a table of list items to find those associated with some foreign key. Rails provides an easy way to seamlessly serialize and deserialize simple objects into YAML for you behind the scenes.

You can accomplish this behind-the-scenes serialization with the `serialize` macro that `ActiveRecord` provides. Use it in your model object, just as you would an association:

```
serialize :favorite_colors
```

You can, and should, also associate an object type with your serialized field. Doing so will allow users of your model to know what to expect out of that field and will also serve as a defense against errors by hard-typing the field. To put a type on the serialized field, just include the class object as the second argument:

```
serialize :favorite_colors, Hash
```

Assume that you want to add a "profile" in your user table that records the user's preferences about various aspects of the site:

```
class AddUserProfiles < ActiveRecord::Migration
  def self.up
    add_column :user, :preferences, :text
  end

  def self.down
    remove_column :user, :preferences
  end
end
```

Next, amend the `User` model object to note that you want the `preferences` column serialized:

```
class User < ActiveRecord::Base
  serialize :preferences, Hash
end
```

And now, booting up `script/console`, you load an existing `User` object and try setting and saving the `preferences` field on it. The following code passes it a regular Ruby hash containing a series of symbols and another embedded hash.

```
>> u.preferences = { :favorite_color => :blue,
?>                   :favorite_steak => :tuna,
?>                   :email => {
```

```
?>                              :spam_occasionally => true,
?>                              :spam_alot => false
>>                          }
>>                      }
=> {:favorite_steak=>:tuna, :favorite_color=>:blue, :email=>{:spam_alot=>false,
:spam_occasionally=>true}}
>> u.save
=> true
```

After saving the `User` object, inspect the value of the saved field as the database sees it to find the YAML representation of the hash you provided in the Rails console.

```
mysql> select preferences from users where id=1;
+------------------------------------------------------------------------+
| preferences                                                            |
+------------------------------------------------------------------------+
:favorite_color: :blue
:favorite_steak: :tuna
:email:
  :spam_alot: false
  :spam_occasionally: true
+------------------------------------------------------------------------+
1 row in set (0.00 sec)
```

Automatically serializing arrays and hashes can have many uses in Rails, from optimizing the lookup of certain pieces of information to storing simple Ruby objects to incorporate in the business logic of your web application as preference settings.

Custom Getters and Setters

ActiveRecord automatically provides getter and setter functionality for all database fields on your `ActiveRecord` objects by inspecting the database, but you can always override these if you need to. A variety of reasons for doing this exist, such as providing custom object serialization, wrapping additional logic around a particular field (such as password encryption), or preventing a database write in some circumstances.

Many applications that allow their users to add text data in a format such as MarkDown or Textile use setter overriding to optimize subsequent reads. They maintain two fields: the author-facing version for creation and editing and the HTML version for display. When the author-facing version is set, an overridden setter automatically translates the text into HTML at write-time. That way, in a typical trade between disk space and execution time, the translation does not have to be done every time someone wants to view the content:

```
class Article < ActiveRecord::Base
  # Assume two fields: body and body_html

  def body=(text)
    self[:body] = text
    self[:body_html] = translate_to_html(text)
  end

end
```

When objects of the `Article` class are used for editing by their author, the body field is accessed to fetch the MarkDown or Textile version of the contents. When the object is used for display to a reader, the `body_html` field is used.

Summary

This chapter showed you some tips and tricks that help streamline database development the same way that you streamline your application code. It covered the basic concept of migrations with a few simple examples and discussed the issue of how to practice team schema development without running into migration collisions. Next, the chapter looked at the issue of data seeding — loading a baseline of data into your database for production use — and described three different ways to package and load seed data. Each way catered to a different size of dataset. Finally, this chapter showed some ways of crafting model objects that use the database above and beyond the abstractions that it provides by default, including Single Table Inheritance, object serialization, and method overrides.

The next chapter takes a look at a topic of critical importance to the long-term viability of a Rails application: testing. Rather than cover the existing unit test framework included with Rails, you'll explore the new discipline of behavior-driven development (BDD) and specification-based tests. The fundamental ideas behind BDD are introduced, as well as a BDD implementation for Ruby called RSpec.

12

Behavior-Driven Development and RSpec

"That's crazy enough that it just might work," one of the technicians said, leaning back in his chair.

They had gathered everyone in the main room of the INOC to go over the plan. Back in front of the larger audience, General Operand had returned to his public persona.

"Of course it will work!" he barked. "Matz says it's flawless." He slapped Matz hard on the back, sending him stumbling a few steps forward.

"Not quite flawless," Matz said as he looked up at the General.

"What do you mean 'not flawless'? You said you were sure!"

"Well, for one thing," Matz explained, "we can't be sure what object types they are programmed to expect unless we can get a copy of their spec documents, which isn't possible in so little time. So we'll have to pick something as unexpected as possible. Something totally random."

In a fitting retaliation, Matz had devised a plan to use the compilers' very inability to dynamically modify code against them. It wouldn't kill the compilers, but it would stun them until revived, which also fit the resistance objectives; compilers were just pawns in this game. As far as General Operand was concerned, the compilers were to be "fought with the care with which you'd fight a brother!"

The plan hinged on the hard-typing of their APIs. They had strict orders, a strict API, and strict callbacks. If the other side was going to fight dirty and take advantage of language features, so would the resistance. They could throw any object they wanted straight into the unsuspecting API and the compilers would crash if it were an object type other than expected.

"Excellent!" the General roared. "We'll just pick something they'd never expect. Bryant! What was that contraption you had in here yesterday?"

"Umm," he was startled again by the General's question. "You mean my humidifier, sir?"

"Exactly — the thing-a-ma-what's-it! We'll use one of those!"

"There's one more thing, General," Matz added reluctantly. "We're going to have to be close."

"How close?"

"Very close. It's going to have to be a callback. . ." He hesitated. "Which means we're going to have to send some agents in there to get captured first."

To see the plan put into action and learn W. Web's fate, visit the book's companion web site at `www.wrox.com`.

Test-driven development (TDD) is an important skill to learn as a developer and one that is especially prized by the Rails community. To the uninitiated, developing through tests seems like extra work at the least and an oppressive corporate-style burden at the most. But as those who follow this practice will tell you, the rewards of TDD far outweigh the work as the size and duration of a project progresses.

TDD is a style of development driven by the premise that you shouldn't write tests just to check the code you write; you should write tests to define the expectations and drive the development of new code. "Test First, Code Second," is a good distillation of the basic message. By writing your tests up front, you are forced into a mentality in which you design code with clean, small divisions of functionality, eschewing long, cryptic methods. If all goes well, the resulting code is not only easy to read and talk about but also defensible because the tests that validate it were developed even before the code itself was.

"If only large-scale projects actually worked that way" is the refrain you might hear from experienced developers when reading the last two paragraphs. Although TDD can be amazingly effective, in truth it is a difficult development style to truly achieve. It is hard to decide up front what to write your tests for, and even after you have decided, you don't always know how fine a grain of capability to test. That is where this chapter hopes to step in with a new style of development that reorients the test-driven mindset toward stories, requirements, and behaviors.

This chapter is about behavior-driven development (BDD), an evolution of the TDD style that overlays an easy-to-understand vocabulary and set of development practices on top of existing expert advice about test-driven practices. These contribute to an overarching developmental story that helps developers define the desired characteristics of an application and identify where and how to test those characteristics.

BDD is rapidly gaining ground in the Rails community as a way to define requirements and expectations, guide development, provide reference examples, and test code all in one package. This chapter will introduce you to BDD and show you how to develop with RSpec, a BDD testing library for Ruby applications.

Behavior-Driven Development

BDD is not a new technology *per se*, but is rather a way to think about and structure your testing and development to maximize your effectiveness as a developer. In the words of `Behaviour-driven.org` (`http://behaviour-driven.org`):

> It must be stressed that BDD is a rephrasing of existing good practice, it is not a radically new departure. Its aim is to bring together existing, well-established techniques under a common banner and with a consistent and unambiguous terminology. BDD is very much focused on "Getting the words right" and this focus is intended to produce a vocabulary that is accurate, accessible, descriptive and consistent.

In the preceding quote, "Getting the words right" refers to a common vocabulary, but the intention applies equally as well to BDD as a whole. Many of the principles of BDD arise directly out of lessons learned from developers experienced in the TDD community. After much reflection, these developers found that writing tests was about far more than checking to see whether a particular piece of code ran correctly, but the way that current testing frameworks are organized does not reveal these extra uses of testing to the casual tester. Most of the testing frameworks available are, in a sense, the raw ingredients required to test, without a story that brings them together in a meaningful way for all to see. BDD is designed as the fast track toward the more evolved virtues of testing, namely so that:

❑ Writing tests is an excellent way to motivate and inform API development.

❑ Writing tests provides documentation for the intended use of your code.

❑ Tests act as a bridge between the nontechnical requirements of a system and their technical implementations.

❑ Well-designed and communicated tests can double as a system specification.

❑ Writing tests is really about describing the expected behavior of the different actors in your system. This final item is the most important one from the philosophical perspective of BDD.

So, from a coding standpoint, BDD involves a set of activities similar to the ones you are accustomed to, but from a process standpoint, it looks and feels very different. These differences aim to put a spotlight on the preceding bulleted ideas right from the get-go.

BDD is all about stories. A story is a unit of discovery used to determine what your application intends to accomplish. The idea is borrowed from the Extreme Programming discipline, in which a user story is a small description of desired functionality from the perspective of a user. In BDD, the language used to define a story is a bit more structured, always taking the form shown in Figure 12-1.

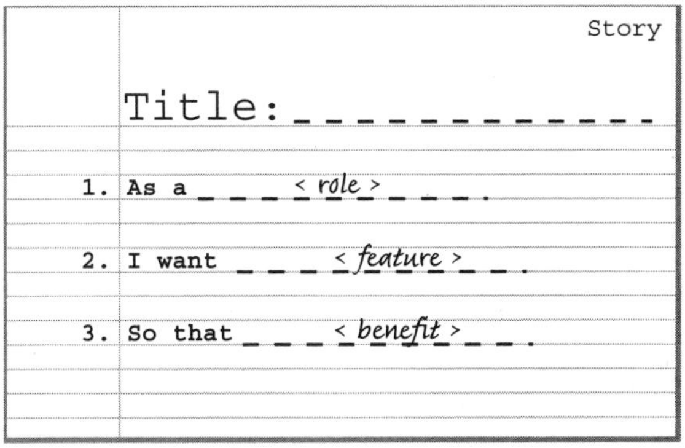

Figure 12-1

So a BDD story defines a role, a feature, and a benefit that will come from that feature. This story provides the basis for a round of development that will turn the story into something possible with your application.

After choosing a story that you would like to pursue, the next step is to decide the acceptance criteria that dictate the conditions under which the story should be possible and the conditions under which it should not be possible. How acceptance criteria are developed varies a bit from framework to framework and developer to developer, so the description given here is designed to align with the RSpec framework discussed later in the chapter. Rails developers using RSpec decompose a story in two different types of objects: scenarios and specs.

❑ Scenarios are similar to integration tests. They are high-level scripts that describe the interactions of many parts of a system.

❑ Specs are most similar to unit tests. A spec describes the expected behavior of a particular object under various conditions.

This decomposition of a story is shown in Figure 12-2.

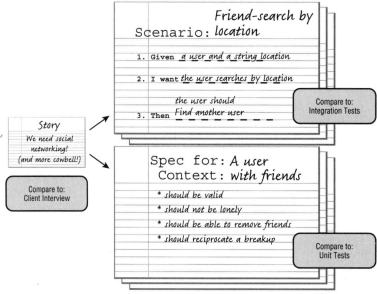

Figure 12-2

Whereas traditional unit testing is aimed at finding a tight mapping between tests and units of code functionality, behavioral testing is aimed at finding a mapping between tests and the specified behaviors that your objects should exhibit when interacting with each other. Sometimes a behavior will involve a small amount of code just as a unit test does, but other times it might not, and in the mindset of a behavior-driven tester, that is okay: If the test fails, you will still be able to track the problem back to the source just as though you had written a unit test for that piece of code. In this way, BDD focuses not on the detailed states of objects but rather the overall interactions between objects.

So far, BDD sounds just like a pencil-and-paper activity to help you identify requirements for the components of your system, but the big benefit is that there are domain-specific languages written on top of Ruby that allow you to write human readable stories and specs that become your coding tests. The rest of this chapter introduces you to RSpec and shows you how to use it to incorporate BDD into your coding.

RSpec: BDD for Ruby and Rails

RSpec is a behavior-driven framework for Ruby applications that supports both object-level specs and application-level stories, the two types of acceptance criteria shown previously in Figure 12-2. Available at http://rspec.info, RSpec enjoys a growing community of both Ruby and Ruby on Rails developers. RSpec integrates into Rails as a series of plug-ins: rspec and rspec_on_rails. These plug-ins provide a number of extra features for your Rails project, including Rails-specific testing helpers and a custom set of generators for use in creating objects on the command line.

You can use RSpec either in tandem with or instead of Rails' default testing framework, and it operates in a separate space so that the two can coexist peacefully. When you install RSpec on a Rails project, it creates the spec/ and stories/ subfolders in your Rails root directory. Within the spec/ folder is a further set of subdirectories reflecting the major components of your application: controllers/, fixtures/, helpers/, models/, and views/.

This chapter addresses only spec-based decomposition (leaving out stories) for two reasons. First, spec-based decomposition is the quickest route to getting a high value from very little learning curve, whereas constructing stories with RSpec is an experimental and more difficult feature at the time of this writing. Second, specs, as with unit tests, are often written before stories (integration tests), so in the introductory materials here it makes more sense to use specs as an example. If you find that this style of coding aligns with your interests, there is plenty more material available at rspec.info.

The Spec Development Cycle

The process of writing a spec begins when you decide on a particular object, or actor, in your application whose expected behaviors you would like to describe. The goal of a spec is to isolate and describe a particular object, so specs should be written separately for models, views, controllers, and helpers. If you are developing specs in conjunction with stories, your spec development will likely be prompted by the fact that the actor in question appears in the story and needs to exhibit certain behaviors in order for the story to complete. The spec for an object is stored inside its own file with the suffix_spec, so a spec for the User model object would be called user_spec.rb.

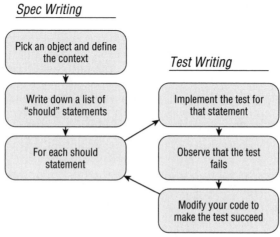

Figure 12-3

After you have decided what you are going to model, you can divide the development process into two separate parts even though they might occur during the same sitting or even within minutes of each other. The first step is development of your behavioral specification at a sentence level. The second step is the expansion of each sentence into a test and the development of the code necessary to pass the test. Figure 12-3 shows this process.

Writing the Spec

The first stage in developing an object with specs is the creation of your specification. The specification is really just the shelled version of the set of tests you hope to achieve, with none of the tests implemented yet. At the end of this stage, you will have an executable document describing the different roles an object in the system plays and a list of the behaviors that the object should or should not exhibit.

The outermost container within a spec is called a *description*. Each description lists either a string-based context or a class object (or both) that it is about:

```
# Description for a class in a particular context

describe Comment, "that is pending" do
   # Required behaviors go here
end

# Description for a particular context not tied to a class

describe "any approval-requiring message" do
   # Required behaviors go here
end
```

In the first case, the description block states that it is about the Comment class in the particular context of a comment "that is pending." The second description is simply about "any approval-requiring message." In this way, the describe container serves as a tool to help you organize your thinking to ensure proper test coverage.

As an example of how to use describe blocks to partition your tests into clusters, imagine that you are implementing a Rails-based blog with a sophisticated comment system. This comment system passes user comments through a gauntlet of approval processes, their status going from PENDING to AKISMET_PASS to APPROVED. A PENDING comment is one that has been added but not checked by Akismet. An AKISMET_PASS comment is one that has passed an Akismet spam check but has not been approved by an administrator, and an APPROVED comment is a spam-free comment that has been approved by the blogger and should be displayed on the page. (Left out are the "bad" states for spam and unapproved comments.) If each of these comment states constitutes a different context that should guide the behavior of the Comment model object, the Comment spec might contain a separate description block for each to help organize the tests required:

```
describe Comment do
   # Required behaviors for all comments
end

describe Comment, "that is pending" do
   # Required behaviors for pending comments
end
```

```
describe Comment, "that has passed Akismet" do
    # Required behaviors for comments that have passed Akismet
end

describe Comment, "that has been approved" to
    # Required behaviors for comments that have been approved
end
```

Within each `describe` block is a series of statements called *examples*. Each example is a sentence about the object being described that states one particular behavior that the object should or should not engage in. Developers who have worked on large software development contracts may have encountered the RSpec notion of examples as "SHALL Statements," a large tree of statements that dictate a system's expected behavior from a high level functional overview all the way down to the specific responses the system should give to particular events and inputs.

> 3.4.2.142 The system SHALL display an error message if a falling cow prevents operation of any of its required features.

Examples in RSpec follow the same idea, except far more fun because you write them as executable code that serves simultaneously as a specification and a test. Each example is written using an object named `it`, which stands for the object whose behavior is being tested. It is really a method that takes a string as an argument that states some expected behavior about the object `it`.

```
describe Comment, "that has passed Akismet" do
    it "should be active"
    it "should be assigned to a moderator for approval"
    it "should have an Akismet response"
end

describe "any component of the system" do
    it "should display an error message if a falling cow causes an exception"
end
```

After you have enumerated all the examples that describe your object's behavior, you have completed the specification step in the development process. When you run an example as a test, each example can result in one of three possible outcomes: pass, fail, and unimplemented. The preceding spec has four unimplemented examples contained in two separate descriptions. To see whether these examples pass or fail, you need to provide tests to implement each one.

Implementing Examples

You can implement an example by providing a block after the `it` statement. Inside the block, place the code necessary to test the behavior that the example describes. In xUnit-style testing frameworks, test developers use various `assert` statements to define the conditions that cause the test to fail. RSpec uses `should` and `should_not` statements. RSpec dynamically adds `should` and `should_not` to the root `Object` class in Ruby, so you can call the method from any object of your choosing.

```
3.should == 3
3.should_not == 2
```

The `should` and `should_not` methods can be used in a variety of ways. Their documentation says it best, so it is copied here, from `rpsec.org`:

```
receiver.should == expected #any value
  => Passes if (receiver == expected)

receiver.should === expected #any value
  => Passes if (receiver === expected)

receiver.should =~ regexp
  => Passes if (receiver =~ regexp)

receiver.should(matcher)
  => Passes if matcher.matches?(receiver)
```

In addition to the preceding operators, RSpec allows you to substitute the method `eql()` for the double-equals operator (which checks whether the two are the same value) and `equal()` for the triple-equals operator (which checks whether the two are the same object).

The `should` and `should_not` methods enforce BDD's actor and behavior-focused mindset. English is a subject-verb-predicate language, so by naming the methods modal verbs, RSpec forces you into a mind-set in which you are focused on the object and its desired behavior instead of just thinking about pieces of data (the way `assert` would encourage). From a design standpoint, this is one of the key advantages of BDD over TDD. Although they both accomplish the same set of operations from the computer's per-spective, the BDD process tricks your mind into trying to compose sentences with your code, therefore affecting the way in which you design and write your tests.

The Sapir-Worf Hypothesis

The Sapir-Worf Hypothesis is the much-debated idea that the structure of language affects the way in which our brain can understand and make decisions about the world. Although it remains unknown how tightly our cognition is bound to the linguistic abstractions we use to describe its inputs and outputs, many believe that there is at least some connection between the two.

Many of the goals and quirks of BDD and Rails development are interesting because they strive to optimize the way we think about and interact with our code just as much as they strive to provide new functionality. Whether they succeed at this or not is for you to decide, but it is interesting to pay attention to the intent *behind* the API and draw parallels between DSLs such as the one `ActiveRecord` provides, BDD and RSpec, and our ideas about human cognition. The point of methods such as `object.should` and `object.should_not` is not so much to make the code easier to read but rather to prime your mind to think in a certain way about the code you are about to write. The result is a very different style of testing.

Matchers

If RSpec allowed examples to state only that objects `should equal` or `should_not equal` other objects, it would be pretty difficult to write a spec that achieved full coverage of the behaviors you would like to describe. The last possibility in the preceding `should` / `should_not` documentation was not an operator but an argument to the method called `matcher`. *Matchers* are a key part of the RSpec framework, and they provide the basis for more complex definitions of what an object should or should not do.

A lot of dynamic programming wizardry allows RSpec to weave in several built-in matchers in sentence-like fashion to your specs. The following table contains a nearly complete list of all the matchers that come bundled with RSpec. For a complete and always up-to-date list, look at the `Spec::Matchers` module in the RSpec documentation, available at `http://rspec.info/rdoc`.

Matcher Method	Tests
`be_{predicate}`	Tests the target's response to the message `predicate?`
	`user.should be_valid`
`be_true` `be_false`	Tests the Boolean value of the target.
	`result.should be_true`
`be_nil`	Tests whether the target is nil.
	`wallet.contents.should_not be_nil`
`be_a_{predicate}(*args)` `be_an_{predicate}(*args)`	Tests the target's response to the message `predicate(*args)`.
	`ted.should be_an_instance_of(Person)`
`be_close(expected, delta)`	Tests whether the target is with `delta` amount of the `expected` value.
	`grenade.longitude.should be_close(50, 10)`
`change(receiver, message, &block)`	*[When* `should` / `should_not` *is called on a Proc]*
	Tests whether the `receiver.message` results in a different value after the Proc was called compared to before. A block may be passed instead of a receiver and message, in which case the block's return value is used to determine whether something has changed.

	`lambda {`
	`  chapter.add_page(page)`
	`}.should change(book, :pagecount)`
	
	`# OR`
	
	`lambda {`
	`  chapter.add_page(page) }.should change { book.pagecount }`

`change( ... )`
`  .by_at_least(x)`
`  .by_at_most(y)`
	[Chained with a change matcher]

	Tests whether the change in the return value of `receiver.message` was at least or at most a certain numeric amount.

Continued

Matcher Method	Tests
	``lambda {
chapter.add_page(page)
}.should change(book, :pagecount).
by_at_least(1)```
	``lambda {
chapter.add_page(page)
}.should change(book, :pagecount).
by_at_most(1)```

`change( ... )`
  `.from(old)`
  `.to(new)`
	[Chained with a change matcher]
	
	Tests whether the value changed from the given "from" value to the given "to" value.
	
	```n = book.pagecount```
	
	``lambda {

chapter.add_page(page)
}.should change(book, :pagecount).
from(n).
to(n+1)```
`have(number).collection`	If the subject of `should` / `should_not` has a collection accessible via the message `collection`, this will test whether the collection size is equal to `number`. ```book.should have(300).pages
Equivalent to
book.pages.length.should == 300```
`have(number).counter`	If the subject of `should` / `should_not` is a collection or a string, the counter is purely "syntactic sugar" for readability's sake and is thrown away. ```[:VA, :MD, :DC].should have(3).states
"Hello".should have(5).letters
[":)"].should have(1).emoticon```
`have_at_least(num)` `have_at_most(num)`	Operates similarly to `have` except with an inequality instead of an exact number. Will not work with `should_not`. ```person.brain.should have_at_most(1)```
`include(*args)`	Tests whether the subject of `should` / `should_not` contains all the provided arguments. ```colors.should include(:red, :blue)
"breakfast".should_not include("gvbdfs")```

Matcher Method	Tests
`match(expression)`	Tests whether the subject matches the provided regular expression. `username.should match(/^[A-Za-z]{5,}$/)`

`raise_error`
`raise_error(ErrorClass)`
`raise_error(Err, msg)`
`raise_error(Err, regexp)`
	Tests whether a Proc raises an error. Optionally allows you to specify which error should be thrown and the message it should contain (or a regular expression that should match the message)
	
	`lambda {`
	`    5 / 0`
	`}.should raise_error(ZeroDivisionError)`

`respond_to(messages)`	Tests whether the option of the `should` / `should_not` call responds to all the messages provided. `person.should respond_to(:name, :save)`

The extensive collection of matchers attempts to cover a wide range of behavior that you might want to test on an object in your system. In the example spec you will build later, you will see how some of these matchers can be applied, but most are somewhat self-documenting in that they are all verbs that make sense in the context of Ruby objects.

If that list wasn't long enough for you, the RSpec Rails plug-in adds even more matchers relevant to your models, views, and controllers — all of which are documented on the RSpec web site.

Custom Matchers

Each application you write will be about a different domain that likely has various rules and abstractions worth creating your own matchers for. A *matcher* is any object that can respond to the following methods (remember that Ruby is duck typed, so an object can be described by its capabilities rather than its class lineage):

```
matches?(actual)
failure_message
negative_failure_message #optional
description #optional
```

So writing a matcher is a relatively painless process. Usually, a matcher should come bundled with a method that creates it so that it can be instantiated in a sentence-like manner as the matchers you have already seen.

Location-based services is one of the coming booms on the Web, so if you are planning a web application that involves geolocations, you might want to create several matchers that help you test your geospatial processing. A "be_within...of" matcher might be implemented as follows (shown completely without error checking, and pretending that the Earth has been projected onto a flat XY plane):

```
class BeWithinMatcher
```

```ruby
def initialize(distance)
  @distance = distance
end

def of(other)
  @other = other
  self
end

def matches?(target)
  @target = target

  x_dist = @target.location.x - @other.location.x
  y_dist = @target.location.y - @other.location.y
  dist = Math::sqrt(x_dist  ** 2 + y_dist ** 2)

  dist <= @distance
end

def failure_message
  "expected #{@target.inspect} to be within #{@distance} units of #{@other.inspect}"
end

def negative_failure_message
  "expected #{@target.inspect} not to be within #{@distance} units of
#{@other.inspect}"
  end
end
```

The `BeWithinMatcher` takes a distance unit in its constructor and allows some other object for comparison to be set with the `of(other)` method. Note how the `of(other)` method returns `self`; this is a common practice among Ruby objects whose methods are meant to be chained together. The `matches?` method takes a target object and uses the Pythagorean theorem to see whether the distance between the locations of two objects is within the distance provided at initialization time.

To allow this matcher to be integrated smoothly into your specs in sentence-like fashion, also add the following method on the root `Object`:

```ruby
def be_within(expected)
  BeWithinMatcher.new(expected)
end
```

And finally, you can test location-aware objects with the new matcher:

```ruby
it "should obey the Pythagorean theorem" do
  # Set up a 3-4-5 triangle with (1,1) as the root
  person1 = Person.new( Coordinate.new(1, 4) )
  person2 = Person.new( Coordinate.new(5, 1) )

  person1.should be_within(5).of(person2)
  person1.should_not be_within(4).of(person2)
end
```

This matcher does not have any notion of units or error checking, but it demonstrates how simple it is to extend RSpec to include domain-specific testing methods to help you minimize code duplication and create specs that are easy to write and come back to later as documentation.

Before and After

Sometimes you would like a certain bit of code to occur before or after each test. In the xUnit testing frameworks, the setUp and tearDown methods support this functionality. In RSpec, this is accomplished with before and after blocks. These methods work just like an it call except they are passed a symbol instead of a String. Passing one of these methods the :all symbol causes the given block to be executed before (or after) all the examples in the description. Passing it the :each symbol causes it to be executed once before (or after) each example in the description. The placement of the before and after calls within the description block does not matter.

```
describe User, 'during the day' do

  before(:all) do
    @user = User.new
    @user.wake_up
  end

  before(:each) do
    @user.wash_hands
    @refrigerator = Refrigerator.get_instance
  end

  it "should eat breakfast" do
    # Have a hearty breakfast, but not TOO hearty!
    lambda {
        @user.eat_breakfast
    }.should change(@refrigerator, :item_count).by_at_most(5)
  end

  it "should eat lunch"  # Unimplemented
  it "should eat dinner" # Unimplemented

  after(:each) do
    @user.clean_dishes
  end

  after(:all) do
    @user.sleep
  end

end
```

In the preceding code, the before and after statements paired with :all get executed as the description of User begins and ends, and the ones paired with :each get executed before and after each example in the description. If you don't pass an argument to the before or after methods, they will assume :each, because this is the option that you will be using most of the time. Note that the RSpec team discourages use of the :all option unless it is particularly needed. On rspec.org they note:

> Warning: The use of `#before(:all)` and `#after(:all)` is generally discouraged because it introduces dependencies between the Examples. Still, it might prove useful for very expensive operations if you know what you are doing.

An Example Trip through the Development Cycle

To demonstrate the last section, you'll explore an example trip through an RSpec development cycle for the cooking site from Chapter 3, "The Server as an Application." Suppose you would like to take the social networking aspects of that site a step further by allowing users to befriend other users. This example narrates the process from story development to spec development to application development that would ensue using BDD.

Part 1: Writing The Story

First, you find a notecard, real or virtual, and record the basic story that captures the new capability you would like to create and the value that it will add. This notecard is shown in Figure 12-4.

Figure 12-4

Even though writing down the story seems like unnecessary bookkeeping, it is an important part of the process. When pursuing the rapid design cycles of agile development, your efforts are more powerful with small, reinforcing self-discipline steps such as this. Even if you are coding by yourself, keep a notepad lying around — it helps you scope the coding tasks in front of you in case you find yourself awake at 4 a.m. wondering how you ended up reimplementing part of `ActiveRecord`.

Part 2: Writing the Specs

In the next part of the RSpec development cycle, you think about how to make this story possible. Many elements of the site need to be developed: Migrations need to be included to add friendship support to the schema; the model needs to contain methods to encapsulate the basic social networking functionality; the controller needs to add an API into this functionality; and the view needs to surface this new feature to the user. For this example, you will remain focused on the model.

You decide that the User object will be the area in your application where the friendship code will surface as a behavior, so the spec for the User object is where the new behavior descriptions will reside. Create a new file called user_spec.rb (if it doesn't already exist) in the spec/models directory of your Rails project. Within this user spec, you will add two new descriptions of a User object's expected behavior: one for a user with friends and another for a user without.

Even though coding the unimplemented spec is fast, pull out your pen again along with two more note-cards and begin to jot a list of the behaviors that each of the two user conditions should adhere to. Leaving the computer screen to write by hand is a good break to take now and then, especially when in design mode. Writing by hand slows down thinking enough for your subconscious to catch up and help out a bit. Figures 12-5 and 12-6 illustrate description cards for the two user conditions.

```
Thing: user
Context: with no friends

* should be valid

* should be lonely

* should have no friends

* should be able to make a friend

* should reciprocate the friendship of others
```

Figure 12-5

```
Thing: user
Context: with no friends

* should be valid

* should not be lonely

* should be able to remove friends

* should reciprocate a breakup
```

Figure 12-6

After you have determined the initial set of behaviors necessary to describe how a User acts in terms of social networking, begin transferring it into the user_spec.rb file.

```
require File.dirname(__FILE__) + '/../spec_helper'

describe User, "with no friends" do

  it "should be valid"
```

```
    it "should be lonely"
    it "should have no friends"
    it "should be able to make a friend"
    it "should accept the friendship of others"

end

describe User, "With friends" do

    it "should be valid"
    it "should not be lonely"
    it "should be able to remove friends"
    it "should reciprocate a breakup"

end
```

Running the spec, you see your two descriptions and nine unimplemented examples. In addition to serving as a test suite, the reports generated by RSpec are an excellent way to get a summary of a particular class from the standpoint of its intended behavior, as shown in Figure 12-7.

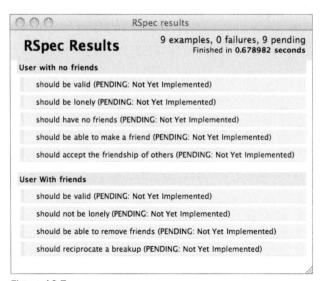

Figure 12-7

Part 3: Initializing and Writing a Basic Test

What order you choose to implement an object's behavioral examples does not matter. RSpec might run them in any order anyway, so it makes sense to take care of the low-hanging fruit first. As you begin to think about how you would implement each test, you will likely realize that the capabilities required for some tests are dependent on those required by others. This, too, will help you decide what order in which to write them.

Before you write any tests, you need to write a `before` block to set up two `User` objects to use in each of the tests. Above the first example, add the following code:

```
before(:each) do
  @harry = User.new
  @sally = User.new
end
```

This code will execute before each test, preparing the variables that you will be testing for proper behavior.

The first example is common to see in a description block for an `ActiveRecord` model object. It tests the conditions under which the model object should be considered valid, which in this case means a newly created `User` with an empty argument list in the constructor. In some ways, this is also an integrity check for the rest of the behavior tests that you will perform, because it will ensure that there are no validation problems with the object you are using for the other tests.

Expand the "should be valid" example into a full test by adding a block that contains the test body.

```
it "should be valid" do
  @harry.should be_valid
  @sally.should be_valid
end
```

You know that the `be_{predicate}` matcher examines the target's response to the `{predicate}?` method call, so `@harry.should be_valid` should pass if `@harry.valid?` returns true.

Never write too many tests before you take the steps to ensure they pass; that way, you minimize the number of issues you deal with at a single time, and you have the added bonus of a feeling of constant, incremental successes as you turn red `FAIL` messages into green `PASS` ones. Running the RSpec tests and observing the result in Figure 12-8, you see that your new test passes, so you can continue with development. Figure 12-8 is black and white, but in the RSpec plug-in for TextMate on the Macintosh, unimplemented tests are shown in yellow, failing tests are shown in red, and passing tests (the top line in the screenshot below, reading "should be valid") are shown in green.

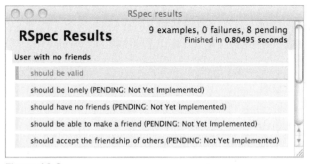

Figure 12-8

Part 4: Writing Behavior Tests That Motivate Development

When you're deciding which example to implement next, dependencies come into play. All the remaining examples require some implementation code that does not yet exist, but "should have no friends" appears to be the least amount of work of the four to achieve a passing score, so you will address that next. Implement it with the following code, which assumes that `User` acts in the standard `ActiveRecord` fashion and maintains a friends association:

```
it "should have no friends" do
  @harry.should have(:no).friends  # Meaning: @harry.friends.size should equal 0
end
```

Recall that `have` creates a `Matcher` object that will inspect the collection returned from the provided method call (`friends`) and pass if the size of the collection is equal to the provided argument. In this case, the test passes if `@harry.friends.length` is zero.

Running the tests once more after you implement this behavior example, you see that it fails, as shown in Figure 12-9.

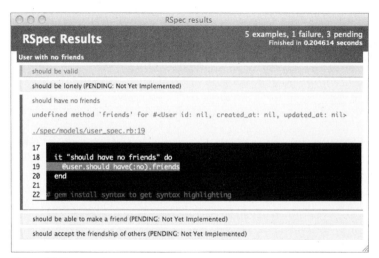

Figure 12-9

Not only does RSpec report the failure, but it also tells you the reason for failure (an undefined `friends` method on the `User` object) and the line in the spec on which it occurred (`@harry.should have(:no)`.`friends`). This is how implementation is motivated by testing: You defined an expected behavior that the `User` object should exhibit and implemented a test to check for that behavior, and now you must implement a feature to make that test pass.

To fix this failing behavior, you need to create an association that enables your `User` object to have a `friends` method that represents the user's collection of friends. First, you need some table to record friendship information. Create a new `Friendship` model and migration using the `script/generate` command, and define two integer fields on the model: `user_id` and `friend_id`. You will use a single `Friendship` object to represent a unidirectional friendship extended from the user with ID `user_id` to the user with ID `friend_id`.

```
ted$ script/generate rspec_model friendship user_id:integer friend_id:integer
```

Now open your `User` model and add a `has_many` association that links users using the `friendships` table as a join:

```
has_many :friends, :class_name => "User",
                   :join_table => "friendships",
                   :foreign_key => "user_id",
                   :association_foreign_key => "friend_id"
```

This association should create the `friends` method required by your behavioral test and should link modifications of that collection to the `Friendship` table in the database. Run the spec again to observe that the example now passes.

Part 5: Completing the Behavioral Test Implementations

The next low-hanging fruit is the "`should be lonely`" example. Now that you have implemented the friends association, determining whether the user is lonely should be a simple `friends.size` check. But first you write the test, thus defining the way you would like to interact with this future bit of functionality. This is why test writing is often said to motivate API development. Here, you will write the test in such a way that your API is expected to provide a `lonely?` method.

```
it "should be lonely" do
  @harry.should be_lonley
end
```

Running the spec to see that it fails, you then add the `lonely?` method implementation on the `User` object:

```
def lonely?
  friends.empty?
end
```

Making new friends, too, should be a simple test. Because of the code that `ActiveRecord` and associations create for you, you do not need this test from a code coverage standpoint — it is superfluous to write tests for code that is a part of the framework. However, it is an important behavior of the `User` object and serves as a test that you implemented the association correctly, so it is worth including:

```
it "should be able to make a friend" do
    lambda {
      @harry.friends << @sally
    }.should change { @harry.friends.size }.by(1)

    @harry.friends.should include(@sally)
  end
```

Running the spec once again, you see that it passes with no further coding required.

Finally, you reach the last behavioral requirement for this `describe` block:

```
it "should accept the friendship of others"
```

Even though your model is built off of a unidirectional friendship object, you would really like friendship to be a bidirectional concept. For simplicity, you will not require any sort of confirmation by the other party, and instead will just enforce the behavior that friendship should be automatically reciprocated.

To implement the test for this, you will first create a new friendship from @sally to @harry and then check to make sure that @harry has reciprocated such that @sally is in his list of friends.

```
it "should accept the friendship of others" do
      @sally.friends << @harry
      @harry.should have(1).friends
      @harry.friends.should include(@sally)
end
```

Running this test, you see that it fails.

From the test output in Figure 12-10, you see that @harry was supposed to have one friend after @sally's friend addition, but instead it had zero. This is expected because it was @sally who added the friend, not @harry, and you haven't implemented the reciprocation yet. You fix this problem by adding a reciprocate_friendship instance method on User that barges into another user's friends list and adds self to it if it isn't already there (how presumptuous!).

```
def reciprocate_friendship(newfriend)
  unless newfriend.friends.include?(self)
    newfriend.friends << self
  end
end
```

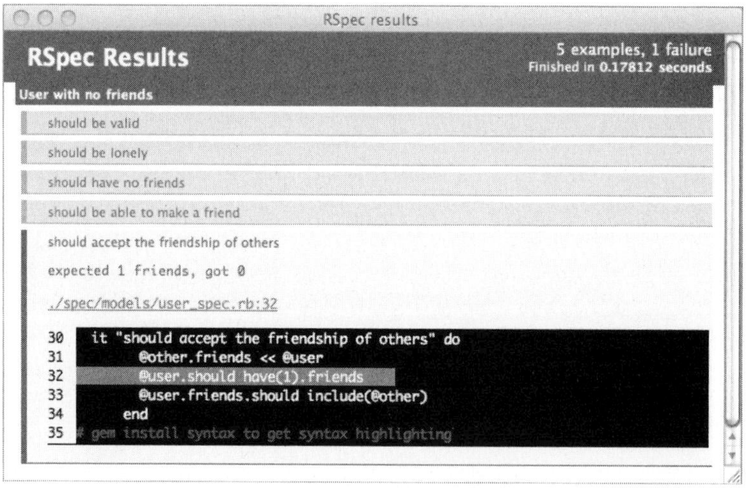

Figure 12-10

Then add a callback to this method on the friends association for *after* a new friend is added (infinite recursion will occur if you do it before):

```
has_and_belongs_to_many :friends,
    :class_name => "User",
    :join_table => "friendships",
    :association_foreign_key => "friend_id",
    :foreign_key => "user_id",
    :after_add => :reciprocate_friendship
```

Running the spec for a final time, you see the display in Figure 12-11, showing all passes.

Figure 12-11

The RSpec not only lets you know when you have accomplished the development goals you set but also serves as a nice way to summarize the behaviors of a described object from a usage standpoint. If a new developer on the project (or an old one, coming back to code written long ago) wanted to know what a User could do, he or she need look only at the spec document. If the developer wants to know how to perform any of the behaviors listed in the spec, the spec implementation serves as a short, simple example of that use case, finishing with a series of should and should_not statements that describe what the expected results will be.

But Wait, There's More

This chapter only scratches the surface of RSpec's capabilities to introduce you to BDD. There is a whole world of features included in RSpec that you can begin to investigate as you become more comfortable with the framework and want to use it more extensively:

- ❑ User stories to tie together and test different system components
- ❑ Mock objects and stubs to help isolate objects for testing
- ❑ Model, View, and Controller-specific testing helpers
- ❑ Continuous build integration and developer tools

For resources on the Web, check out the RSpec home page at http://rspec.info/. Geoffrey Grosenbach's PeepCode (http://peepcode.com) also has several excellent webcasts for sale that contain narrative walkthroughs of many of RSpec's features from beginning to advanced.

Summary

BDD is an enjoyable and effective way to develop any application, and RSpec's Ruby DSL for BDD makes it especially powerful for Rails developers. Using RSpec does not require many new tricks or add heavy time commitments to your coding because it is a reorganization of many of the tasks that you probably already pursue in a less unified manner.

When you develop a project in this new way, you start with the overall goals, or stories, that you would like to accomplish. Each of these motivates specs for the various objects in your system, each containing behavioral examples of the object in various contexts. These examples are transformed into unit-like tests that perform the steps necessary to achieve a particular behavior and verify that it did (or didn't) happen. The development of tests, in turn, motivates development on the actual object being tested so that it can perform the behavior being asked of it.

In addition to providing the benefit of continuous testing for your Rails application, RSpec is a powerful design and communication tool. Spec design informs the interface choices that you eventually make about your objects to support their required behavior. The spec itself forms a living document, both of the system's capabilities and of a reference implementation for each capability. And the half-implemented spec serves as a roadmap to guide your development tasks toward completion.

Index

U

V

W